Indian Population Decline

Indian Population Decline

The Missions of Northwestern New Spain, 1687–1840

Robert H. Jackson

University of New Mexico Press
Albuquerque

Library of Congress Cataloging-in-Publication Data

Jackson, Robert H. (Robert Howard)
Indian population decline : the missions of northwestern New Spain, 1687–1840 / Robert H. Jackson. — 1st ed.
p. cm.
Includes bibliographical references and index.
ISBN 0-8263-1505-4
1. Indians of New Mexico—New Spain—Population. 2. Indians of Mexico—New Spain—Missions. 3. Indians of Mexico—Diseases—New Spain. 4. Jesuits—Missions—New Spain—History—Sources.
5. Ethnohistory—New Spain. 6. Epidemics—New Spain—History—Sources. I. Title.
F1219.J28 1993 93-39274
304.6′0972—dc20 CIP

First Edition

Contents

List of Maps, Graphs, Tables

Maps

Population Graphs

Tables

Acknowledgments

The intellectual genesis of this study dates to my experience as a youngster in the fourth grade public schools, where I was first exposed to the history of the frontier Indian missions in northwestern New Spain (Mexico). My parents supported my early interest in the missions by taking me on several trips, through the coastal valleys of central and southern California, to visit the mission sites in California.

I owe an important debt to a number of teachers and colleagues who supported my interest in the history of the missions at different stages in my intellectual formation. David Sweet and Edward Castillo of the University of California, Santa Cruz, provided me with invaluable guidance, and began the process of my transformation from an avocational to a professional historian with an expertise in the missions. Both Sweet and Castillo were instrumental in my obtaining several small research fellowships while at Santa Cruz, which helped to finance the early stages of research. Murdo MacLeod was my mentor and friend at the University of Arizona, where I completed a Master's thesis on the demography of the missions of northern Sonora and Baja California. Robert McCaa of the University of Minnesota introduced me to the computer program *Populate.*

Several colleagues have collaborated with me at different stages in my research on the missions. Archaeologists David Huelsbeck and Paul Farnsworth worked with me on detailed studies of several Alta California missions. Erick Langer coauthored an important article that compared missions in Alta California and southeastern Bolivia, and laid out a number of theoretical issues useful in the analysis of the historical processes that occurred in the missions. Kieran McCarty, O.F.M., and Charles Polzer, S.J., both of the University of Arizona, shared ideas and sources with me.

The staff of a number of archives and libraries provided invaluable assistance during the course of my research. I am particularly grateful to the staff of the Bancroft Library, University of California at Berkeley, The Santa Barbara Mission Archive-Library, the Monterey Diocese Chancery Archive, the San Francisco Archdiocese Chancery Archive, the Los Angeles Archdiocese Chancery Archive, the Archives of the University of Santa Clara, and the Library and Special Collections Library at the University of Arizona.

Finally, I owe a debt of gratitude to my wife Ana, and children Robert, Marjorie, and James, who have put up with the hours spent in analyzing sources or in front of the computer, typing. Without them I could not have completed this project.

Indian Population Decline

When all were peaceful a second time [following a second Indian revolt], God disclosed a new field of endeavor as customarily exists during general contagious epidemics. His Divine Majesty sent two successive [epidemics], *punishment for repeated apostasy and transgressions.* These [epidemics were] so catastrophic that of a thousand and some souls there remain but 449, reduced from three neighboring pueblos. From this reduction [congregation] were secured the greater glory of God, [the] well-being of their souls, and other temporal and spiritual fruits. This was evident during the last epidemic which, although doleful, was not as grievous as the first because, by communicating more easily, [they] were able to care for their bodies and souls.

—Antonio Tempis, S.J., Santiago de las Coras
Mission, Baja California, 1744

Introduction

One consequence of sustained European contact with the native populations of the Americas after 1492 was the introduction of a new series of Euroasiatic diseases, such as smallpox and measles. Under the impact of recurring epidemics of contagious diseases, and forced changes in social and economic organization, culture, and worldview, the native populations of the Americas experienced demographic collapse; a drastic reduction in the number of people; and, in many instances, a resulting social disintegration. Epidemics swept throughout North and South America, affecting all native populations, but the rates of depopulation were the greatest for those groups more closely integrated into colonial state structures and well-developed patterns of regional or interregional trade. Epidemics most commonly followed in the wake of the mules and wagons that carried goods, or were hidden in the bodies of settlers moving to establish new communities.

Historians and social scientists have analyzed and debated the causes and manifestations of Indian demographic collapse almost from the very beginning of the European occupation of the Americas. In recent years, two basic types of academic studies have been written: monographs that engage in the "numbers game," efforts to establish contact-population sizes using a variety of sources including accounts and descriptions written by the first conquerors and colonists, tribute and tax records, archaeological records of settlement sizes, and estimates of the carrying capacity of the land based upon specific forms of exploitation; and more conventional historical demographic studies, which reconstruct the patterns of fertility and mortality of discrete populations using censuses and sacramental registers of baptisms, burials, marriages, and confirmations. The numbers game has generated perhaps the greatest debate, because of its implications for larger historical and political interpretations of economic, political, and social development, including the validity of the "Black Legend" of Spanish colonialism.

The Black Legend view of the Spanish conquest of the Caribbean and American mainland in the sixteenth century incorporates the assumption that the destruction of the Indians resulted from the cruelty and exploitation of the Spaniards. This interpretation first emerged in the writings of Bartolomé de las Casas in the mid-sixteenth century. Spain's European enemies used his condemnation of the abuse of Caribbean natives by Spanish colonists as potent propaganda. The "White Legend" attempts to present a sanitized version of the Spanish conquests in the Americas, and to minimize the negative impact of the conquest on the Indians while stressing what is considered to be the positive aspects of Spanish colonization, namely the introduction of a "superior" culture and religion. Assumptions about the complexity of Indian civilization have also influenced early population estimates. Those who advocated relatively small Indian populations in the late fifteenth century stress the simplicity of Indian society: denigrating the cultural and artistic achievements of the principal sedentary Indian civilizations, frequently in an effort to minimize the impact of European conquest and colonization of the Americas.[1]

Although useful because they establish the parameters of the degree of demographic collapse, studies that attempt to estimate contact-population levels do not explain the dynamic of the process of depopulation, the life history of native populations prior to the arrival of the Spaniards, and the modifications of Indian life-styles that contributed to the collapse of the native populations. The basic assumption is that epidemics wiped out millions of people in the wake of the European conquest. However, they do little to explain the specific cause or causes for the demographic collapse of the native population. What specific patterns of epidemic mortality can be identified, and in all cases was epidemic disease the primary cause of demographic collapse? What other biological and nonbiological factors contributed to the elevated mortality rates that were responsible for the collapse of Indian populations? What factors prevented a rebound or a gradual recovery from epidemic mortality, as occurred, for example, in Europe following the great bubonic-plague outbreak of the mid-fourteenth century and subsequent severe mortality crises?[2] Was mortality uniform across age and gender? These and other questions frame this study, which offers a detailed examination of the process of demographic collapse in the mission communities of northwestern New Spain (colonial Mexico), the regions known as the Pimería Alta in northern Sonora, Baja California, and Alta California. This book provides a case study of the causes and manifestations of the demographic collapse of a discrete New World Indian population for which the documentation is relatively complete.

Beginning in 1591, Jesuit missionaries established missions among the semisedentary agriculturalists and hunter-gatherers of Sinaloa, and later Sonora and Baja California. The implementation of the colonial policy of *congregación,* the resettlement of dispersed populations into spatially compact communities, had as its goal the transplanting to the northern frontier of colonial social, economic, and cultural patterns developed by the Spanish in central Mexico. Enculturated Indians would form the lower levels of a hierarchical society rigidly stratified along racial lines, and would provide a fiscal and economic base for the colonial state and frontier society through the payment of tribute (a poll tax), labor for the development of mines and other enterprises, and markets for goods. However, the establishment of missions accelerated the process of demographic collapse, which most likely had already begun in the decades following the Spanish conquest of central Mexico in 1521. The mission frontier expanded northward to the Pimería Alta region in the 1680s, although the northern Pima had already been in intimate contact with the Spanish frontier society of Sonora for at least fifty years; to Baja California in the late 1690s, and to Alta California in the late 1760s, as one aspect of a general reorganization of the colonial frontier under the direction of *visitador general* José de Gálvez.

The process of Indian demographic collapse in northwestern New Spain has received attention from a number of scholars, although the types of sources used and the general quality of the results varied from study to study and few studies offer a comparative evaluation of demographic collapse. Of the three regions examined here, the process of demographic collapse in the Pimería Alta has garnered the least amount of attention. Anthropologist Henry Dobyns published a study that examined demographic change in the Indian mission of Tucson and in the military garrison of the same name.[3] Dobyns made extensive use of censuses and other primary sources, but did not have access to sacramental registers of baptisms, burials, and marriages that generally provide the most detailed information on the vital rates of a population. Nevertheless, Dobyns does present a good overview of demographic change and, particularly, a flavor for frontier life and the pace of warfare with the Apaches and other hostile Indians.

The process of depopulation in the Baja California mission has been the subject of a number of studies. Two historical geographers, Peveril Meigs and Homer Aschmann, wrote detailed monographs on the ecology, economy, and demography of the missions in two parts of the peninsula.[4] Both studies made extensive use of sacramental registers and censuses, but their analysis did not transcend a description of the general patterns of mortality and, in the case of Aschmann's monograph, the age and gender structure of the mission populations. Moreover, because of their early date of publication (1935, 1959), both authors were unable to make use of the new methodologies of historical demography being developed in Europe, especially family reconstitution. Nevertheless, both studies were very significant contributions to the field. Sherburne Cook provided a general overview to the impact of epidemic disease from the 1690s through 1773, and estimated the size of the population in the peninsula prior to the establishment of the missions in a short study published in 1937.[5] A more recent article, based upon an analysis of aggregate totals of baptisms, births, and burials at selected Baja California missions, established a chronology of major epidemic episodes in the peninsula, and levels of population decline from the 1690s through the early nineteenth century.[6]

The study of the Alta California missions generated and continues to generate the greatest controversy, primarily because of the conflicting interpretations of a militant group of supporters of a "White-Legend" view of the history of the missions and the role of the Franciscans in the Spanish colonization of the region, and the more balanced and better documented view of academically oriented scholars. Sherburne Cook, who worked with Woodrow Borah at the end of his career, wrote a series of monographs that attempted to establish population levels in California in 1769, and documented the causes of demographic collapse. In an initial series of monographs first published in the 1940s, Cook explored a variety of factors that contributed to the rapid decline of the Indian population of California between 1769 and 1900. In the study of the Alta California missions, Cook focused on biological and nonbiological factors, including epidemic and endemic disease including syphilis, diet, warfare, and what in modern terms would be characterized as psychological disorientation caused by the stresses of mission life. Cook also examined the use of corporal punishment, as a means of maintaining social control, and forms of resistance, including flight from the missions. Cook also, in a tentative fashion, documented the age and gender structure of the mission populations. Cook concluded that elevated mortality was the primary cause of the demographic collapse of the Indian populations living in the missions, and that birthrates dropped. Finally, Cook suggested that regional variations occurred within the vital rates of the mission populations.[7] Cook did not employ original sacramental registers, and he relied upon abstracts made from original documents destroyed in 1906, which were found in the Bancroft Library (University of California, Berkeley) and which some scholars, largely for nonacademic, political reasons, maintain are not reliable. Nevertheless, this early series of monographs established an outline for future studies of the history of the Indian-European interface in California. Most scholars continue to test and refine Cook's initial conclusions, and—as is the case in this present study—confirmed many of Cook's early interpretations.

In a volume of essays written at different times and published in 1976, Cook updated his earlier estimates of the size of the Indian population in 1769, and the number of Indians in the state at different points in the nineteenth century. However, Cook introduced no new ideas on the causes of demographic collapse.[8] Cook's last major contribution to the historical demography of the Alta California missions was a collaborative effort written with Woodrow Borah and included in volume three of *Essays in Population History*.[9] Cook and Borah analyzed original mission sacramental registers for the first time, and constructed life tables that predicted rates of survival of the Indians living in the missions, both converts relocated to the mission communities and children born there. The conclusions presented in this essay largely substantiated many of Cook's earlier interpretations on the causes and manifestations of Indian demographic collapse in the missions, a fact that many of Cook's detractors tend to ignore. Cook and Borah also compared the vital rates of the mission populations with contemporary European populations, although, because of the different methodologies employed in the creation of the data sets cited, this comparison is less convincing.

The works of Cook mentioned above, while in some instances methodologically weak, have set the tone for subsequent research on the Alta California missions. Advocates of the "White-Legend" view of the missions attempted and continue to attempt to construct arguments that challenge Cook's interpretation, or to quibble over the meaning or reliability of some sources. Criticisms of Cook's conclusions generally appear within the context of efforts to present a sanitized but distorted view of the history of the missions consistent with the efforts to publicize and sell the canonization of Junipero Serra, O.F.M., at both the academic and popular levels.[10] More serious scholarship, especially in the 1980s, refined and expanded upon many of the issues raised by Cook, often using sources and methodologies not available when Cook completed his initial research in the 1930s and 1940s. In spite of the Columbus quincentenary and Hispanophiles and boosters of the Catholic church railing against "Serra-bashers" and a nonexistent resurgence of the "Black Legend," one fact remains unchanged. Most recent research supports many of Cook's early conclusions.

Recent studies of the Alta California missions have built upon the foundation of Cook's early work, but have brought different approaches to the question of the causes and manifestations of demographic collapse in the missions. Anthropologists have employed parish registers to reconstruct social relations as well as demographic patterns using a modified version of family reconstitution.[11] A second series of studies explore the formation of the mission communities and the instability in the mission populations, the age and gender structure of the mission populations as related to patterns of recruitment of converts, and the vital rates of the mission populations.[12] Finally, the ethnohistory of the mission populations has received recent attention, and contributes to the understanding of Indian demographic collapse by showing the specific sociocultural changes enforced in the missions by the Franciscan missionaries.[13]

One last area of inquiry has been the extent of, the chronology of, and the mortality toll caused by epidemics, especially the pandemics of the sixteenth century. There has been considerable debate recently over the impact of epidemics on native populations in the Americas, and the severity and chronology of early epidemics. Henry Dobyns and several other scholars engaged in a debate in the pages of the journal *Ethnohistory,* over the identification of epidemic chronologies and estimates of epidemic mortality.[14] In many ways, this debate reflects an older approach to the study of epidemics and depopulation based upon a reading of contact-period accounts, and trying to tease and interpret information from accounts that are at best ambiguous. In a recent article, historical geographer Thomas Whitmore provided a new method for evaluating the long-term impact of epidemic disease on native populations, which demonstrates the usefulness of computer simulations and computer-generated data in the study of demographic collapse, applied in this case to the Valley of Mexico.[15] In another article, Woodrow Borah provided a useful overview of the study of epidemics in the Americas, and areas for future research. Borah's extensive bibliography includes many studies of borderlands regions.[16]

Studies of the historical demography of northwestern New Spain generally focus on a single region encapsulated within the broader literature on Latin American population studies. Few studies attempt a comparative analysis that compares and contrasts the similarities and dissimilarities in the demographic patterns of different populations.[17] Moreover, most studies do not have a solid foundation in the literature on the historical demography of early modern Europe, which provides a convenient comparison for the demographic patterns of Indian populations as well as important methodological insights.[18] Studies of early modern European populations focus on patterns of fertility and less on mortality, and on the factors, economic and sociocultural, that modified family formation. Finally, they offer important insights on mortality, especially disease-related mortality and patterns of infant and child mortality.

This study analyzes the demographic collapse of the Indian populations congregated ino three groups of missions located in northwestern New Spain (the Pimería Alta and the Californias), presented in a comparative content within the larger region being studied, and also with contemporary American and non-American populations. This study also provides new insights into the process of demographic collapse by employing a relatively new methodology, inverse projection, to analyze a large body of primary sources, including mission sacramental registers. Sophisticated demographic statistics generated for different populations allow for an in-depth evaluation of the causes and manifestations and regional variations in the process of demographic collapse, and the application of the same methodology to contemporary populations provides data for a valid comparison of patterns of mortality and fertility. Finally, this study not only contributes to the literature on colonial Latin America, but because of its comparative content, it will be useful for scholars engaged in research on non-American populations, and especially non-European populations in formal colonial setting.

The study consists of four chapters. Chapter 1 outlines the process of the formation of the mission communities through the implementation of congregation; the resettlement of dispersed Indian populations into spatially compact villages; and the dissolution of the mission communities in the early nineteenth century, when government support for the mission programs ended. The second chapter discusses the degree of population decline in the Pimería Alta, Baja California, and Alta California missions, and includes detailed case studies of the vital rates of individual mission communities and an analysis of the age and gender structure of the mission populations. I use censuses and sacramental registers to reconstruct fluctuations in population levels in the missions, and the vital rates of the mission populations. Chapter 3 explores the causes of demographic collapse, with emphasis placed on the Alta California missions, which evidenced a pattern distinct from the patterns documented for the Pimería Alta and Baja California missions. Finally, Chapter 4 offers a comparative discussion of demographic patterns within the larger region of northwestern New Spain, and selected contemporary non-American populations.

This is not a history of the missions, but rather an analysis of the vital rates and demographic patterns of specific mission populations. I do not discuss the personalities of individual missionaries, and I outline the implementation of colonial policies only insofar as they illustrate aspects of the central themes of this monograph. Finally, the conclusions drawn in this study reflect only on the populations of the mission communities, and not on the larger and relatively undocumented populations that remained outside the Spanish colonial mission system. The quality of the sources for the missions and the dearth of comparable information for the nonmission populations dictates this approach. Moreover, I do not attempt to establish Indian population levels prior to the establishment of the missions, nor do I use population figures and rates of decline in the missions to estimate changing population levels for the larger nonmission populations. My objective is to provide a detailed evaluation of the discrete Indian populations living in the missions.

A Note on Methodology

The core of this monograph consists of an analysis of the vital rates of individual mission communities in the Pimería Alta and the Californias. I use the inverse-projection methodology, developed by historical demographer Ron Lee, to reconstruct the vital rates of the mission populations based on aggregate totals of births, burials, and population.[19] The microcomputer program *Populate,* which employs inverse projection, provides a flexible and efficient way of analyzing a large volume of quantitative data. *Populate* produces sophisticated demographic statistics based on the analysis of quinquennium totals of births, deaths, and population.

Several caveats to the use of *Populate* must be introduced. First, the program produces better results with better quality and more complete data. This is particularly imprtant in relation to population figures, and especially the base populations for each quinquennium upon which the calculation of vital rates is based. A slight error in the base population can skew the resulting demographic statistics. Second, the program works better with larger populations. The analysis presented here is based upon raw data taken from individual missions, many with substantial populations and a fairly complete run of population figures taken from censuses and other sources. However, I have put together several composite data sets made up of information on a number of missions. These composite data sets are used to validate the statistics generated for the individual missions. Finally, the underregistration of births and deaths in the sacramental registers can also skew the results of the analysis, although a close reading of the sacramental registers of the mission communities of northwestern

New Spain and nonmission parishes in other parts of colonial Spanish America indicate that the mission registers are relatively complete, especially in the baptisms of children born at the missions. There were no economic factors, such as fees charged by secular parish priests, which served as disincentives for people to go before a priest to register births, marriages, and burials. Moreover, the special evangelical mission of the missionaries, coupled with the obligation to report the material and spiritual results of the mission enterprise, contributed to a more accurate registration of vital events. Finally, in many instances, particularly in the Californias, two missionaries were stationed at a single mission, so it was easier to keep track of people.

The analysis of the mission sacramental registers produces several indices of vital rates. Crude birth-and-death rates per thousand population document relative rates of fertility and mortality. The gross reproduction ratio measures the production of children of a population. The net reproduction ratio records the net growth of a population. A ratio of 1.0 indicates the doubling of the population over a generation, and a figure of 0.5 a halving of the population. Finally, the mean life expectancy at birth measures the length of survival of a newborn. The case studies of the data of individual mission communities is based upon an evaluation of these statistics, and, in order to maintain the validity of the comparison, the analysis of the nonmission and non-American populations is based upon the same statistics generated by *Populate.*

I

The Formation and Dissolution of the Mission Communities

Throughout the colonial period, Spanish officials implemented programs and policies to change the social structure and economy of New Spain. For example, beginning in the late sixteenth century, civil and religious authorities enforced the policy of *congregación,* the resettlement of Indian populations in nucleated settlements.[1] Epidemics during the first decades following the Spanish conquest of Mexico left many communities depopulated or underpopulated, and the survivors frequently lived in dispersed settlements. The congregation of the Indian population entailed the foundation of new communities populated by the residents of numerous smaller and dispersed communities. The formation of large nucleated communities facilitated the conversion to Catholicism of the Indians, because many priests felt it a burden to have to visit many small dispersed communities in a large parish. Moreover, it was also easier for royal officials to collect tribute and organize labor drafts in the new larger communities.

The formation of mission communities along the northern frontier of New Spain followed the same basic principle. The Spanish attempted to replicate central Mexican patterns of exploitation of the Indian population and Spanish rural-village society in the north,[2] but first they had to create sedentary communities among semisedentary and nomadic populations: the semisedentary and agriculturalist northern Pimas in northern Sonora; the nomadic hunter-gatherers of Baja California; and the semisedentary hunter-gatherers in coastal Alta California, who practiced sophisticated wild-food resource management. Patterns of *congregación* differed in the three regions examined here, but in each case, patterns of resettlement to the mission communities are critical for an understanding of the demographic collapse of the Indian populations living in the mission communities.

This chapter outlines the implementation of *congregación* that led to the formation of the mission communities; the continued repopulation of the missions through the resettlement of non-Christians from outside the missions; and the dissolution of the mission communities in the early nineteenth century, largely as a consequence of changes in government policy. The Jesuits and Franciscans stationed in the Pimería Alta missions of northern Sonora and the Alta California establishments repopulated the missions through continued *congregación*. The Jesuits, Franciscans, and Dominicans stationed in the Baja California missions, on the other hand, were unable to repopulate the missions there following the *congregación* of the local Indian populations, because the Indian population was small to begin with and there was no significant pool of potential converts living outside the missions. The first section documents the formation of mission communities and the phenomenon of ethnic mingling in the Pimería Alta; the second section discusses the formation of the Baja California mission communities; and the final section concentrates on the resettlement of Indian converts to the Alta California missions and the rapid dispersion of the mission populations, following the secularization of the mission communities and beginning in 1834.

Conversion and Ethnic Mingling in the Pimería Alta Missions

In 1687, Jesuit missionary Eusebio Kino established the first mission in northern Pima territory in Sonora. The missions among the northern Pimas were the northernmost extension of a Jesuit missionary enterprise begun in the 1590s in central Sinaloa, following some sixty years of sporadic contact with the Spanish. In the late seventeenth century, the different northern Pima groups living in *rancherías,* seasonal villages, had a decentralized political system, and practiced varying degrees of agriculture.[3] The advanced sedentary Hohokm culture had apparently declined prior to the arrival of the Spaniards in the sixteenth century. The Jesuit program in Sinaloa attempted to transform the northern Pimas and other groups into a more sedentary community peasantry along the lines of the corporate indigenous communities in central New Spain. Despite periodic revolts and other forms of active and passive resistance, the Jesuit missionaries achieved some success in attracting converts to their missions. What attraction did the missions have for the northern Pimas? Traditional Eurocentric interpretations stress the attractiveness of superior Iberian material culture and Catholicism, especially livestock and new crops.[4]

A recent study offers an alternative explanation for the apparent early Jesuit success in Sinaloa and Sonora.[5] According to Reff, the early six-

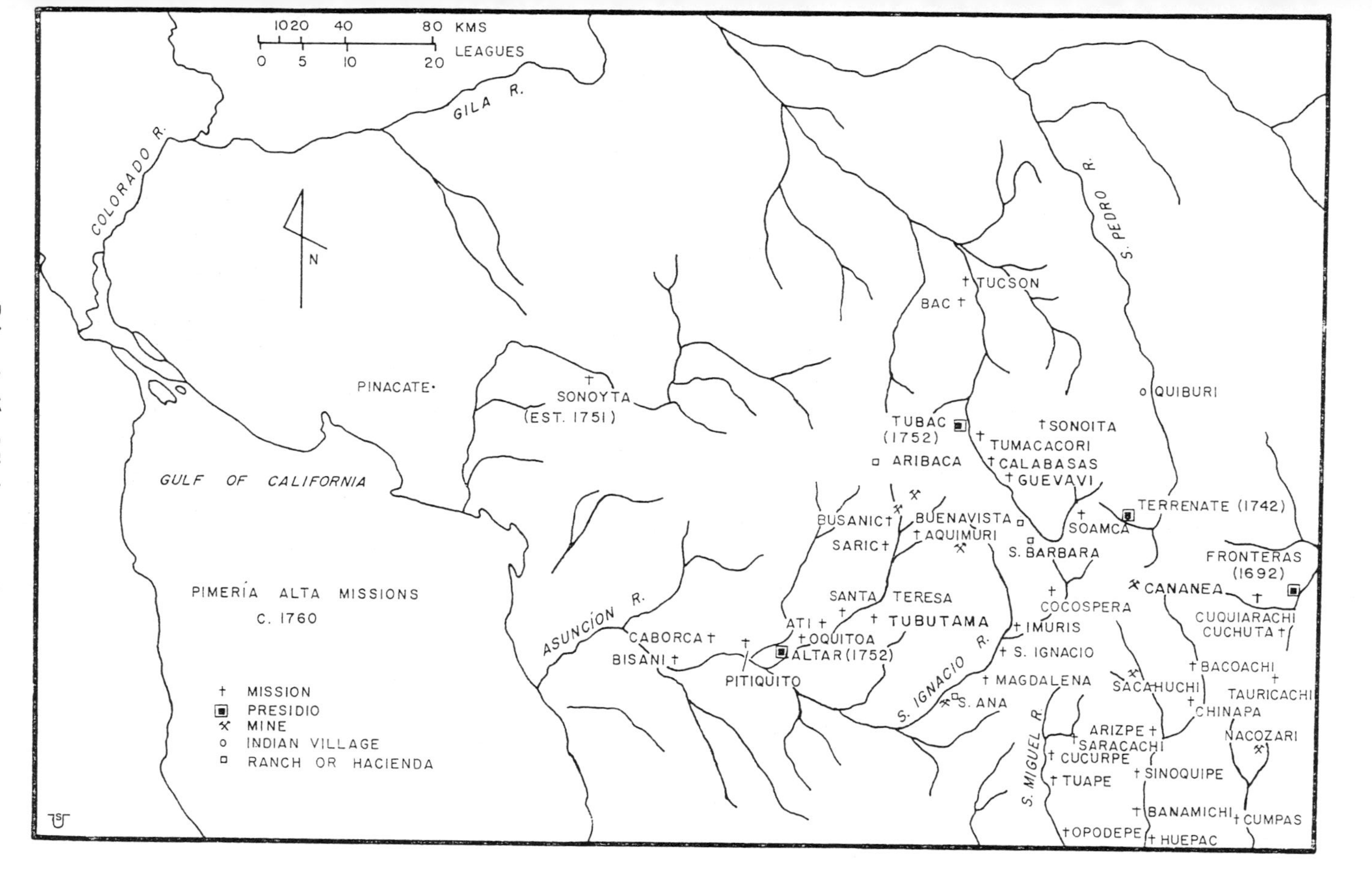

Primería Alta Missions, c. 1760

teenth-century accounts of the first Spanish contacts with northern Pimas and other Sonoran groups described more advanced political organizations and larger permanent villages. Although the Hohokam culture may have entered a period of gradual decline in the fourteenth and fifteenth centuries, sedentary agricultural villages still existed in northern Sonora. The builders of Casa Grande and elaborate irrigation systems in the Gila River Basin still lived in permanent villages. Drastic cultural and political change occurred only in the sixteenth century, following the impact of newly introduced Euroasiatic disease, such as smallpox and measles, which killed thousands of Indians. Northern Pimas abandoned large villages in favor of dispersed *rancherías,* which inhibited somewhat the spread of disease. Following more than a century of social and political disintegration, the Jesuits offered a point of reference for reorganization. Reff's hypothesis offers a dynamic interpretation of social and cultural change among the Indian populations of northwestern New Spain, replacing an older view of static and unchanging populations.

Epidemics in the sixteenth and seventeenth centuries spread along aboriginal and, later, Spanish trade routes undermining the stability of northern Pima society. Through *congregación,* Jesuit missionaries re-created permanent agricultural communities in the principal river valleys in northern Sonora and, when disease depopulated the communities, repopulated the missions by resettling northern Pima converts. The *congregación* of the northern Pimas occurred in several phases related to the availability of missionaries and the willingness of the viceregal government in Mexico City to finance the missions and provide military garrisons to protect the Jesuits.

The process of conversion or organization of the northern Pimas into a system of missions communities can be chronologically divided into four periods, based upon the availability of missionaries and changes in the political climate and official policy: first expansion during the ministry of Jesuit Eusebio Kino (1687–1711); retrenchment in the face of shortages of missionaries (1711–1732); several attempts at expansion of the number of missions as the government sent more missionaries to northern Sonora and met with growing resistance by Pima tribelets still outside the control of the missionaries (1732–1767); and the Franciscan period (1768–c. 1830), characterized by a pattern of the repopulation of the existing mission villages with Papago converts from the desert west of the river valleys, who depended upon seasonal food resources generally available only in the mission villages.

While the Jesuits converted the Pima tribelets that occupied the principal river valleys in the region, a process nominally completed by the 1750s if

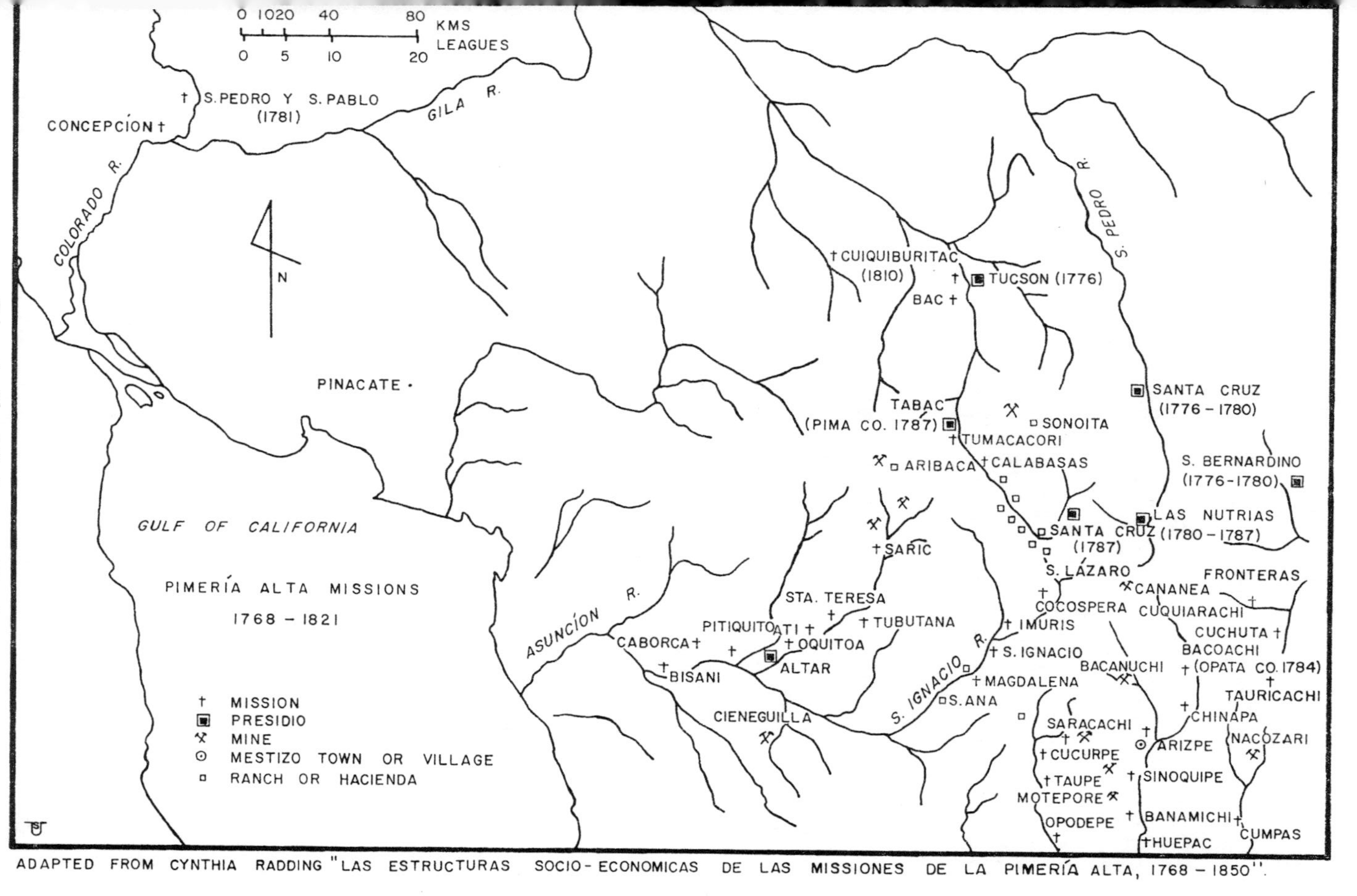

Primería Alta Missions, 1768–1821

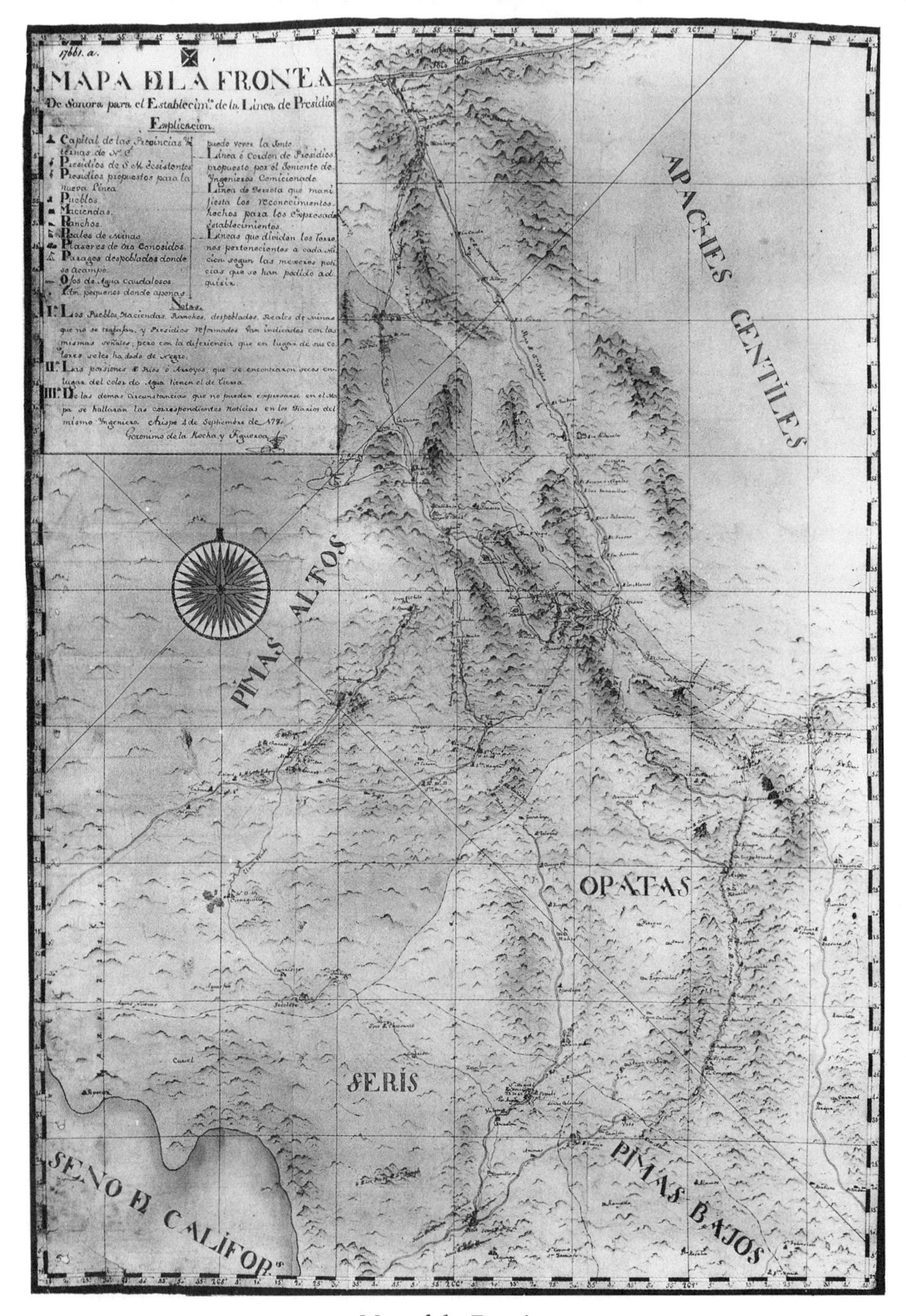

Map of the Frontier

not before, the Black Robes and later the Franciscans continued to settle the Pima group, which they identified as Papagos, into the missions during the colonial period and, to a lesser extent, following Mexican independence in 1821. Missionaries themselves or mission Indians entered the *Papagueria* to bring converts back to the missions. Some Papagos voluntarily sought baptism. In other cases, the Jesuits and Franciscans enticed or pressured Papagos who came to work in the river-valley communities on a seasonal basis. As the mission populations declined under the impact of disease and other factors, the missionaries repopulated the mission communities with Papago converts who increasingly formed a larger percentage of the mission populations. Few sacramental registers survive from the early years of Jesuit missionary activity because of their destruction during the 1695 Pima revolt, and the loss of many documents related to the history of northern Sonora following Mexican independence. Nevertheless, a number of generalizations can be made. From his base at Dolores mission (established 1687), Kino and a handful of Jesuits began the process of converting the Pimas, and Kino himself undertook numerous explorations of the vast Pima territory as far as the Colorado River region. Kino's contemporaries included Agustín de Campos, S.J., stationed at San Ignacio between 1693 and 1736; Daniel Januske, at Tubutama from 1694 to 1696; and Francisco Saeta, who died at the hands of rebels at Caborca in 1695.[6]

In twenty-four years of active missionary work in the Pimería Alta, Kino and his associates established the basis of a rather extensive network of missions, although the conversion of the Indians was superficial at best and especially so in the villages not staffed by resident missionaries. The Jesuits assigned *cabecera* status to a number of existing Pima villages, and designated other population centers as *pueblos de visita,* using the same administrative system implemented by the Spaniards in central Mexico in the sixteenth century. The following table summarizes the ecclesiastical organization of the Pimería Alta missions and the dates of the first recorded baptisms at a given village (see Table 1.1).[7]

Only one sacramental register survives from the early period of Jesuit missionary activity, a baptisms register for Santa María Magdalena *visita* of San Ignacio mission in the years 1698–1718. A notation on the first page of the baptismal register states that between 1693 and 1695, prior to the Pima revolt, missionary Campos baptized 223 people at San Ignacio and its satellite villages. It appears that the Pimas allowed Campos to resume his ministry only in 1698, or at least Campos did not return to San Ignacio until that year.

Table 1.1 Ecclesiastical Organization of the Pimería Alta Missions

Cabecera	Year	Visita	Year
Dolores de Cosari	1687	Remedios	1687
		Cocospera	1687
San Ignacio	1687	Magdalena	1687
		Ymuris	1687
Tubutama	1689	Santa Teresa	1689
		Oquitoa	1689
Caborca	1689	Busanic	1689
		Pitiqui	1689
Saric	1689	Aquimuri	1689
		Busanic y Tucubavia	1698
Guevavi	1691	Sonita	1691
		Tumacacori	1691
Bac	1692	Tucson	1692
		Cuyoabagum	1699
Soamca		San Lazaro	1689
		Bacoancas	1689
Sonoyta	1697		

Source: Charles Polzer, S.J., *Precepts of the Jesuit Missions* (Tucson, 1976), p. 37.

The record of baptisms for the years 1698 to 1711 is suggestive of patterns of conversion in the first years of missionary activity in the region. One important element of the acculturation program was the instruction and baptism of adults. Between 1698 and 1708 Campos baptized 106 adults (roughly, age eleven and above); 43 in 1700; and 20 in 1708. Baptisms of newborns and the children of converts totaled 105 between 1698 and 1711. No evidence in the register indicates that Campos relocated Papago converts to Magdalena, so it can be assumed that in 1698 the Jesuit resumed the conversion of the Pimas living at Santa María Magdalena, which had been interrupted by rebellion in 1695.[8]

Several detailed mission reports from 1744 record the number of baptisms from the beginning of the conversion at each establishment through the year 1744. Gaspar Stiger, S.J., also stationed at San Ignacio, reported a total of 3,722 baptisms at the three villages of the mission district, San Ignacio, Magdalena, and Ymuris, from the date of the foundation of the missions to 1744.[9] After Kino's death, Campos assumed responsibility for those villages without resident missionaries, which inflated the count of baptisms recorded in the San Ignacio baptismal register. Domingo Cossio, S.J., stationed at Dolores, reported a total of 2,435 baptisms between 1687 and 1744.[10] In 1720, Luis Velarde, S.J., who replaced Kino at Dolores, noted that between 1716 and 1720 he baptized 66 children and 3 adults in three villages under his jurisdiction, and 129 in villages to the north of the mission.[11] In other words, the volume of baptisms recorded in the Dolores mission baptismal register declined after Kino's death, and the bulk of the recorded baptisms were of Indians living in villages other than Dolores, Remedios, and Cocospera, the three villages that made up the mission district.

The Jesuits exposed large numbers of Pimas to the rudiments of Christianity and European culture, but only at a superficial level. The understanding of complex Catholic doctrine was limited, and the Black Robes hardly modified the socioeconomic structure of most Pima villages in the first decades of their ministry. Indoctrination in the mysteries of the faith and lessons in the supposed benefits of European-style agriculture and other economic activities had little effect when not reinforced by the daily teachings of a resident missionary. The impressive numbers of baptisms does not imply a profound change in the lives of the Pimas who did not live under the day-to-day direction of the Jesuits.

Not all Pimas accepted the missionaries, and some factions in several Pima tribelets actively rejected the intervention of the Black Robes. In the first years of Kino's ministry, the tribelet identified by the Spaniards as the Soba, who occupied the area around Caborca, actively resisted the Spanish advance. In about 1688, one Captain Fuente organized a punitive expedition that was to enter Soba territory, but Kino intervened to mediate a peaceful solution to the conflict, which temporarily removed the threat of conflict.[12] Hostility to the new regime and resentment of the activities of Opata catechists stationed in the missions erupted into a full-blown revolt in 1695. The uprising, initiated by Indians from Tubutama and Oquitoa in the Altar Valley, began at Tubutama with the murder of three Opata servants, and missionary Januske barely escaped along a little-used trail. The rebels caught up with Francisco Xavier Saeta at Caborca and killed him, while Campos reached safety at Dolores. Kino patched together a peace, but it took several years for the Jesuit ministry to return to prerevolt conditions.[13]

Kino died in 1711.[14] For the next twenty years, the Pimería Alta missions remained understaffed because of a shortage of Jesuits in New Spain. The number of Jesuits was insufficient to meet requests for Black Robes in central Mexico, let alone provide missionaries for the northwestern frontier. For at least eight years (1712–1720), only two missionaries worked in the Pimería Alta—Campos at San Ignacio and Luis Velarde (1714–1737) at Dolores.[15] Additional personnel reached northern Sonora sporadically. In 1720, Luis Gallardo, S.J., and Luis Marciano, S.J., arrived in the Pimería Alta, but Marciano left soon afterward. After replacing Campos for a short period of time at San Ignacio mission, Gallardo was sent to Tubutama mission, where he remained until his death in 1736.[16] Nevertheless, the acculturation program remained limited in scope.

Campos remained active during this period, visiting and baptizing Pimas in the river-valley settlements north and east of San Ignacio. In April and May of 1720, for example, the Black Robe baptized 81 at Tubutama, Oquitoa, and Caborca, all villages without missionaries. In the following year, Campos visited Guevavi, San Cayetano, Xoporica, and San Francisco del Bac in the Santa Cruz Valley. In the winter of 1724, the Jesuit visited the Santa Cruz and San Pedro valleys during a major smallpox epidemic, where he baptized 157 people. Campos also maintained contacts with the Gileños living to the north, in the Salt and Gila River valleys. In 1726, for example, Campos visited the Santa Cruz and Gila River valleys.[17] Nevertheless, the contacts between the Jesuits and most of the northern Pima tribelets continued to be limited as in earlier years, and the degree of social, cultural, and economic change small.

In 1731, Jesuit officials in Mexico sent a handful of missionaries to northern Sonora, in an attempt to accelerate the acculturation of the northern Pimas. Four Jesuits arrived in the Pimería Alta to staff dormant missions. Phelipe Segesser was assigned to San Francisco Xavier del Bac mission, located in the Santa Cruz Valley. Gaspar Stiger replaced Campos at San Ignacio; Ignacio Keller staffed Santa María Soamca mission, located in the Santa Cruz Valley; and Juan Bautista Grazhofer went to Guevavi mission, also located in the Santa Cruz Valley. However, two of the Jesuits left the scene fairly quickly. Grazhofer died under mysterious circumstances, and Segesser left the Pimería Alta because of poor health.[18]

Officials in Mexico City expressed more interest in the development of the Sonora frontier in the 1730s and 1740s, and attempted to replace those Jesuits who died or had to leave the frontier missions. Jacobo Sedelmayr, S.J., for example, arrived at Tubutama in 1736, and remained in the Pimería Alta for the next sixteen years. Sedelmayr continued the exploration of the western desert begun by Kino, and he attempted to expand the mission program to encompass a larger part of the Pimería Alta.[19] Alexander Rapicani, S.J., arrived at Guevavi mission in 1737, and José Molino, S.J., went to Dolores mission in the same year.[20]

The first major expansion of the mission system was in the Santa Cruz Valley. Three of the newly arrived Jesuits reestablished missions at Soamca,

Bac, and Guevavi. No Jesuit consistently lived at Bac until the 1750s, however, and the village remained a distant *visita* of Guevavi. Consequently, the acculturation of the Pimas living there remained superficial at best. In 1751, Sedelmayr reported that the Indians were not well instructed in Catholic doctrine, and that there were no *temastianes* (catechists) to teach at least the rudiments of the new religion.[21]

The baptismal registers of Soamca and Guevavi survive, shedding light on the process of conversion and acculturation in the Santa Cruz Valley and surrounding areas. Ignacio Keller assumed responsibility for the groups in the northeastern Pimería Alta without missionaries, and counted the San Pedro and Gila valleys located north and east of the Santa Cruz Valley as lying within his district. In three visits to the Gila River in 1736, 1737, and 1743, for example, Keller baptized 104, 139, and 106 Gileños, respectively.[22] In 1735 and 1743, Keller recorded the population of the satellite villages located on the San Pedro River and in the area between the two valleys. The population of the villages dropped between 1735 and 1743, with one village disappearing entirely from the record; and there was a marked sexual imbalance, a deficit of women, with a female:male ratio of 1:1.06 in 1735 and 1:1.17 in 1743—all evidence of the demographic collapse of the Indian population.

The Jesuits began the process of reducing the Pimas living in the Santa Cruz Valley into a smaller number of settlements, following the long-established colonial policy of *reducción/congregación;* and eventually they concentrated the population in the central village (*cabecera*) and satellite villages (*visitas*). Using data abstracted from the extant Guevavi mission baptismal register, anthropologist Henry Dobyns documented the consolidation of the population of the middle Santa Cruz River Valley into a handful of villages. In some thirty years, the Jesuits congregated the population of twelve rancherías, an estimated twenty-four hundred people, into four villages; Guevavi the *cabecera,* and the three *visitas* of Tumacacori, Calabazas, and Sonoyta. The resettlement and baptism of both adults and children from Toacuquita–Doacuquita ranchería at Calabazas *visita* in 1756 typified the process.[23]

The Jesuits attempted to expand the missionary program in the Pimería Alta in the late 1750s, although with limited success due to growing hostility toward the Jesuit program and the growing threat to subsistence security posed by increased Spanish settlement in the region. In 1756, five German Jesuits arrived in the Pimería Alta, to be assigned to new missions: Bernardo Middendorf, Francisco Hlava, Miguel Gerstner, Ignacio Pfefferkorn, and Joseph Och.[24] Middendorf remained at Tucson for several months before hostile Pimas drove him off.[25] Hlava and Gerstner attempted to establish a ministry among the Sobaipuri Pimas living in the San Pedro Valley, but they also encountered opposition from a group accustomed to Christianity from a distance, as well as access to the material benefits of contact with Spanish colonial society and military aid against their enemies, but not the social and economic chanes which would have resulted had they allowed a resident missionary and military escort to remain. Following their failure among the Sobaipuris, Gerstner was assigned to Guevavi mission and Hlava to Cocospera.[26]

Ignacio Pfefferkorn remained longer in the Pimería Alta than his companions of 1756, working among the Pimas congregated at Ati-Oquitoa

Table 1.2 Population of the *Visitas* of Soamca Mission in 1735 and 1743

1735			
Pueblo	**Male**	**Female**	**Total**
San Pedro	34	31	65
Santa Cruz Bavisi	21	30	51
San Juan de Quiburi	59	56	115
Santiago Optuavo	82	54	136
San Andres de Seug Baag and San Cisnas de Seug Tubaris	120	120	240
San Pablo de Baihca	119	116	235
San Thadeo de Babocomarig	56	56	112
Total	491	463	954

1743			
Pueblo	**Male**	**Female**	**Total**
Tavarison	36	36	72
Bavisi	37	35	72
Quiburi	41	42	83
Optuavo	81	59	140
Seug Tubaris and Seug Baag	126	79	205
Bobocomarig	132	137	269
Total	453	388	841

Source: Ms., Santa María Soamca Baptismal Register; Bancroft Library, University of California, Berkeley.

mission in the Altar Valley.[27] Baptismal registers begun by Pfefferkorn for the two villages survive, and they document the activities of the Jesuit missionaries stationed in the older Pimería Alta missions among Pimas long since reduced to mission life. In addition to directing the exploitation of communal mission resources known as temporalities, namely agricultural land and perhaps artisan activities such as weaving, the Black Robe ministered to the spiritual needs of the military garrison stationed at Altar presidio as well as to those of the Pima population of the villages in his jurisdiction. Pfefferkorn baptized the children of the inhabitants of Ati and Oquitoa and a small number of recent Papago converts. The bulk of the baptisms registered at the two villages were recently born infants. Between 1757 and 1827 Pfefferkorn and his successors baptized 357 people, including 266 children born at the mission, or 75 percent of all baptisms.[28] Baptisms at Oquitoa totaled 545 from 1757 to 1841, including 376 births, or 69 percent of the total.[29]

In 1767, King Carlos III ordered the expulsion of the Jesuits from the Spanish empire for reasons of state, and the Franciscans of the Apostolic College of Santa Cruz de Querétaro replaced the Black Robes in the Pimería Alta. The region changed considerably during the eighty years of Jesuit tenure. Disease and other factors greatly reduced the size of the converted Pima population living in the missions, and recent converts, generally classified as Papagos, increasingly comprised the bulk of the mission populations, as seen in contemporary censuses. In 1801, for example, the population of Tucson *pueblo de visita* consisted of 213 Papagos, 26 "Pimas," and 7 Gileños.[30]

Jesuits and, later, Franciscans stationed in the Pimería Alta repopulated the missions by resettling individual or groups of Papago converts to the mission villages. For example, the missionaries persuaded or pressured Papagos who came to the mission villages on a seasonal basis, to work in the harvests and to trade, to remain. Most Papagos came to the mission in small numbers, but the missionaries also baptized large groups. In 1724, for example, Campos baptized 112 Papagos at San Ignacio, and Gaspar Stiger, S.J., baptized another 107 at the same mission in 1756.[31] In 1796, Juan Bautista Llorens, O.F.M., stationed at San Francisco Xavier del Bac mission, relocated 134 Papagos to Tucson.[32]

Tubutama missionary Jacobo Sedelmayr, S.J., was particularly active in reducing Papagos to mission life in the 1740s. In 1745, Sedelmayr resettled 140 Papagos to Tubutama and Santa Teresa, and left 2 youths at a second *ranchería* to instruct the Indians.[33] In the following year, Sedelmayr resettled another 250 Papagos to Tubutama.[34] In 1747, the Jesuit Sedelmayr took 200 people from a *ranchería* located near the Gulf of California, west of Caborca mission, to Ati.[35]

In addition to relocating Pima tribelets living in the *Papagueria* to the missions, the missionaries also converted individuals who came to the missions on a seasonal basis. The seasonal migration of Pimas to the river valleys, a pre-Hispanic pattern that persisted following the arrival of the Jesuits, not only expanded the mission labor force at a critical point in the agricultural cycle, but also gave the missionaries an opportunity to persuade Papagos to remain. In 1729, Campos noted in the San Ignacio baptismal register that on "January thirteenth [I] baptized without solemnity, because they were sick from measles, the following [twenty-two] adults . . . [who] are from various inland *rancherías*, and had come here to work."[36] "These [Papago] Indians," wrote Father Visitor Juan Antonio Balthasar, S.J., "from sheer hunger, leave their native haunts in order to work in the missions and steal whatever they can. With this they go back to their own land and remain there for the rest of the year."[37] As late as the 1790s, Papagos continued to migrate seasonally to the missions.[38]

The Jesuits established a short-lived mission in 1751 at Sonoyta, west of Caborca at the only site in the *Papagueria* described as being capable of supporting a mission community with an agricultural base.[39] Kino first recognized the potential of the site, and proposed the establishment of a mission there. "The post and *ranchería* of San Marcelo [Sonoyta]," Kino wrote in 1700, "is the best there is on this coast. It has fertile land, with irrigation ditches for good crops, water which runs all the year, good pasture for cattle, and everything necessary for a good settlement, for it has very near here more than a thousand souls."[40]

As outlined above, plans to expand the number of Pimería Alta missions circulated in the 1740s, and officials decided to suppress Dolores mission (established in 1687) and transfer the endowment to a new mission.[41] In 1745, *visitador general* Juan Balthasar, S.J., reported a total of only thirty families at Dolores and its satellites, the *visitas* Remedios and Cocospera, or a total population of some 105 people. Balthasar proposed closing the first two settlements and moving the entire population of the two villages to Cocospera, and to establish a new mission. Sedelmayr initially favored establishing the mission in the San Pedro Valley or at the Gileño *rancherías* located near Casa Grande.[42]

Officials selected Sonoyta to be the site of the new mission, and Sedelmayr made efforts to have the *ranchería* prepared for its first resident missionary. In January of 1751, Sedelmayr reported that the Indians had already built and prepared a house and kitchen, and he assigned Caborca missionary Thomas Tello the task of directing the planting of wheat and perhaps corn.[43] In May of the same year, Tello visited Sonoyta a second time to check on the state of the crop and on other preparations for the arrival of the first resident missionary; to take 2 youths from Sonoyta to Caborca for training as catechists; and to return 150 fugitives from Caborca and the other missions, who had taken refuge at Sonoyta.[44]

In the spring of 1751, the German-born Enrique Rhuen arrived at Sonoyta. However, Rhuen barely had a chance to establish himself at the new mission before being killed in a rebellion that attempted to wipe out the Spanish presence in the region. The Jesuits and, later, the Franciscans never attempted to establish a mission among the Papagos that would ensure the continued survival of the Papagos as a people with a distinct culture, and they merely continued to resettle Papago converts in the existing missions. As a consequence, many Papagos avoided mission life and prolonged contact with disease, which proved to be so disastrous for the residents of the mission villages. Sonoyta itself continued to exist as a Papago settlement at least until the 1770s, although not with the same number of residents as reported in earlier years. In October of 1775, Altar presidio Captain Bernardo de Urrea visited a number of Papago *rancherías,* including Sonoyta. Urrea and his company remained at the village for several days, and counted a population of eighty-three people.[45]

The resettlement of Papagos to the existing missions was an important, if not the single most important, element of the acculturation program in the Pimería Alta after 1751. A 1797 report summarized baptisms of recruits at selected missions from the arrival of the Franciscans in 1768 to 1796. The report records the baptism of 437 Papagos at six of the eight Pimería Alta missions, with the largest number resettled at Caborca, Bac, and Tumacacori. The populations of the last three named missions remained large in relation to the other missions until the collapse of the mission system in the 1820s and 1830s. The report also documents the growing ethnic diversity of the population of the Pimería Alta. The Franciscans baptized 143 *nijora* slaves from the Colorado River region (see below), plus another 70 converts from the same area who were identified by their tribal affiliation, 82 Gila Pimas, and 17 Seris and 20 Apaches who were most likely war captives (see Table 1.3).

Other Sonora ethnic-racial groups appear in the mission records. There was migration between missions in different parts of Sonora, and to the mining camps, farming hamlets, and ranches inhabited by the growing Spanish-mestizo population. Yaquis and, to a lesser degree, Opatas and Nebomes (southern Pimas), settled or were resettled to the Pimería Alta

Table 1.3 Baptisms of Converts at Selected Pimería Alta Missions, 1768–1796

Mission	Papago	Pima	Nijora	Apache	Seri	Pima	Yuma	Jalchedon	Cajuenche
Caborca	111	23	117	2	17	1	3	2	1
Bac	209		5			58	32		
Tubutama	44						21		
Saric	7		5	3			4		
San Ignacio	1		7	3					
Tumacacori	65		9	12			7		

Source: Daniel Matson and Bernard Fontana, trans. and ed., *Fray Bringas Reports to the King* (Tucson, 1977), pp. 135–50.

missions and surrounding communities as catechists, servants, and laborers. Moreover, prominent settlers benefited from the constant warfare on the Sonora frontier and a regional slave trade to bring war captives into their households. Local officials placed Apache and Seri children under the care of settler families in order to promote their acculturation. Settlers also promoted a trade in war captives known as *nijoras,* from the Colorado River region. The Jesuit and Franciscan missionaries stationed in the missions baptized the children of the different Indian ethnic groups in the region, as summarized in Table 1.4.

A second important pattern was the settlement of Spanish-mestizo colonists in northern Sonora, and the transformation of the frontier society and the ethnic-racial composition of the population of many of the mission villages. In a number of the older missions, colonists who settled in the mission villages overwhelmed and marginalized the surviving Pima population, and, in most instances, usurped Pima lands. In the case of Ymuris *visita* of San Ignacio mission, for example, settlers completely displaced the Pima population. In the Altar Valley communities, settlers numerically outnumbered Pimas, and most likely, they successfully competed for land and water resources. In 1801–1802, 158 Pimas and 260 settlers lived in the five missions in the valley, in addition to the settlers living in ranches and small mining camps in the area. On the other hand, several villages retained a large Pima population because of the resettlement of Papagos. For example, the Pima population of the three villages of Caborca mission was 353, mostly recent converts; 105 settlers living in the mission villages; and 360 and 31, respectively, in the two villages of San Francisco Xavier del Bac mission (see Table 1.5).[46]

Table 1.4 Baptisms of Different Ethnic Groups Recorded at Selected Pimería Alta Missions

Mission	Years	Pima	Opata	Yaqui	Seri	Apache	Nijora	Nebome	Yuma
Cucurpe	1684–1711	4	444	2	12	0	0	0	0
Cucurpe	1686–1703	1	82	14	5	0	0	1	0
Magdalena	1698–1718	258	0	0	0	6	1	0	0
Magdalena	1744–1776	211	1	5	0	5	17	0	0
Magdalena	1810–1830	24	1	91	0	3	0	0	11
San Ignacio	1720–1762	2,625	4	37	10	10	70	0	0
Soamca	1732–1768	1,641	0	1	0	10	8	0	0
Soamca	1743–1753	361	0	0	0	1	0	0	0
Guevavi	1741–1763	1,144	2	4	1	10	20	0	1
Tumacacori	1773–1825	290	1	9	0	18	5	0	19
Ati	1757–1827	347	0	3	0	1	13	0	2
Oquitoa	1757–1841	533	3	4	0	7	19	0	8
Oquitoa	1778–1830	3	0	43	0	0	7	0	3
Caborca	1764–1838	1,121	22	66	2	1	55	0	100
Tubutama	1768–1833	241	3	13	0	2	12	0	9
Tubutama	1804–1837	24	6	20	0	0	0	0	1
Bisanig	1768 1803	296	1	1	0	1	23	0	0
Pitiqui	1772–1845	325	2	68	7	0	36	1	8
Cocospera	1822–1836	64	0	0	0	0	0	0	1
Total		9,513	512	381	37	75	286	2	163

Source: Altar Parish Archive, Altar, Sonora; Bancroft Library, University of California, Berkeley, California; and Magdalena Parish Archive, Magdalena de Kino, Sonora.

Table 1.5 The Population of the Pimería Alta Missions, 1801–1802 by Ethnic/Racial Group

Community	Pima	Yaqui	Opata	Apache	Seri	Colorado R.Groups	*Gente de Razón*
Bac	114	0	0	2	0	11	31
Tucson	246	0	0	0	0	0	0
Tumacacori	65	1	2	0	0	10	29
Cocospera	65	9	7	0	0	1	16
San Ignacio	41	12	6	0	0	3	44
Magdalena	64	0	1	0	0	1	8
Terrenate	0	0	0	0	0	0	67
Ymuris	0	5	0	0	0	0	95
San Lorenzo	1	0	1	0	0	2	46
Santa Ana	0	4	0	0	0	2	105
Saric	19	0	1	1	0	6	8
Tubutama	23	13	2	3	0	6	117
Santa Teresa	17	0	0	0	0	0	0
Ati	48	2	0	0	0	16	131
Oquitoa	51	0	0	0	0	7	4
Caborca	181	10	8	0	5	32	71
Pitiqui	85	3	0	0	2	4	9
Bisanig	87	4	0	0	0	1	25
Total	1,107	63	28	6	7	102	806

Source: Individual Parish Polls, Archivo General Eclesiastico de la Mitra de Sonora, Hermosillo, Sonora.

During the first seventy years of the Jesuit ministry in the Pimería Alta, the missionaries achieved some success in reducing a segment of the northern Pima population to a semblance of village life in nucleated mission communities, although shortages of personnel limited the scope of the planned program of acculturation to those villages located in the principal river valleys with the greatest agricultural potential. Growing stresses of cultural and social change within the mission villages, coupled with resource competition between Indian and settler and increased raiding by hostile Indian groups, generated resistance to the acculturation program in the 1750s, which stalled efforts to expand the number of missions. By the 1760s and 1770s the Jesuit and, later, the Franciscan missionaries altered the strategy by placing more emphasis on repopulating the existing mission villages through the resettlement of Papago converts.

ructure of northern Sonoran society changed during the course of nteenth century, with the expansion of the settler population and evelopment of a market economy based upon mining and ranching agriculture, which supplied the populations of the mining centers with od and leather. Prospects for commercial agriculture created competition between settlers and mission Indians over access to water and land, and the decline of the Pima population left lands traditionally cultivated by Pimas underutilized and thus subject to usurpation by settlers. Settlers brought war captives, slaves, and Indian workers from central and southern Sonora into their households and economic operations, thus contributing to the ethnic and racial diversity of the region. The Pima population increasingly became marginalized both socially and spatially within the mision communities, and in the nineteenth century the surviving northern Pimas were absorbed into the growing mestizo population in Sonora. Biological and cultural *mestizaje* (mestizoization) in the missions, mining camps, ranches, and farming hamlets, together with the decline in numbers of the northern Pima population, led to the transformation of Sonoran society in ways not originally envisioned by the Jesuit missionaries.

Between 1818 and 1822, agricultural production in the fourteen Pimería Alta mission villages totaled 5,942 *fanegas* of wheat (a *fanega* equals 2.6 bushels), but only 313 *fanegas* of corn, which was the principal grain grown by the northern Pimas prior to the arrival of the Spaniards.[47] The dramatic change in northern Pima agricultural production seem to indicate two possible patterns: that the Indians remaining in the missions geared production for a local market-oriented economy, either on their own initiative or under pressure from the Franciscan missionaries or civil officials; and that patterns of consumption may have changed, with the Indians eating more wheat than corn, which seems to indicate a significant change in northern Pima culture. These interpretations raise a third possible question: How ethnically Pima were the "Pimas" living in the missions?

The children of some Pimas passed from the ranks of the "*republica de indios*" to the mass of the *castas* (Afro-mestizos and Indo-mestizos) through the process of *mestizaje* (cultural or biological miscegenation). Furthermore, "ethnic mingling", intermarriage among different Indian groups, also occurred. The evidence suggests that *mestizaje* occurred on a small scale in the Pimería Alta, but it is difficult to quantify a social process that was subtle and was mentioned on the basis of a highly subjective criteria in different documents that described the characteristics of the frontier population. The church did not legitimize all interracial or interethnic pairings, and as such, the record of mixed unions does not always appear in the sacramental registers. Moreover, *mestizaje* most commonly took place in the mining camps, ranches, military garrisons, and farming communities, when Pimas and other Indians lived among the racially and ethnically mixed northern Sonora settlers, but only fragments of the sacramental registers from these settlements survive.

An examination of samples of marriages abstracted from extant marriage registers from selected Pimería Alta missions shows that few mixed marriages took place under the auspices of the church. For the purposes of this analysis, ten-year samples of marriages are examined from several missions, with the data divided into five discrete categories: marriages between Pimas and Pimas, between Pimas and other Indians, between Pimas and non-Indians, between non-Indians and Indians, and Indian marriages that failed to specify the ethnicity of the couples. For purposes of comparison, data from the farming community of Santa Ana, located in the Pimería Alta, is included. Of a sample of 256 marriages only 4 (1.6 percent) involved Pimas and non-Pimas, and another 28 (11 percent) between Pimas and other Indians. There is no clear evidence from Santa Ana of unions between Pimas and non-Indians because the parish priest generally used the category *Indian* without specifying the ethnic identification of the Indians (see Table 1.6).

Table 1.6 Interracial and Interethnic Marriages at Selected Pimería Alta Missions and the *Puesto* of Santa Ana

Mission	Years	Pima–Pima	Pima–Other Indian	Pima–Razon*	Razon–Indian	Unspecified
Tumacacori	1771–1781	34	1	1	0	28
Pitiquito	1791–1810	17	2	1	0	1
San Ignacio	1768–1778	29	5	1	0	5
Caborca	1769–1779	54	8	0	0	16
Caborca	1790–1800	34	11	1	0	8
Santa Ana	1778–1795	0	1	0	5**	7
Total		168	26	4	5	65***

**Gente de Razón* was a generic term for settlers, as distinguished from mission Indians.
**This category may include marriages between Pimas and non-Indians.
***Cases of marriages in which the ethnic/racial identity of the marriage partners is not recorded, but the majority probably were marriages between Pimas and Pimas.
Source: Robert H. Jackson, "Causes of Indian Population Decline in the Pimería Alta Missions of Northern Sonora," *The Journal of Arizona History* 24 (1983), p. 419.

Detailed parish and mission censuses prepared at the end of the eighteenth century indicate that mixed unions may have been more common in the Pimería Alta than the marriage records show. Several of the 1796 and 1801 censuses record families of Pimas and non-Indians, and Pimas with Yumas, Opatas, and Yaquis. The census data show a higher instance of Pimas establishing unions with other Indians. Sixteen of the unions sampled (7 percent) were of Pimas and other Indians, and six (2.6 percent) marriages of Pimas and non-Indians. Moreover, in the case of mixed unions, ethnic or racial identification followed that of the father. Children who were biologically mestizos could be and were classified by the missionaries as being Pimas. This being the case, an argument could be made that the populations of the less populous Pimería Alta missions, those with only a small number of recent converts, had become, by the first two decades of the nineteenth century, biologically and perhaps culturally mestizo, but the Franciscans continued to categorize them as Pimas (see Table 1.7). It was through this biological process and the related cultural transformation that the Pimas still living in the missions could be absorbed into the growing frontier mestizo-settler population in northern Sonora following the collapse of the mission system in the 1820s after Mexican independence.

Whereas *mestizaje* occurred on a limited scale in the missions, it was the fluid social conditions in the mining camps in northern Sonora, which attracted seasonal labor from the Pimería Alta and other Sonora missions, that most likely contributed to and facilitated the establishment of mixed unions, both legitimate and illicit in the eyes of the church.[48] *Mestizaje,* in

Table 1.7 Mixed Unions at Selected Pimería Alta Missions in 1796 and 1801, as Recorded in Parish Censuses

Mission	Year	Total Families	*Pima–Razón*	Pima–Indian
San Ignacio and its visita	1801	117	2	4
Tubutama	1796	47	1	0
Tumacacori	1801	26	1	7
Cocospera	1801	28	2	1
Saric	1801	9	0	4
Total		227	6	16

Source: Robert H. Jackson, "Causes of Indian Population Decline in the Pimería Alta Missions of Northern Sonora," *The Journal of Arizona History* 24 (1983), p. 420.

both its biological and cultural manifestations and patterns of seasonal and permanent migration to the mining camps and other settler communities in northern Sonora, contributed to the relative and actual decline of the mission populations.

The Baja California Mission Frontier, 1697–1840

Beginning in 1697, the Jesuits and, later, the Franciscans and Dominicans developed an extensive system of missions in Baja California. Differences in the social and economic organization of the Indian tribelets were encountered in Baja California, and ecological considerations modified the development of the program of acculturation. Whereas in the Pimería Alta mission system the missionaries organized mission communities at existing settlements, the missionaries in Baja California created villages from scratch at sites suitable for agriculture with materials for building construction. However, the Baja California mission frontier was different in several respects from the northern Sonora mission frontier. There was little in Baja California to attract large numbers of settlers, so the peninsula establishments developed in relative isolation. In contrast to patterns documented for northern Sonora, little ethnic mingling or cultural and biological *mestizaje* occurred in the Baja California missions. Moreover, since the Indian population in Baja California was small and the missionaries established communities throughout the peninsula, Jesuit, Franciscan, and Dominican missionaries were unable to repopulate the existing missions with new recruits once they completed the congregation of the Indian population in the district assigned to each mission.

There were few sites suitable for agriculture in the arid Baja California peninsula, and most mission communities, particularly those with sizable populations, did not grow enough food to support the entire population at the mission community (*cabecera*). Therefore, the Jesuits organized a rotational system under which the population of outlying settlements came to the *cabecera* on a regular basis to receive religious instruction and food.[49] In the satellite villages, the Indians continued to hunt and collect food as they had done prior to the arrival of the missionaries, and most likely, they continued to practice their traditional religious beliefs. The level of religious instruction was superficial at best, and some missionaries even complained about the persistence of pre-Hispanic religious beliefs.[50] On the other hand, missionaries stationed at some missions claimed a high level of understanding of Christian doctrine by the converts.[51]

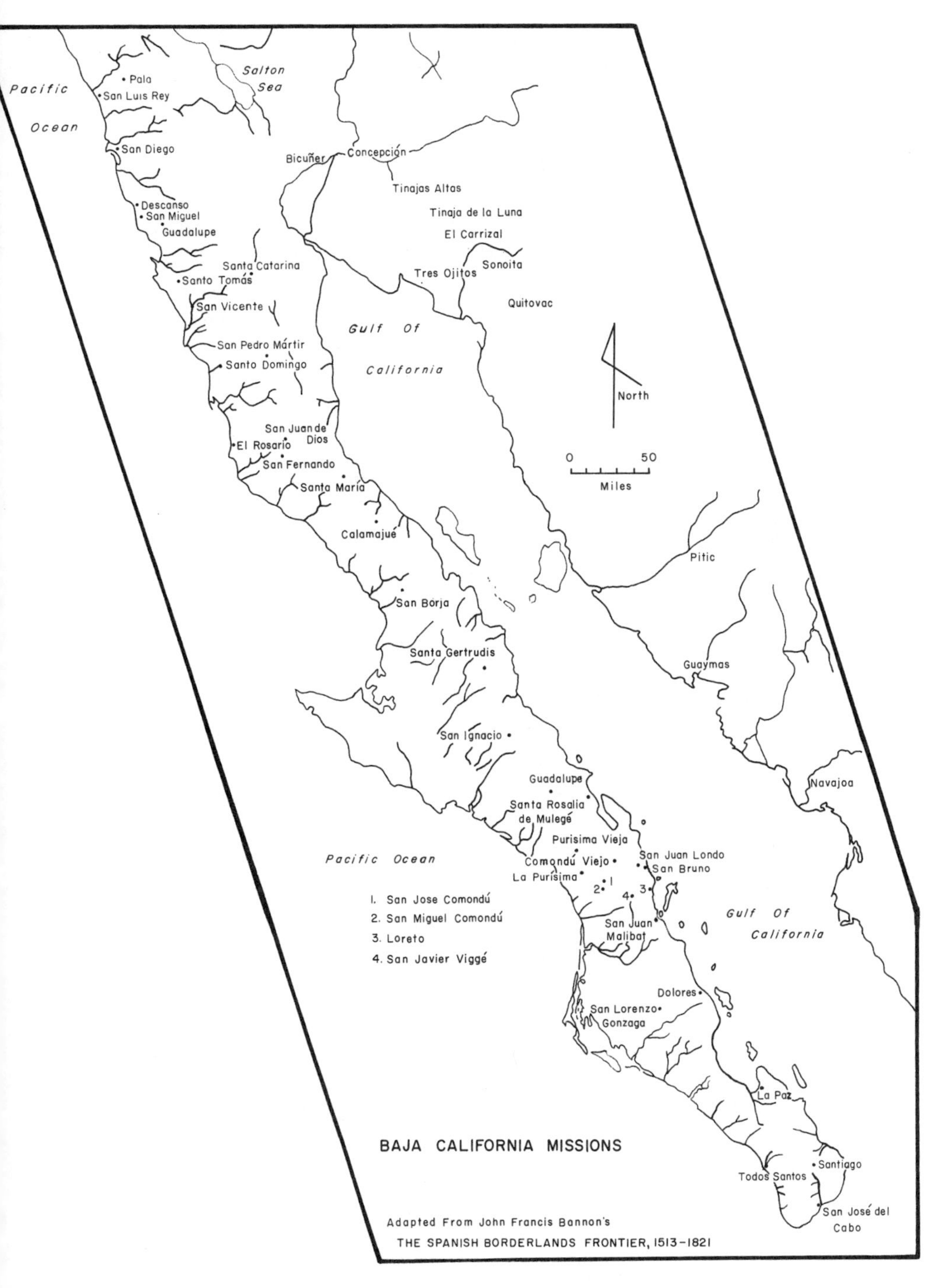

Baja California Missions

In the early stages of the mission program in Baja California, the bulk of the Indian population resided in satellite villages. In 1726, for example, Jesuit missionary Everard Helen counted 1,707 converts living in thirty-two *rancherías.*[52] Most of the satellite settlements were villages only in name, and they had no improvements in the way of Spanish-style housing or irrigation systems for agriculture. However, there were exceptions. For example, Jesuits directed the development of agriculture and the construction of buildings at San Miguel Cadandogmo, a *visita* of San Francisco Xavier mission that eventually became a mission with a resident missionary because of the agricultural potential of the site.

As the Indian populations declined, the missionaries congregated the survivors into a smaller number of villages and eventually relocated the remaining population to the *cabeceras.* There were also instances of the transfer of Indians to the jurisdiction of other missions. In 1728, following the establishment of San Ignacio mission, the Jesuits transferred twelve *rancherías* from the jurisdiction of Guadalupe mission to that of the new establishment, leaving the missionary stationed at the former mission responsible for twenty *rancherías.*[53] In 1771, the entire population of Guadalupe mission lived at the *cabecera,* although some crops were still grown at the sites of two former *visitas.*[54]

The period in which the congregation of the Indian populations was completed varied in the different parts of the peninsula. In the central part of Baja California, where the Jesuits established eight missions in the first half of the eighteenth century, the congregation of the Indian populations had been largely completed by 1768. Between 1728 and 1769, the Jesuits and Franciscans organized four mission communities in the Central Desert region. In the 1770s and 1780s, the Dominicans completed the congregation of the Indian populations and, as the numbers of converts died, relocated a larger percentage of the Indians at the *cabecera.* From the 1720s to the late 1730s the Jesuits established six missions in the southern part of the peninsula. Severe epidemics and two revolts rapidly reduced the number of converts, and in 1768 civil officials redistributed the converts living in the missions to a smaller number of establishments in a final congregation plan. Between 1774 and 1834, the Dominicans established nine mission communities on the northern Pacific Coast section of Baja California. The congregation of Indians in the mission communities was an ongoing process in the Dominican establishments until the collapse of the mission system in the late 1830s, following the passage of a secularization decree for the Baja California mission by a liberal Mexican congress.[55]

The Alta California Mission Frontier, 1769–1840

In 1769, a Spanish expedition organized in Baja California established a mission and military garrison at the port of San Diego. Over the following seventy years, Franciscan missionaries founded twenty-one mission communities and numerous satellite settlements in Alta California. As in Baja California, the Franciscans in Alta California selected mission sites on the basis of their suitability for agriculture and ranching, and the availability of building materials. However, the damper climate and greater water resources allowed the Franciscans to develop large-scale agriculture in Alta California and, in most cases, to congregate all or a large percentage of the Indian converts at the *cabecera*. A part of the Indian population lived and worked in outlying farms and ranches, generally identified in contemporary documents as *ranchos* or *labores*. In several of the missions found in the drier sections of Alta California, *ranchos* located at some distance from the *cabecera* became significant population centers. For example, San Antonio de Pala was a *rancho* of San Luis Rey mission, with a large resident population.[56]

Ecological conditions varied within the area of effective Spanish control along the coast of Alta California, but in general, the agricultural-ranching economies of the missions could support a larger percentage of the Indian population at the *cabecera* than was the case in Baja California. Moreover, surpluses produced in the missions may have been used as one way of attracting new converts, and the replenishment of the labor supply through the recruitment of converts became a critical element in the continued development of the mission economies. In contrast to the pattern observed in the Baja California missions, where a decline in total numbers occurred once the bulk of the local Indian population was congregaed into the missions, the Franciscan missionaries stationed in Alta California successfully resettled new converts from *rancherías* located at greater distances from the *cabecera* to replace those who died. The demographic collapse of the Indian populations living in the missions was masked during periods of active recruitment. The population in the missions grew despite the fact that these populations were not viable and could not expand or maintain existing levels through natural reproduction.

The method of recruitment has generated controversy among scholars, especially with the argument that the military working closely with the missionaries applied levels of coercion to force Indians to relocate to the missions. One important Indian response to mission life was flight on an individual basis, in small groups, or in large groups. According to one document prepared in 1817, a total of 3,205 Indians successfully fled from fifteen Alta California missions, which works out as an average of 5.95 percent of the cumulative total of baptisms at the fifteen establishments, with a high of 15 percent at San Carlos mission.[57] Spanish and Mexican officials and missionaries responded by organizing expeditions to recapture fugitives and punish tribelets that sheltered the fugitives. Between 1800 and 1841 there were at least fifty-one major expeditions into the Sacramento and San Joaquín valleys.[58] Although not absolutely conclusive, the evidence strongly suggests that the military expeditions did bring pagans back to be resettled at the missions.

The population of the missions fluctuated from year to year, as the missionaries established new missions and repopulated the existing establishments. Two distinct phases of recruitment and population growth appear in the record. Between 1769 and 1804, the Franciscans established nineteen missions and congregated the bulk of the Indian populations living in the coastal region into the missions. Over the next ten years, the populations dropped as the number of recruits brought into the missions was insufficient to replace the growing number of converts who died. The mission populations grew again after 1815, as the Franciscans began congregating larger numbers of converts from tribelets living further inland, such as the Miwoks and the Yokuts from the Sacramento and San Joaquín valleys and the Cahuillas from the interior valleys east of San Diego, San Luis Rey, and San Gabriel missions. The Franciscans also established two new missions during this period. The expansion of the mission populations abruptly ended in the mid-1820s, as the interior groups more effectively resisted the recruitment efforts of the Franciscans and as large-scale flight increasingly threatened the security of the missions and reduced the size of the mission labor force. Moreover, certain Central Valley tribelets adopted a more active form of resistance to the missions and the growing settler population, and initiated raids on the herds of mission livestock, especially horses, which provided food and greater mobility. The decline of the mission populations accelerated with the exodus of more than half of the Indians living in the missions prior to and following the implementation of the 1834 secularization decree, which removed control of the missions from the hands of the Franciscans.

An examination of population levels in the seven missions located immediately south of San Francisco Bay demonstrates the instability of the mission populations. Between 1775 and 1790, the mean population of the first three missions established in the area (San Carlos, San Antonio, and San Luis Obispo, founded between 1770 and 1772) rose from 247 in the first year to 801. In the 1790s, the Franciscans established four new missions and intensified their recruitment efforts. The Indian population living in the missions rose from 2,403 in three establishments, in 1790, to 5,936 in seven establishments fifteen years later. The mean population of the seven missions was 848 in 1805. The number of recruits entering the missions dropped after 1805, and the population of the seven missions declined to 4,476 and a mean of 639 in 1820, 3,041 and a mean of 500 in 1830, and 1,224 and a mean of 175 in 1839(see Appendix 4).

The fluctuations in the population of the seven missions discussed above resulted both from patterns of congregation and mortality. During periods of the resettlement of large numbers of converts to the mission communities, the populations grew, but then declined when the number of Indians brought to live in the missions dropped. Appendix 5 summarizes baptisms, burials, and population at the seven central Alta California missions, distinguishing between births recorded in the missions and the baptism of converts congregated to the mission communities.

The Franciscans stationed at San Carlos mission (established in 1770) actively recruited converts from the Monterey Bay region, Salinas Valley, and Carmel Valley between 1771 and 1799, and a final wave of converts from 1804 to 1808. During the first period, the Franciscans baptized 1,294 converts, an average of 46 per year, and recorded a population of 886 in 1795, which was the highest recorded population at the mission. During the second phase of recruitment, from 1804 to 1808, the Franciscans baptized 138 converts, an average of some 27 per year. After 1808, the Franciscans did not resettle Indians to the mission community.

There were two distinctive phases of recruitment at San Antonio mission (established in 1771): the congregation of the local Indian population between 1771 and 1810, and the relocation of Yokuts from the Central Valley between 1834 and 1838. During the first period, the Franciscans baptized 2,026 converts resettled to the mission, an average of nearly 52 each year. In 1805, 1,296 Indians lived in San Antonio, the largest number recorded in the history of the mission. Between 1834 and 1838, the Franciscans baptized 66 Yokuts, an average of 13 per year. However, it is not clear if the Yokuts settled at the mission or were put to work on the ranches being established in the Salinas Valley and nearby areas.

The pattern of congregation at San Luis Obispo (established in 1772) was similar to the pattern described for San Antonio. The Franciscans relocated converts to the mission from 1772 to 1813, and again in the mid-1830s. During the first period (the record for the years 1783 and 1784 is incomplete), the Franciscans baptized 1,426 converts, or an average of nearly 38 per year. In 1804, 961 Indians lived at San Luis Obispo, the largest recorded population. In the years 1834 to 1838, 178 Indians, most likely Central Valley Yokuts, received the waters of baptism, an average of some 36 per year.

The Franciscans established two new missions during the fall of 1791. The first was Santa Cruz, located on the northern shore of Monterey Bay. The missionaries resettled Indians to the mission throughout its history, but two distinctive phases of congregation appear in the record. From 1791 to 1811, the Franciscans baptized 988 converts from the Monterey Bay area and nearby inland valleys, an average of some 49 each year. The largest number of Indians recorded at the mission was 523 in 1795, while the Franciscans continued to congregate the Indian population in the immediate environs of the mission. Between 1813 and 1839, the Franciscans baptized another 411 converts from the inland valleys east of the mission and the Central Valley, or an average of some 16 per year.

In 1791, the Franciscans also established Soledad mission, located in the middle Salinas Valley. Three phases of congregation can be seen in the Soledad mission baptismal registers. From 1791 to 1813, the Franciscans stationed at the mission baptized 1,209 converts recruited in the Salinas Valley and surrounding areas, an average of 55 per year. Another 280 converts, 35 per year, received baptism from 1815 to 1823. Finally, from 1828 to 1835, 155 converts, mostly Yokuts, were baptized, averaging 19 per year. The largest number of Indians recorded at the mission was 688 in 1805.

In 1797, the Franciscans established two more missions in central Alta California: San Juan Bautista, located in the San Benito Valley, and San Miguel, in the upper Salinas Valley. There were two distinct phases of congregation at San Juan Bautista mission. From 1797 to 1808, the Franciscans baptized 1,493 converts, or 124 per year. From 1810 to 1834 another 1,138 conerts received baptism, an average of 47 per year. However, the Franciscans baptized the largest group, Yokuts from the Central Valley, during the 1820s. In 1823, 1,248 Indians lived at San Juan Bautista, the largest recorded population.

The Franciscans stationed at San Miguel baptized the bulk of the Indian population in the upper Salinas Valley between 1797 and 1816. During these years, 1,392 converts received baptism, averaging 73 per year. The largest recorded population at San Miguel was 1,078 in 1814. The Franciscans baptized a handful of converts in the 1820s, and 261 Central Valley Yokuts, an average of 65 per year, between 1832 and 1835.

In all seven cases, the Franciscans completed resettling the local Indian population in the mission communities in twenty to thirty years. After about 1815 the Franciscans, working closely with the military, began relocating Central Valley Yokuts in the missions. However, Yokuts baptized after 1834 may have been brought to work on the ranches being created by settlers from mission lands once the secularization process began. Patterns of congregation were similar at the other fourteen missions in Alta California.

In 1810, independence wars began in central Mexico, and continued for the next eleven years. In 1821, Mexico became independent, and politicians influenced by liberal ideology questioned the need for the frontier missions. Policies implemented in the 1820s and 1830s resulted in varying degrees in the dissolution of the mission communities. The following section outlines the impact of these policies on the mission communities in the Pimería Alta, Baja California, and Alta California.

Secularization and the Dissolution of the Mission Communities

In 1813, the liberal Spanish Cortes (the parliament) legislated the secularization (the conversion of missions to parishes and the distribution of mission property to Indian converts) of frontier missions in Spanish America as a measure in fostering the integration of Indian converts in colonial society. However, the restoration in 1814 of Ferdinand VII led to the suspension of all laws enacted by the Cortes, and the viceregal government in Mexico City never enforced the law.[59] After Mexico became independent in 1821, there was increasing discussion of the secularization of the missions.[60] Moreover, there was growing anti-Spanish sentiment in Mexico, which led to two expulsion decrees in the late 1820s that forced many Spanish-born missionaries to abandon the frontier missions.[61] Finally, in 1833, a short-lived liberal congress decreed the secularization of surviving frontier missions, especially those in the Californias.[62]

The anticlerical and anti-Spanish Mexican policies of the 1820s and 1830s had a different impact on the frontier missions in northwestern Mexico. In the Pimería Alta, the growth of the settler population and the continued decline of the northern Pima population in the first three decades of the nineteenth century resulted in the marginalization of the surviving Pima population, the transformation of many of the Pimería Alta missions into settler communities, and the absorption of the remaining northern Pimas into the growing frontier mestizo population that also took much of the land formerly assigned to the missions. The 1827 Spanish expulsion decree led to the exodus of Franciscans from the apostolic college of Santa Cruz de Querétaro, the missionary college that staffed the Pimería Alta missions, and shortages of missionaries in northern Sonora. Finally, the chronic fiscal difficulties of the newly independent Mexican government resulted in the underfunding of the military garrisons in Sonora and the end of government subsidies for Apache bands that had accepted peace and a form of reservation life in the late eighteenth and early nineteenth centuries. Apache raiding of northern Sonora began again, forcing the abandonment of exposed communities. Early in 1849, for example, the Indian population of Tumacacori abandoned the former mission because of Apache attacks.[63]

The collapse of the Baja California missions following Mexican independence was similar in some respects to the case of the Pimería Alta missions. With the exception of the northern Dominican missions, the Indian population in the peninsula missions was substantially reduced in number by the early and middle nineteenth century, and was increasingly marginalized by the growing mestizo-settler population. In 1829, 646 converts lived in seven northern missions, and a mere 19 at San Fernando (established in 1769). In 1857, the settler population of San Ignacio mission (established in 1728) was 281, and 1,091 at San José del Cabo (established in 1730). In the same year, 26 and 3 people, respectively, lived in Santa Gertrudis (established in 1751) and in San Fernando.[64]

The decline of the Indian population led to the closure of two missions in 1794–1795, because the number of converts was too small to justify the cost of stationing a missionary in the communities. The government transferred the population of two closed missions to other missions.[65] Between 1822 and 1825, the government suppressed the older missions. Different sources give the date for the suppression of the missions as 1822, 1823, or 1825.[66] An 1825 *reglamento* implemented by California governor Echeandia attempted to emancipate the converts in the missions, removed control of mission temporalities from the hands of the Dominican missionaries, and distributed mission property to the Indians. The Dominicans protested Echeandia's measure.[67] Despite efforts to apply the 1833 secularization decree to the remaining missions in the peninsula, the northern missions continued to operate under the spiritual and temporal supervision of the missionaries at least until 1840, when one of the last Dominicans was driven from the missions by hostile Indians, and 1849, when the last mission was finally abandoned.[68] Nevertheless, the expulsion of Spaniards in the late 1820s made it difficult to staff the Baja California missions, and as early as 1822 the remaining Dominicans complained about not having received government stipends for several years.[69]

The growing number of settlers in Baja California, and not the few surviving Indians who continued to live in the former missions, benefited from the secularization of the missions. As was the case in the Pimería Alta, settlers received government grants of land from the lands originally assigned to the missions. As early as the 1790s, soldiers and settlers received former mission lands; but it was only with the passage of colonization laws by the Mexican government, which were designed to populate northern frontier territories, that settlers and soldiers received title to those extensive tracts of former mission lands. In northern Baja California, for example, prominent settlers from San Diego and Los Angeles received former mission lands. Further south, the descendants of soldiers stationed in the missions operated ranches.[70]

The Pimería Alta and Baja California missions were already declining when the Mexican government enacted anti-Spanish and anticlerical measures. The Alta California missions, on the other hand, still flourished, and thousands of Indians still lived in the establishments. The 1820s and 1830s legislation had a more drastic impact on the missions.

The Alta California missions survived the Mexican-independence wars relatively untouched, but they were specifically targeted for closure by liberal-minded politicians, under the leadership of Valentín Gómez Farias, who briefly controlled the national government in 1833. The so-called Pious Fund, the endowment for the California-mission enterprise originally set up by the Jesuits in the early eighteenth century to finance the cost of missions in Baja California, became a target for politicians who favored disentailing church wealth in Mexico, while liberals who advocated integrating Indians in society supported secularization of the missions.[71] From the standpoint of Mexican liberals, the disentailment of the wealth of the Alta California missions was generally successful, since the partition of the mission estates played an important role in the growth of the Alta California economy and opened lands for the colonization of a strategic, but underpopulated and thus vulnerable, frontier region. However, the intnt of liberal reformers was deflected by a second political development: the establishment of autonomy in the mid-1830s by local politicians who directed the implementation of the secularization decree in its later stages. Were the Indian converts fully integrated into the emerging frontier society?

The historiography of the Alta California missions generally focuses on a single aspect of the secularization process, the civil administration of the mission estates following the removal of Franciscan control over the temporalities (mission economies and labor supply), and the appropriation by prominent colonists and politicians of much of the mission lands, goods, and livestock.[72] Until recently, the discussion of secularization concentrated almost exclusively on the partition of the mission estates, while the fate of the former converts received little if no attention.[73]

The implementation of the secularization decree in Alta California, beginning in 1834, did not signal an immediate change in the legal status of the converts living in the mission communities. The legal emancipation of the mission Indians, their conversion from the status of state wards to free citizens, was a gradual process that began in the late 1820s, but was not completed until after 1840. However, the breakdown of social control in the missions in the 1830s, with the transition from control by the missionaries to state-appointed administrators, contributed to an exodus of Indians from the missions.

Prior to 1834, the Mexican government experimented with a loosening of social controls in the missions by emancipating a small number of more acculturated converts. Emancipation had a dual meaning. Not only were the Indians freed from the control of the missionaries, but they were also legally able to take their place in Mexican society as free citizens with the right to settle where they pleased. In concrete terms, one of the most immediate changes brought about by emancipation was the right to refuse to labor in the communal projects in the missions and, at least theoretically, not to be subjected to whippings and other forms of corporal punishment and imprisonment on the orders of the missionaries. The first emancipation decree of July 25, 1826, emancipated a small number of converts living in the mission communities within the jurisdiction of the San Diego, Santa Barbara, and Monterey presidios. In 1828, the government extended the initial emancipation decree to the missions in the jurisdiction of San Francisco presidio, excluding the recently established San Rafael and San Francisco Solano missions. The initial emancipation plan also called for the establishment of a community of free Indians near San Fernando mission—a plan that was never carried out.[74] Most, if not all, of the emancipated Indians migrated to the emerging towns in the province. For example, emancipated Indians settled in the growing town of Monterey and nearby ranches, as reported in the annual reports prepared by the missionaries stationed at San Carlos mission.[75]

The impact of the presecularization emancipation decrees can be measured by documenting changes in the number of Indians living at the seven nonmission settlements in Alta California prior to 1834. There was an increase in the number of Indians living at the seven communities from 154 in 1825 to 427 in 1830, and then a decline of from 435 in 1832 to 406

Table 1.8 Population of Indians Living at Non-Mission Settlements in Alta California

Settlement	1825	1830	1832	1834
San Diego Presidio	52	78	65	67
Montery Presidio	37	67	89	52
San Francisco Presidio	10	48	30	27
Santa Barbara Presidio	9	8	11	13
Los Angeles	23	198	189	178
San José	15	20	40	60
Branciforte	8	8	11	9
Total	154	427	435	406

Source: Ms. "Mission Statistics," Bancroft Library, University of California, Berkeley.

two years later (see Table 1.8). Los Angeles was the single largest center of nonmission Indian settlement, which was related to the larger number of emancipations in the southern missions. In 1825 a mere 23 Indians reportedly lived at Los Angeles, but the number increased to 311 three years later in 1828 (see Table 1.9).

Table 1.9 Population of Indians at Monterey Presidio and Los Angeles, 1825–1837

Year	Monterey Presidio	Los Angeles
1825	37	23
1826	35	25
1827	27	27
1828	51	311
1829	48	253
1830	67	198
1831	110	162
1832	89	189
1833	63	201
1834	52	178
1836	39	—
1837	65	—

Source: Ms. "Mission Statistics," Bancroft Library, University of California, Berkeley.

Table 1.10 Population of Adult Male Indians at Monterey Presidio and Los Angeles, 1825–1837

Year	Monterey Presidio	% of Total Population	Los Angeles	% of Total Population
1825	12	32	5	22
1826	14	40	6	24
1827	10	37	7	26
1828	30	59	198	64
1829	26	54	152	60
1830	33	49	107	54
1831	71	66	64	40
1832	40	45	61	32
1833	31	49	67	33
1834	35	67	52	29
1836	28	72	—	—
1837	40	62	—	—

Source: Ms. "Mission Statistics," Bancroft Library, University of California, Berkeley.

A close examination of the patterns of Indian settlement at Monterey presidio and in Los Angeles sheds further light on the short-term impact of the 1826 and 1828 emancipation decrees. Between 1827 and 1828 the Indian population in both settlements increased, with the greatest increase occurring in Los Angeles. The numbers gradually declined in subsequent years, however, as Indians apparently left the area. The Indian population of Monterey nearly doubled between 1827 and 1828, but did not reach a presecularization high of 110 until 1831 (see Table 1.9). The majority of the Indians leaving the missions in the late 1820s were adult males. At Los Angeles, for example, adult males constituted 22 percent of the total Indian population in 1825, but they increased to 64 percent in 1828. Similarly, the percentage of adult males in the Indian population of Monterey ranged from 49 percent to 72 percent between 1828 and 1837 (see Table 1.10). Where the adult males who left Los Angeles between 1829 to 1834 went is not known, although many probably went to work on ranches being created in the region by prominent local politicians and colonists.

The second stage of emancipation began in May of 1833, as local politicians discussed the secularization of the missions. Governor José Figueroa (1833–1835), over the objections of the Franciscans, provisionally decreed the emancipation of a larger number of the converts still living primarily in the southern missions. The 1833 decree also set in motion a social experiment at San Juan Capistrano mission (established in 1776). In October of the same year, the governor emancipated all of the Indians living at the mission and created a *pueblo de indios,* a formal pueblo inhabited by former mission Indians. The governor justified this experiment on the grounds that the Indians at the older establishment were sufficiently acculturated to take their place in society. The creation of the *pueblo de indios* entailed the distribution of mission lands to the Indians, generally lands that they had already exploited for their own subsistence needs. In the following year, the provincial government initiated the secularization of San Juan Capistrano mission, and appointed a civil administrator to manage the Indians. The return of the Indians to a form of subjugation similar to the coercive social controls previously exercised by the Franciscans disrupted the development of the Indian pueblo. In the late 1830s, the Indians at San Juan Capistrano complained about the administrator, especially his attempts to get the Indians to work for his personal benefit and the benefit of local ranchers. Moreover, the Indians complained about the granting of mission lands and goods to prominent settlers and politicians. Discontent led to desertion from the community. In 1834, 861 Indians lived at San Juan Capistrano, and in 1840 there were 500, of whom only some 100 were residents of the Indian pueblo proper. The provincial government dissolved the Indian pueblo in July of 1841, and distributed the pueblo lands between the remaining Indians and local settlers, in an effort to promote the development of a more stable community.[76]

The immediate result of the 1833 emancipation decree was to reduce the labor force available to the missionaries, since most of the newly liberated converts refused to work under the same coercive labor system in the missions. For example, the Franciscans stationed at San Luis Rey mission reported in June of 1833 that many, if not most, of the recently emancipated converts refused to work on the communal mission projects.[77]

The two presecularization emancipation decrees freed many Indians living in the missions, but Indians who continued to live at the missions after 1834 remained for all intents and purposes as wards of the state, under the control of the administrators appointed under the terms of the 1833 secularization decree to replace the Franciscans. Moreover, the 1826, 1828, and 1833 decrees had more of an impact on the Indians living in the older southern missions, and they did not substantially alter the status of many converts. For example, the majority of Indians living at Santa Cruz mission (established in 1791) during the years 1835 to 1840 continued to work in communal labors, under the direction of the state-appointed administrators.[78] At the same time, the unauthorized exodus of converts from the missions in 1835 and 1836, as the civil admnistrators took charge of the missions, alarmed local officials. A May 25, 1836, decree issued by interim governor Mariano Chico (1836) attempted to stop the out-migration with only limited success, but it probably delayed the further emancipation of Indians still living in the missions, particularly in the more recently established northern missions.[79]

In the years 1839–1840, the provincial government sent Anglo-California settler and rancher William Hartnell on an inspection tour of the missions. Hartnell recorded complaints in the diary and official report prepared following his inspection of the missions. Although the surviving copy of the diary and report is incomplete, it does record the request for emancipation presented by Indians in several missions.[80] A number of emancipated Indians continued to live in the missions, such as the twenty-two emancipated adults reportedly at San Buenaventura (established in 1782), who were 11 percent of all adults living there. Indians still living in Soledad (established in 1791), Santa Cruz (established in 1791), San Francisco (established in 1776), and San Rafael (established in 1817) missions, in the northern part of the province, petitioned for their emancipation and the distribution of remaining communal property. At San Rafael mission, Hartnell specified that the "Old Christians"—the more acculturated converts—were the ones who specifically requested emancipation.

Although incomplete, the evidence indicates that either a blanket or more limited emancipation was granted to the Indians who still lived at the missions in 1840, following Hartnell's inspection tour. According to one document, Governor Juan Bautista Alvarado (1836–1842) emancipated the Indians at Santa Cruz mission in 1840.[81] Guadalupe Vallejo, brother of the commander of the northern military district, Mariano Vallejo, emancipated the Indians of San Rafael mission, which he administered. Writing in December of 1840, the Franciscan stationed at the ex-mission of San Rafael complained that Vallejo's emancipation of the Indians had caused most of the Indians to leave.[82]

The different emancipation decrees contributed to, but were not of themselves responsible for, the general exodus of Indians from the missions; and the out-migration from the missions clearly stands as evidence of the rejection by many converts of their role in the mission economies and of the social policies implemented by the Franciscans. Official reports written by the Franciscans still assigned to the ex-missions after 1834 and by other government officials, such as William Hartnell, uniformly discussed the exodus from the missions. Most of the surviving annual reports prepared in 1840 by the missionaries commented on the dispersion of the mission populations, and the patterns of out-migration. For example, Jesús González, O.F.M., stationed at San José, noted that "almost the majority [of the Indians that formerly lived in the mission] are wandering with the Gentiles, [in the] Ranches, and [the other] Missions."[83] The Franciscan stationed at San Antonio wrote that "[i]n the number of [Indians listed in the census] is included those who are wandering in the Ranches, or [have] fled to the tulares[.]"[84] José Quija, O.F.M., stationed at San Rafael, wrote:

> On October 26, Sor. Don Guadalupe Vallejo [emancipated] all of the Neophytes of this Mission, with whose permission they could go where they wanted, as a consequence of which the Mission has remained only with my servants . . . the rest have gone to various ranches and some to the *gentilidad*[.][85]

Contemporary sources record several distinctive patterns of out-migration from the missions: an exodus away from the area of effective Mexican control on the coast; resettlement as laborers on the ranches being carved out of former mission lands by prominent local politicians and settlers; and migration to the emerging towns in the province. I focus here on patterns of migration within the area of effective Mexican control in Alta California. Most of the converts who remained under Mexican jurisdiction probably went to work, on a seasonal or permanent basis, on the growing number of cattle ranches as all categories of laborers, including vaqueros, agricultural laborers, skilled craftsmen, cooks, and household servants. The majority of the converts probably left the missions in search of employment, whereas some may have been directly recruited from the missions. For example, a census of the population of San Antonio mission, conducted about 1840, records that one Señor Aguilar took two Indian families, six individuals, to San Luis Obispo mission. The census provides little information beyond this, but Aguilar may have taken the Indians to work for him.[86]

Former mission Indians found work on the ranches from the very beginning of implementation of the emancipation and secularization decrees in the late 1820s and the 1830s, and they were extremely mobile. A detailed census of the jurisdiction of the municipality of Monterey, including ranches in the Salinas and Pajaro valleys, lists Indians, both converts and individuals seized on military and paramilitary raids to the Sacramento and San Joaquin valleys, as living on a number of ranches (see Table 1.11). William Hartnell had eighteen former mission Indians living and working on his Rancho Patrocinio, the largest number on any of the ranches in the jurisdiction. All told, there were fifty-nine former mission Indians and four gentiles living on nine ranches. The Indians working on the Salinas Valley ranches had migrated a considerable distance. There were individuals listed in the census as having come from Santa Clara mission in northern Alta California, and La Purísima, Santa Inés, San Fernando, and San Gabriel missions in the south. In the early stages of the process of secularization, Indians were a significant but not dominant source of labor on ranches in the Monterey area, and a number of ranches did not even employ Indian workers. Social and economic differentiation in early nineteenth-century Spanish and Mexican California led to the growth of an incipient Hispanic working class, and much of the labor on the ranches was provided by non-Indians.[87]

Former mission Indians also migrated to the growing towns, where they lived in *rancherías* on the outskirts and served as a pool of day labor or found more stable employment and lived in the households of prominent settlers as servants and cooks, and in other capacities. In 1836, six former mission Indians and one "gentile" lived in Monterey town.[88] By 1839 the exodus of Indians from the missions, in general, and the specific migration to the towns caused considerable alarm for civil officials. For example,

Table 1.11 Indian Laborers on the Ranches in the Jurisdiction of Monterey in 1836

		Indian Laborers	
Ranch	**Owner**	**Converts**	**"Gentiles"**
Patrocinio	William Hartnell	18	0
Pilarcitos	José Arco	9	0
La Nación	Francisco Mesa	1	0
Alisal	Feliciano Soberanes	5	0
Natividad	Manuel Butron	6	2
Vergeles	Eusebio Boronda	2	0
Sausal	Martín Olivera	8	2
Buenavista	José Estrada	5	0
San Francisquito	?	5	0
Total		59	4

Source: José Estrada, "Padrón general que manifiesta el numero de havitantes que ecsisten en la municipalidad de Monterey [en] 1836," Bancroft Library, University of California, Berkeley.

William Hartnell received complaints about the flight of the Indians and resulting labor shortages from the administrators of the ex-missions San Diego, San Luis Rey, and San Juan Capistrano. Many of the Indians had gone to Los Angeles. On June 11 and 14 of 1839, Hartnell wrote to the prefect of Los Angeles, asking that fugitive Indians be returned to San Luis Rey and other missions.[89]

Finally, there was a limited pattern of migration from the northernmost missions alluded to by Hartnell in his inspection diary. The division of the region north of San Francisco Bay into Spanish-Mexican and Russian spheres of influence did not disrupt established trading patterns between coastal and interior tribelets. In the 1830s, the Franciscans stationed at San Rafael mission reported that numbers of the Indians under their charge were absent at the Russian settlement at Ross, and they documented one instance of a local Indian woman who married an Aleut, went to the Russian colony in Alaska, and later settled at San Rafael mission.[90] Following secularization, Indians from San Rafael, and perhaps from San Francisco Solano mission as well, also went to work for the Russians at Fort Ross as agricultural workers.[91]

How many former converts left the missions in the twelve years following the initial implementation of the secularization decree? There are postsecularization population counts and estimates that serve as the basis for the calculation of the degree of the exodus from the missions, although the population figures are not as accurate as the censuss prepared during the period of Franciscan administration of the missions. The very fact that converts left the missions in large numbers, or left settlements around the missions on a seasonal basis to work in the towns or ranches, made it difficult to prepare accurate censuses. For example, William Hartnell recorded a population of 70 Indians at Santa Cruz mission in 1839, while the Franciscan stationed there counted 102 in the following year. Other evidence suggests that as many as 148 to 160 Indians lived in the Santa Cruz area in 1840. Former mission Indians lived at the mission site and in a number of small *rancherías* located close to the mission complex, but they left their settlements periodically to work on nearby ranches.[92]

San Juan Bautista missionary José Anzar, O.F.M., succinctly described the problems in trying to enumerate, in 1840, the number of Indians living in the missions as well as those the Franciscans and civil officials still considered to be residents of the missions:

> It is not possible to take an exact count of the number of Indians because [they are] all very dispersed in the other missions and as fugitives in their land.[93]

San José missionary Jesús González, O.F.M., added that "[t]he Indians that are [enumerated] above are not currently congregated here[.]"[94] The general trend was toward a decline in the numbers of Indians remaining in the neighborhood of the former missions, due to disease—a severe small-pox outbreak in 1838—and to out-migration. In 1842, some forty-three hundred were counted in, as well as in the immediate neighborhood of, the twenty-one establishments, amounting to less than a third of the number of converts in the missions prior to secularization in 1834. However, the postsecularization population counts do not provide a suitable basis for a calculation of the relative importance of out-migration and high mortality rates as causes of the decline in the number of Indians living in and around the ex-missions.

A projection of the vital rates of the population of the twenty-one missions shows that the missions' population would have continued to decline at a rate of about 4 percent per year had the missions not been secularized. In total numbers, there would have been some 11,845 converts in 1840 and 9,321 in 1845. Censuses in 1839 and 1842 reported substantially lower Indian populations at the former missions, with 7,246 in the former year and 4,372 in the latter. On the basis of the projection, I calculate that as many as 43 percent of the Indians living in the missions in 1834 had left by 1839, and the number of converts leaving the missions increased by another 17 percent by 1842. The mean annual rate of out-migration was 8.6 percent between 1834 and 1839, and 5.6 percent from 1839 to 1842. Altogether, 60 percent of the decline in the mission populations over the eight years following the implementation of the secularization decree resulted from the exodus of converts.[95]

A significant number of former converts lived at the missions or in the immediate neighborhood of the missions following secularization; and in some locations, they continued to work until 1840 in the communal labors at the missions, and under the direction of the state-appointed administrators. The administrators attempted to maintain the same forms of coercive social controls as existed during the Franciscan regime prior to secularization, including the use of corporal punishment.[96] However, many of the converts who remained at the mission under the control of the administrators agitated for the change in their legal status—namely, emancipation, as outlined above, and the distribution to them of lands and other mission properties to which they were entitled under the terms of the 1833 secularization decree. Moreover, the Indians complained about the granting of lands from the mission territories as ranches to non-Indian settlers.[97] The process of the distribution of mission lands and goods to former mission Indians varied from establishment to establishment, but distinctions can be made between those mission communities where the government attepted to establish Indian pueblos, as at San Juan Capistrano, and the other missions where prominent local settlers retained control over the secularization process and distributed mission lands and goods to only a small number of Indians and on an individual basis. The course of secularization at Santa Cruz missions is illustrative of the majority of cases in which the government did not attempt to establish Indian pueblos.

The Indians living at Santa Cruz missions remained under the control of the appointed administrators until they were emancipated in 1840 by Governor Alvarado. Prior to 1840, the converts complained on numerous occasions about abuses by the administrators. For example, Russian-born José Bolcoff, placed in charge of the ex-mission in the late 1830s, reportedly took roof tiles and other building materials for use in structures being built on his own ranches.[98] Much of the mission lands and movable goods were lost prior to 1840, but enough remained to reward the more acculturated Indians who remained in and near the ex-mission and worked on the ranches and town growing up around the mission. Twenty-five Indians owned small plots of former mission lands during the years 1834–1849, including ten individuals who communally exploited a parcel known as "San Pedro Regalado" as late as 1847. However, most of the Indian landowners sold their lands to Mexican and Anglo-American settlers in the 1840s, 1850s, and 1860s.[99] Similarly, Indians received sections of mission buildings, particularly residences in the dormitories built under the direction of the Franciscans to house Indian converts. Again, though, the recipients of sections of buildings sold their interests to Mexican and Anglo-American settlers.[100] In the 1860s, few Indians lived in the predominantly Anglo-American town of Santa Cruz growing around the mission site, and, as was also the case in the Pimería Alta and Baja California mission communities, the surviving Indians formed a part of a marginalized work force in Santa Cruz County.

Conclusions

The colonial policy of *congregación* created nucleated mission communities in northern Sonora and the Californias on the model of the central Mexican corporate peasant communities. Moreover, the mission communities continued to exist until the breakdown of the colonial order in the early nineteenth century, and the implementation of new policies designed to integrate the Indian into Mexican society. However, the expulsion of Spanish-born missionaries and the secularization of the missions caused the dissolution of the mission communities in all three regions, which indicates the fragility of the artificial bonds that held the communities together. Unlike the central Mexican corporate communities, which had their own internal dynamic that survived changes in government policy, the mission communities in northwestern Mexico were artificial entities that collapsed once the government had dismantled the mission system. The collapse of the mission communities was particularly evident in Alta California.

However, demographic factors had already undermined the stability of the mission communities. In all three regions studied here, the Indian populations living in the missions were not viable and did not grow through natural reproduction, and the size of the mission populations only grew during periods of active recruitment. The following chapter examines the vital rates of the mission populations, the manifestations of the demographic collapse of the Indian population congregated in the missions.

Demographic Collapse of the Mission Population

With sustained contact between the Old World and the New World after 1492, the Indian populations of the Americas collapsed under the impact of newly introduced Euroasiatic disease and other factors. The Indian populations of the mission communities in northern Sonora and the Californias declined following the establishment of missions, although the process of demographic collapse already may have begun in the early sixteenth century, as epidemics spread northward from central New Spain. The collapse of the mission populations continued into the first decades of the nineteenth century, and in the case of Alta California the Indian population continued to decline until the end of the century.

This chapter documents the degree of demographic collapse in the missions, and the vital rates of the mission populations. The first section outlines overall population trends in the missions, which, however, do not show, in every instance, the degree of population decline since the missionaries continued to repopulate the mission communities with new converts. The second, third, and fourth sections provide detailed case studies of the vital rates of the missions, based upon an analysis of data abstracted from parish registers and contemporary censuses.

The Degree of Demographic Collapse of the Mission Populations

Superficially, it appears that the decline of the population of the Pimería Alta missions was a gradual process that perhaps did not reach the same levels as in neighboring frontier provinces. An examination of data extracted from extant censuses shows fluctuations in the mission populations, but numbers of Pima converts continued to live in the mission villages as late as the 1820s and 1830s. The mission communities continued to appear in the record as populous settlements. On closer examination, however, the evidence indicates that mortality rates were equally high in the mission villages, and, as documented in the previous chapter, the missionaries repopulated the existing communities by resettling converts.

The northern Pima population may have experienced depopulation in the years following the first Spanish intrusion into New Spain in 1519. Epidemic disease was most likely transmitted into the region along established trade routes, over which communities in Sonora and Sinaloa obtained goods produced in central Mexico. A recent estimate of contact population for the Pimería Alta and an estimate of the 1700 population give an indication of the degree of depopulation prior to the establishment of the first missions in the region. There may have been as many as fifty-thousand northern Pimas in 1519, and some twenty-three thousand in 1700. This indicates a decline in numbers of 54 percent.[1]

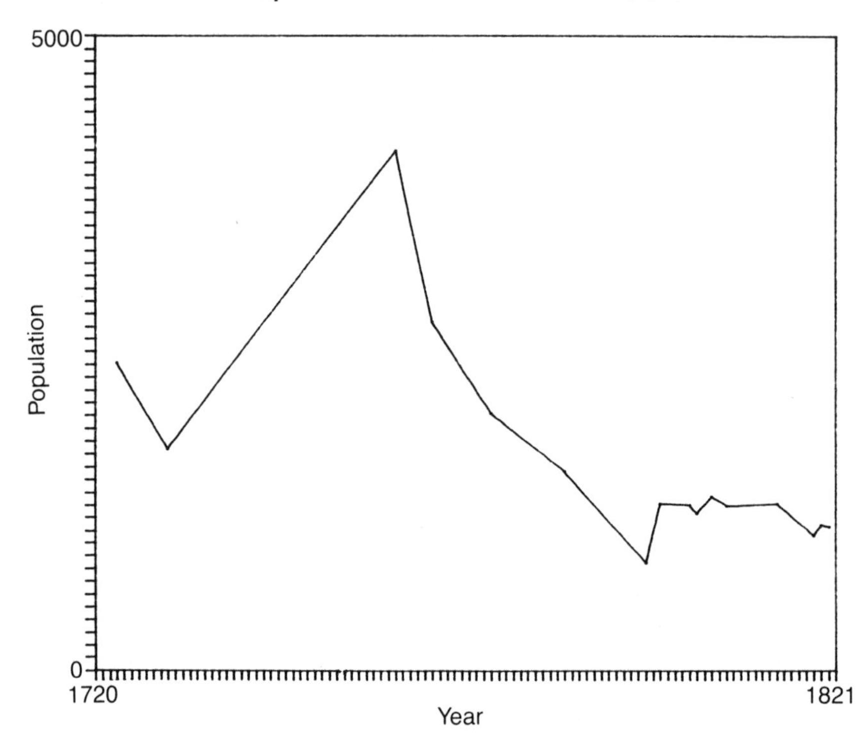

Accounts written in the years following the establishment of the first mission in the Pimería Alta recorded estimates of the size of the populations of the villages located in the valleys where the Jesuits established missions. Although not precise, these estimates can serve as the basis for calculating short-term population decline. However, these estimates document the villages of only a part of the Pimería Alta.

In the early 1690s, some 8,600 Indians lived in the area of the Pimería Alta where the Jesuits organized the system of mission villages. Over the next seventy years, the numbers declined by about 53 percent to 4,088 living in twenty-two villages, although the actual rate of decline was greater as the missionaries repopulated the mission villages by resettling converts from the *Papagueria* and other sections of the Pimería Alta. The population of the missions continued to decline over the next sixty years, although at a slower rate, and the Jesuit and Franciscan missionaries reduced the surviving population into a smaller number of villages. There were 2,018 in sixteen villages in 1774, following several devastating epidemics in the 1760s and early 1770s, and 1,293 in fourteen villages in 1806. The numbers increased slightly, to 1,315, in 1813 as a result of increased resettlement of Papagos, but then dropped in subsequent years (see Table 2.1).

Patterns in Baja California were different from those in the Pimería Alta. Although somewhat isolated from the mainland, epidemics spread to Baja

Table 2.1 Population of the Pimería Alta Missions in Selected Years

Year	Number of Villages	Population	Index (c. 1690=100)	Mean Population
c. 1690	33	c. 8,645	100	262
1761	22	4,088	47	186
1766	21	2,738	32	130
1774	16	2,018	23	126
1784	15	1,560	18	104
1797	14	1,312	15	94
1806	14	1,293	15	92
1813	14	1,315	15	94
1820	14	1,127	13	81

Source: Appendix 2; Herbert Bolton, trans. and ed., Kino's Historical Memoir of the Pimería Alta (Berkeley and Los Angeles, 1948), pp. 118–20, 205–9, 232–33, 245, 276, and 279; and Ernest Burrus, S.J., Kino and Manje Explorers of Sonora and Arizona (Rome and St. Louis 1971), pp. 167–70, 182–83, 190–91, 198–99, 215–17, and 252.

Table 2.2 Population and Baptisms, from Founding to 1744, of Eight Baja California Missions in 1744

Mission	Year of Founding	Total Baptisms to 1744	Population in 1744	% of Decline
Loreto	1697	1,199	150	87
San Francisco Xavier	1699	1,726	352	80
Mulege*	1705	1,358	326	76
Comondú	1708	1,563	513	77
La Purísima	1718	1,890	535	72
Guadalupe*	1720	2,599	701	73
Santiago	1721	1,749	449	75
San Ignacio	1728	2,746	1,196	56
Total		14,830	4,222	72

*A part of the population was transferred to the jurisdiction of a neighboring mission prior to 1744.
Source: Robert H. Jackson, "Indian Demographic Patterns in Colonial New Spain: The Case of the Baja California Missions," *PCCLAS Proceedings* 12 (1985–1986), p. 39; and Ernest Burrus, S.J., and Felix Zubillaga, S.J., ed., *Misiones Mexicanas de la Companía de Jesús,* 1618–1745 (Madrid, 1982), pp. 267–69, 243–53.

California following the establishment of missions in 1697. The population of the peninsula collapsed in about a century. Estimates of the population of Baja California in 1697 vary from 48,000 to 60,000.[2] The rate of depopulation varied within the peninsula, but, in general terms, the number of Indians living in the missions declined during the first four decades of the eighteenth century and then expanded in the 1750s and 1760s. A series of reports prepared in 1744 recorded the total number of baptisms from the date of the establishment of each mission, as well as providing the population in 1744. Reports for eight missions recorded a total of 14,830 baptisms, but only a population of 4,222 (see Table 2.2). Roughly three-quarters of the Indians congregated in the eight missions prior to 1744 had died.

The population increase of the 1750s and 1760s can be attributed to two factors: the establishment of new missions and the congregation of thousands of converts in the new missions; and growth due to natural increase at several of the older missions. The population of San Francisco Xavier increased from 352 in 1744, to 380 in 1755, and 448 in 1762. Similarly, the population of Guadalupe grew from 472 in 1755 to 544 in 1768 (see Appendix 3).[3]

Table 2.3 Population of the Baja California Missions in Selected Years

Year	Number of Missions	Population	Index (1755=100)	Mean Population
1755	13	5,974	100	460
1762	14	6,300	106	450
1768	15	7,149	120	477
1773	14	4,116	69	294
1782	16	3,056	51	191
1795	17	3,319	56	195
1798	18	3,114	52	173
1800	18	3,156	53	174
1804	18	2,815	47	156

Source: Appendix 3.

The expulsion of the Jesuits from Baja California in 1768 and the expansion northward in 1769 to Alta California accelerated the rate of demographic collapse. The movement of personnel through the peninsula facilitated the spread of contagious disease; and severe epidemics in 1769 (measles), 1771–1772 (unidentified), and 1781–1782 (smallpox) killed more than half of the Indians living in the missions. Despite the establishment of new missions by the Dominicans after 1774, the Indian population of the missions fluctuated but continued to decline. The average population per mission dropped (see Table 2.3). In 1800, some 5,900 Indians survived in Baja California, both inside and outside the missions, and 1,200 in the 1840s.[4] Although estimates of contact population differ, it is clear that the Indian population in Baja California declined by more than 90 percent in the century and a half following the establishment of the first permanent mission in the peninsula.

As outlined in the previous chapter, the Franciscans stationed in the Alta California missions congregated Indians by moving them to the mission communities from the districts surrounding the missions, as well as from considerable distances. Estimates of the Indian population of California vary, but some 60,000 people lived in the coastal sections where the Franciscans established missions.[5] In addition to the local population, the Franciscans resettled some 10,500 Indians to the missions from the Central Valley and the San Joaquín–Sacramento River

Table 2.4 Population of the Alta California Missions in Selected Years

Year	Number of Missions	Total Population	Index (1790=100)	Mean Population
1790	11	7,711	100	701
1795	13	10,998	143	846
1800	18	13,628	177	757
1804	19	19,060	247	1,003
1810	19	18,680	242	983
1815	19	19,485	253	1,026
1820	20	21,063	273	1,053
1825	21	20,301	263	968
1830	21	18,135	235	864
1832	21	18,117	235	863
1834	21	15,225	197	721
1839*	21	7,246	94	345
1842*	21	4,372	57	280

*Poulation following secularization of the missions.
Source: Appendix 4.

Delta, and 3,500 converts from the region north of San Francisco Bay.[6] In southern Alta California, the Franciscans recruited among the Cahuillas and other interior groups.

The total population of the missions grew until 1820, when 21,063 converts, or an average of 1,053 Indians, lived in twenty establishments. Over the next fourteen years the numbers of converts dropped, largely as a result of the growing inability of the missionaries to attract new converts. By 1834, 15,225 Indians lived in the missions, or an average of 721. As discussed in the previous chapter, secularization and the breakdown of social control in the missions led to the dispersion of the mission populations (see Table 2.4).

The populations of the individual missions experienced high rates of mortality, rates that were in the long run higher than birthrates. However, there was considerable local and regional variation in vital rates between th three areas studied here, as well as within the three regions. Moreover, epidemics affected mission populations differently. Epidemics in the Pimería Alta and in Baja California significantly raised death rates, whereas death rates were chronically high in the Alta California missions. The following sections offer case studies of the collapse of individual mission populations as shown by birth and death rates.

Demographic Collapse in the Pimería Alta

The vital rates of the Pimería Alta mission communities were determined by several factors: (1) the frequency and virulence of epidemics; (2) patterns of infant and child mortality; and (3) patterns of repopulation of the mission communities. Epidemics generally killed the most susceptible members of society, individuals not previously exposed to a given contagion. In the case of the Pimería Alta mission communities, young children and recent converts previously not exposed to a contagion would be at greatest risk. During periods of active recruitment, the mission populations included increased numbers of high-risk people.

Three detailed case studies illustrate in more detail the dynamic of depopulation in the Pimería Alta. The case studies are of Tumacacori, Caborca, and Ati missions. The first case study is of Guevavi-Tumacacori mission, located in the middle of the Santa Cruz River Valley.

Anthropologist Carl Sauer estimated an aboriginal population of some 5,500 in the Santa Cruz River Valley, when the Jesuits established the first mission in the Pimería Alta; and Henry Dobyns arrived at a figure of 2,400 for the middle section of the valley that contributed converts to the mission.[7] Although no Jesuits served in the Santa Cruz Valley missions until the 1730s, the northern Pimas living in the Santa Cruz Valley came in contact with Christianity and Spanish material culture. Moreover, epidemic disease reduced the Indian population in numbers, prior to the establishment of a permanent Jesuit presence in the valley in 1732. A 1732 document estimated a population of 4,200 Pimas living in the three missions in the valley, but this total apparently included the population of the satellite villages of Soamca missions, including the Sobaipuri Pimas from the neighboring San Pedro Valley.[8] The missionaries stationed at Guevavi-Tumacacori mission reduced the bulk of the local population to mission life within ten to fifteen years, but they continued to resettle converts, including Papagos, from the surrounding territory.

Despite the resettlement of converts and the congregation of a large population in a smaller number of villages, the population of the Santa Cruz Valley missions declined in the 1740s and 1750s. In 1761, 507 Pimas lived in the four villages of the mission (see Table 2.5). In the same year, the governor of Sonora ordered the relocation of the surviving Sobaipuri Pimas from the San Pedro Valley to the Santa Cruz Valley missions.[9]

In addition to disease, Apache raids had depleted the population of the Sobaipuri northern Pimas. However, the abandonment of the San Pedro Valley exacerbated the problem of warfare. With the removal of the

Sobaipuris, Apache raiders were able to penetrate deeper into Sonora, and the Santa Cruz Valley now became a battlefield.

The relocation of the Sobaipuris contributed to the process of repopulating the missions. The largest group of some 250–400 people were moved to Tucson *visita* of Bac mission, and at least 30 went to Soamca.[10] However, the relocation of the Sobaipuris did not reverse the trend of population decline in the Santa Cruz Valley missions. A total of 488 converts lived in the four villages of Guevavi-Tumacacori mission in 1766, and 310 two years later, in 1768 (see Table 2.5). Following the Jesuit expulsion, the Franciscans further congregated the surviving population by moving it from four villages to one village, Tumacacori. Guevavi, the former *cabecera*, was abandoned because the resident missionary preferred to live at Tumacacori, which was closer to the soldier-settler population of Tubac presidio.[11] An Apache raid in July of 1770 left nineteen dead at Sonoyta, which forced the abandonment of the village bcause of its exposure to Apache raids.[12] Finally, the Franciscans depopulated Calabazas *visita* at some point in the 1780s, most likely because of the continued decline of the population in conjunction with the pressure of Apache

Table 2.5 The Spatial Distribution of the Population of Guevavi-Tumacacori Mission 1754–1820

Year	Guevavi	Tumacacori	Aribac	Sonoita	Calabazas	Total
1754	80	40	108	88	0	316
1761	101	199	0	91	116	507
1766	82	122	0	139	145	488
1768	53	70	0	110	77	310
1774	0	98	0	0	138	236
1784	0	95	0	0	0	95
1795	0	119	0	0	0	119
1796	0	98	0	0	0	98
1797	0	69	0	0	0	69
1801	0	78	0	0	0	78
1802	0	76	0	0	0	76
1804	0	82	0	0	0	82
1806	0	83	0	0	0	83
1813	0	119	0	0	0	119
1818	0	105	0	0	0	105
1819	0	123	0	0	0	123
1820	0	121	0	0	0	121

Source: Appendix 2.

raids.[13] The surviving Pima population continued to drop until only 121 remained in 1820 (see Table 2.5).

Two methodologies are used to document the collapse of the northern Pima population of Guevavi-Tumacacori mission. A family reconstitution provides a detailed life history of 123 children born at the mission between 1773 and 1825. The majority of the children in the sample (73 percent) did not survive the first five years of life; they were victims of dehydration caused by diarrhea, childhood diseases and contagious epidemics, and other ailments. A mere 7 percent lived beyond the age of ten. However, it should be pointed out that there are potential weaknesses in the methodology. Not all children born in the mission during the years under study are included in the sample, although the majority are. Some individuals were lost because of gaps in the parish records. Others born in the 1810s

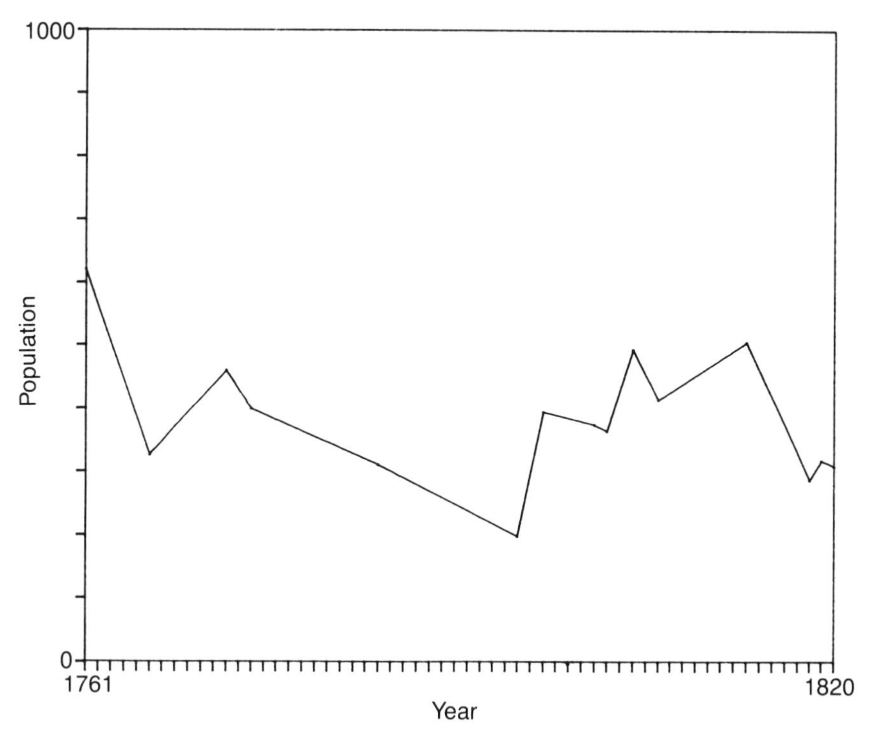

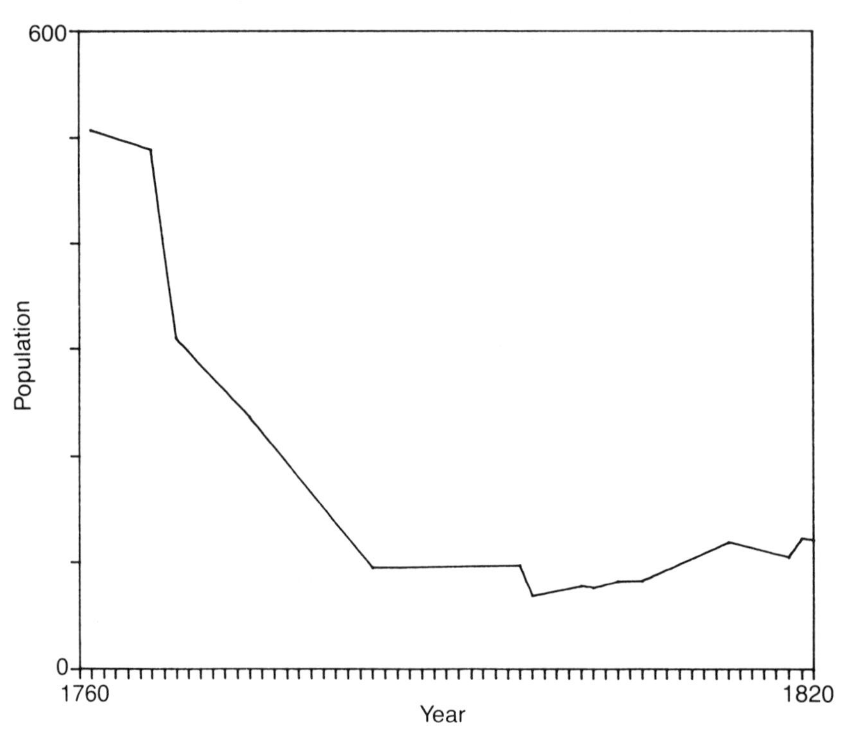

and 1820s disappear from the record because of the loss of the post–1825 parish registers for Tumacacori. Nevertheless, the sample and the conclusions based upon the family reconstitution are valid.

Aggregate data abstracted from the extant Guevavi-Tumacacori sacramental registers are used to reconstruct crude birth and death rates, gross and net reproduction ratios, and life expectancy. Pima women living at Tumacacori bore children, and birthrates were high, as evidenced by a mean crude birthrate of 48 per thousand population and a mean gross reproduction ratio of 2.73. However, death rates were consistently higher than birthrates, with the exception of one quinquennium, averaging 60 per thousand population. The net reproduction ratio averaged .66, which indicates a steady but gradual mean rate of decline over a generation of 34 percent. The average mean life expectancy at birth was 15.2 years, which,

Table 2.6 Patterns of Infant and Child Mortality at Tumacacori Mission, 1773–1825

Cohort	Number of Deaths by Cohort	Percentage of Sample
0–1	56	46
1–5	33	27
5–10	26	21
10+	8	7
Total	123	101

Source: San José de Tumacacori baptismal, burial, and marriage registers; Tucson Diocese Chancery Archive, Tucson, Arizona.

despite the results of the family reconstitution reported above, reflects the fact that some children did survive childhood (see Table 2.7).

The second case study is Caborca mission, located in the western section of the Pimería Alta. The records are incomplete, but they still lend themselves to limited analysis. As noted above, the influx of converts resettled at the *cabecera* and two *visitas* slowed the rate of decline in the size of the population of the three mission villages, but it did not reverse

Table 2.7 Tumacacori Mission Demographic Statistics, 1775–1825

Year	Population	CBR	CDR	GRR	NRR	Life Expectancy
1777	93*	45	64	2.61	.52	12.6
1782	86*	42	53	2.29	.58	16.0
1787	94*	57	59	3.10	.81	16.6
1792	95*	57	53	3.26	1.05	20.4
1797	69	36	48	2.20	.66	18.8
1802	76	60	65	3.89	.90	14.7
1807	76*	50	82	3.05	.39	8.4
1812	79*	48	68	2.57	.44	11.0
1817	108*	32	58	1.57	.30	12.3
1822	122*	54	49	2.77	.92	21.0

*Population estimate generated by *Populate*.
Source: San José de Tumacacori Mission baptismal and burial registers, Diocese of Tucson Chancery Archive, Tucson, Arizona.

the trend of demographic collapse. However, the influx of women of child-bearing age pushed birthrates up, averaging 75 per thousand population and a mean gross reproduction ratio of 4.11 for three quinquennium (flaws in the data abstracted from extant baptismal and burial registers may inflate the vital rates calculated by *Populate*).

Periodic epidemics and high rates of infant and child mortality still undermined the viability of the Indian population living in the mission villages. Epidemics in the last Jesuit years reduced the population of Caborca and its *visitas*. In 1764, for example, 94 converts died at Caborca, while in the same year the Black Robes baptized 34. The population of the community experienced a net loss in population of 60. In the following year, there was a net gain in population of four. A second epidemic in 1766 decimated the Indian population, killing 68.[14] The population of the three villages dropped by 48 percent, from 1,060 in 1761 to 551 in 1766, but then recovered to a level of 1,060 two years later, in 1768, which indicates that a part of the population decline in the early 1760s was also due to the flight of Indians trying to escape the impact of epidemics and, to a lesser degree, of Apache raiding. Natural reproduction and the resettlement of converts alone cannot account for the rapid increase in the size of the population of the three villages between 1766 and 1768.

Registers of baptisms and burials survive for Caborca mission in a fragmented state, and only fifteen years of vital statistics can be analyzed(1764–1768, 1785–1794). Nevertheless, the data summarized in Table 2.8 do give an indication of the dynamic of demographic change at Caborca. Birthrates were high in the mid-1760s and during the years 1785–1794, and they were also reflected in high gross reproduction ratios (there may be some inflation in these figures due to underegistration in censuses, particularly in the 1784 census, which provides the base population for the 1785–1789 quinquennium). High rates of mortality, and particularly infant and child mortality, wiped out much of the increase in numbers through natural reproduction. Mortality in the first year of life ranged from 62 percent to 90 percent, and children under the age of ten comprised between 23 percent and 12 percent of the total population. The evidence suggests that conditions grew worse in the late 1780s and early 1790s, as shown by higher crude death rates and lower net reproduction ratios. In the long run, the population of Caborca declined, although the process may have accelerated in the late eighteenth century. Mean life expectancy at birth declined (see Table 2.8).

The final case study is Ati, located in the Altar Valley. Ati was one of two villages organized ecclesiastically as a single mission district. In the Fran-

Table 2.8 Demographic Statistics of Caborca Mission, 1764–1768, 1785–1794

Year	Population	CBR	CDR	GRR	NRR	Life Expectancy
1766	530*	64	83	3.75	.57	9.8
1787	106*	85	116	4.87	.40	5.6
1792	81*	77	153	3.71	.07	1.5

*Population estimate generated by *Populate.*
Source: La Purísima Concepción de Caborca baptismal and burial registers; Altar Parish Archive, Altar, Sonora, and the Bancroft Library, University of California, Berkeley.

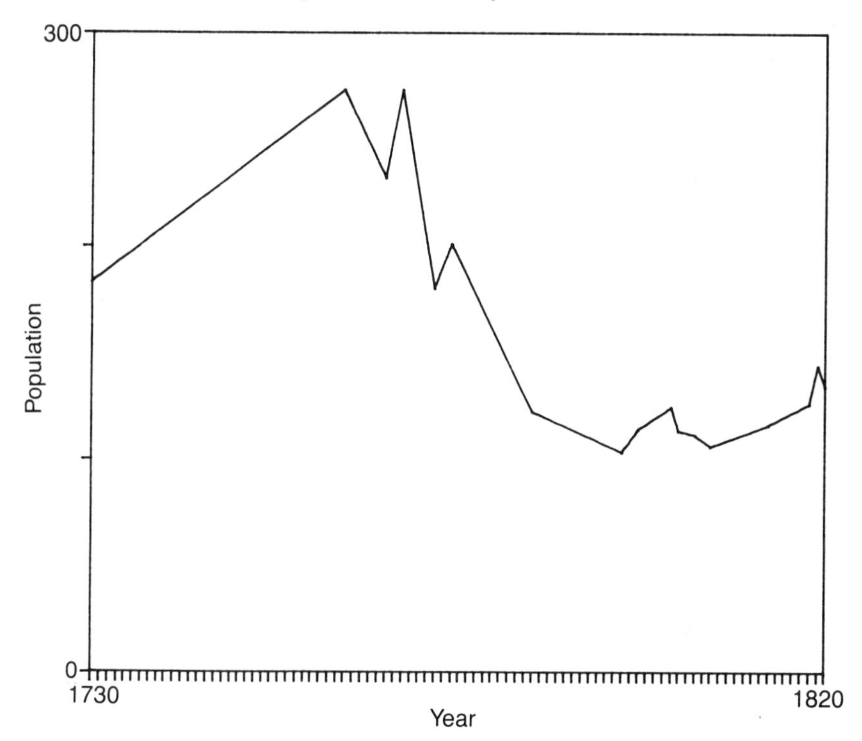

ciscan period, the resident missionaries switched their residence, and thus *cabecera* status, between Ati and Oquitoa; and after 1800, they lumped the population of the two villages together when reported in the censuses, which posed a methodological problem in estimating the base population for each quinquennium of data for analysis by *Populate*. For the purposes of the analysis of the demographic statistics of Ati, the population of the village has arbitrarily been taken to be 50 percent of the recorded population of both villages when they are combined in the census returns. However, inaccuracies can result when an overly high or low base population is estimated, especially for small populations such as Ati, where the vital rates are particularly sensitive to slight variations in the base population. Nevertheless, the results of the analysis indicate that potential inaccuracies are minimal, probably limited to one quinquennium, as indicated in Table 2.9.

The 1730 census is the first that recorded individual village populations. In that year, Ati and Oquitoa had a combined population of 183. The population fluctuated in subsequent years, but it experienced an upward trend as a result of the push in the 1740s and 1750s to recruit Papagos. It was 273 in 1761, 232 in 1766, and 273 again in 1768. After 1768, however, the population began a period of decline. The numbers stood at 201 in 1774, 122 in 1784, 124 in 1801, and 106 in 1806; but then they increased to 134 in 1820 (see Appendix 2).

The analysis of the demographic statistics of Ati village indicates a pattern of high infant and child mortality, combined with periodic and traumatic epidemics, which substantially raised death rates and lowered life expectancy. Birthrates were high, averaging 42 per thousand population and a mean gross reproduction ratio of 2.21. However, death rates were also chronically high, and, with the exception of one quinquennium, they were consistently higher than death rates. The crude death rate averaged 73 per thousand population, but it went as high as 156 per thousand population during the 1778–1782 quinquennium as a consequence of a severe smallpox outbreak in 1781. The net reproduction ratio averaged .42, or a 48 percent rate of depopulation over a generation; but it dropped as low as .02, during the 1781 smallpox epidemic, and .05, during a second smallpox outbreak in 1816. Life expectancy fluctuated, but it averaged 13.2 years (see Table 2.9).

In all three case studies examined above, the Indian populations congregated in the missions experienced net decline, but at different rates. Epidemics were traumatic episodes that substantially raised death rates, but generally they occurred only one a generation, with a duration of a year

Table 2.9 Ati Mission Demographic Statistics, 1773–1827

Year	Population	CBR	CDR	GRR	NRR	Life Expectancy
1775	87*	67	81	3.94	.67	11.0
1780	63*	38	156	1.83	.02	1.1
1785	49*	73	53	3.28	1.01	19.4
1790	48*	59	92	2.76	.31	7.4
1798	50*	40	52	2.41	.62	16.6
1803	45*	27	57	1.49	.21	9.4
1809	50*	24	44	1.36	.39	17.9
1814	52*	54**	130	2.61	.05	1.5
1820	70*	20	31	1.21	.46	25.1
1825***	66*	21	33	1.22	.42	22.3

*Population estimate generated by *Populate*.
**Possible error in the data due to an overly large population estimate for 1811 that serves as the base population for the 1812–1816 quinquennium.
***Population estimate generated by *Populate*.
Source: Ati Mission baptismal and burial registers; Altar Parish Archive, Altar, Sonora, and the Bancroft Library, University of California, Berkeley.

or two. For example, there were severe smallpox outbreaks in the Pimería Alta in 1764, 1781, and 1816. However, chronic endemic disease was equally important as a factor in the decline of the Indian population, and in particular, it raised infant and child mortality rates to the point that over several generations the populations simply did not reproduce in sufficient numbers to make up losses caused by the increased mortality rates in the missions. A conjunction of factors, then, caused the demographic collapse of the northern Pima population.

Demographic Collapse in Baja California

The discussion of demographic collapse in Baja California is based on six case studies: Santa Rosalia de Mulege (established in 1705); San José de Comondú (established in 1708); Santa Gertrudis (established in 1752); San Fernando de Velicata (established in 1769); Rosario (established in 1774); and Santo Domingo (established in 1775). Although patterns varied from one mission community to another, the case studies examined here are representative of general patterns observed in all of the Baja California missions.

The Jesuits established Santa Rosalia de Mulege mission in 1705, on the banks of the Rio Mulege, the largest river in Baja California. Even today Mulege has the aspect of an oasis, with hundreds of date palms descended from trees initially introduced by the missionaries in the eighteenth century and producing a fruit that constitutes the single most important agricultural export from the community. The surrounding mountains, in contrast, are dry with different types of xerophytic vegetation. The Mulege River is one of a number of streams that have cut narrow valleys through the surrounding mountains and plateau.

Although established at a site with an abundant supply of water, the amount of arable land available was insufficient to support the resettlement of the entire mission population at the *cabecera* in the first stages of the acculturation program. The first surviving report describes conditions in 1730. In that year, the population of 346 lived at the *cabecera* and in several satellite villages. The population dropped over the next thirty-eight years,

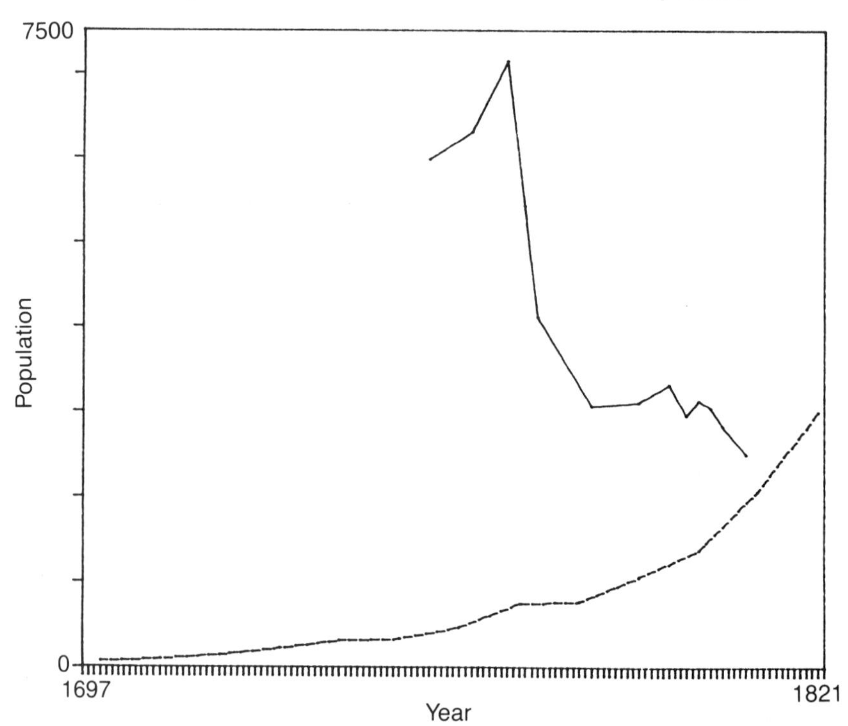

with a population of 281 reported in 1762 and 245 in 1768. The population of Mulege continued to decline following the Jesuit expulsion, despite efforts to repopulate the mission community by moving converts to Mulege from missions with less agricultural potential. In 1795, the government ordered the closing of Guadalupe mission (established in 1720), and relocated the surviving population from that mission to Mulege and Comondú. The relocation of Indians from Guadalupe to Mulege accounts for the increase in the mission population from 55 in 1794 to 88 in the following year. The population continued to decline in subsequent years. There were 72 Indians living at Mulege in 1800, 66 in 1804, and 39 in 1808.[15]

The population of Mulege mission stabilized in the early 1770s, but then it began a final phase of nearly continuous decline following the 1781 smallpox epidemic, which killed many women of child-bearing age and resulted in numerous remarriages during the years immediately following the epidemic. The demographic crisis from 1768 to 1782 lowered the mean life expectancy at Mulege from 19.6 years during the quinquennium (1773–1777) to a mere .9 (ten months, twenty-four days) between 1778 and 1782. The population dropped at a rate of almost 20 per thousand over five years, and if similar levels of mortality had been maintained over a generation, the population would have experienced a 99 percent decline, as indicated by the low net reproduction ratio. The population of Mulege recovered somewhat after 1783, and averaged a mean life expectancy of 6.3 years. The mean rate of decline over a generation dropped to 76 percent. This high rate of decline occurred despite high birthrates. The gross reproduction ratio averaged 2.66 (see Table 2.10).

In addition to the high mortality among adults caused by epidemics, there was a pattern of chronically high infant and child mortality rates at Mulege mission, as indicated by the low net reproduction ratio in the years after 1778. A family reconstitution of the population of Mulege mission between 1771 and 1835 further illustrates patterns of infant and child ortality. A sample is drawn from a group of 75 women who bore at least one child between 1771 and 1835, but were married prior to 1821. Age at death is calculated for 143 children born at the mission. Of the total, 50 percent died before reaching their first birthday, another thirty-three percent died between the ages of one and five, 11 percent from the ages of five to ten, and 6 percent of the children contained in the sample lived beyond the age of ten.[16]

The Jesuits established San José de Comondú mission in 1708, at a site later known as Comondú Viejo, and, about 1737, relocated the mission to a second site with more arable land in a narrow valley with a permanently running stream cut into the surrounding plateau. Relocation in the late

Table 2.10 Mulege Mission Demographic Statistics, 1730–1807

Year	Population	CBR	CDR	GRR	NRR	Life Expectancy
1730	346					
1755	294					
1768	245					
1771	180					
1773	165					
1775	175*	60	55	3.67	1.14	19.6
1780	109*	55	206	2.64	.02	.9
1782	75					
1785	73*	58	69	2.48	.38	10.0
1790	58	65	110	2.71	.15	3.9
1795	88	59	71	2.73	.51	12.0
1800	72	46	100	2.59	.15	4.1
1805	55*	29	101	1.77	.03	1.6
1808	39					

*Population estimates generated by *Populate*.
Source: Santa Rosalia de Mulege Mission baptismal and burial registers, Glesson Library, University of San Francisco, available on microfilm at the Bancroft Library, University of California, Berkeley; and Robert H. Jackson, "Demographic Patterns in the Missions of Central Baja California," *Journal of California and Great Basin Anthropology* 6 (1984), pp. 96–97.

1730s also led to the abandonment of a short-lived mission named San Miguel, which operated at a nearby site as an independent establishment from at least 1730, if not earlier.

The earliest extant report dates from 1744, and recorded a population of 513. The numbers dropped after 1744, despite the continued resettlement to Comondú of Guaicuras from the northern Magdalena Desert in the 1730s and 1740s. There were 350 converts in 1768; the population dropped to 216 in 1771, following a devastating measles epidemic in 1769, which killed 160 people; but then, the population rose to 284 in 1773, following the relocation to Comondú of Indians from Santa Gertrudis and San Francisco de Borja missions. Finally, the population stood at 80 in 1782, following a virulent smallpox epidemic, and the numbers continued to decline in subsequent years.[17]

Mean life expectancy at birth averaged 13.3 prior to the Jesuit expulsion, but it then fell to .9 (eleven months, three days) between 1766 and 1785. During the same years, the population experienced a net decline of between

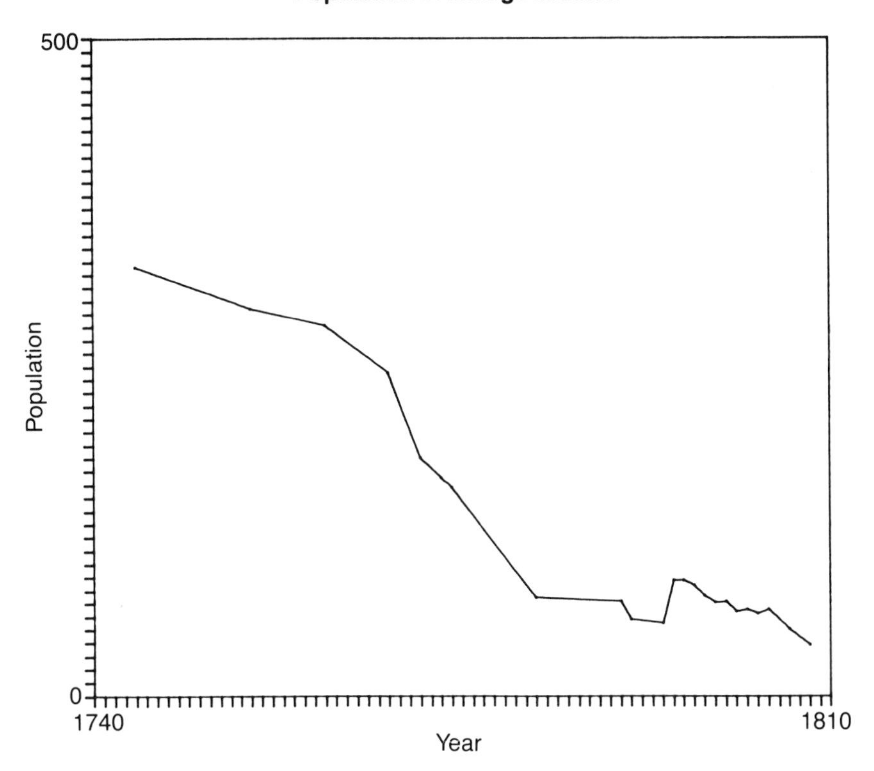

9 to 20 per thousand, and a mean decline of 98 percent had the same mortality rates been sustained over a generation. The gross reproduction ratio averaged 2.70. The population of Comondú did not recover following the demographic collapse of 1768 to 1782. Life expectancy, for example, averaged only 1.3 years (see Table 2.11). In 1790, 67 Indians continued to live at Comondú, with the numbers dropping to 21 in 1800, and to 36 in 1808.[18]

The Jesuit expansion in Baja California stalled after 1728 in the southern reaches of the Central Desert, following the establishment in that year of San Ignacio mission. In addition to problems of finding funding to support the establishment of the next mission to the north, the Jesuits had to take special care in identifying the few sites in the Central Desert with sufficient water to support even limited agriculture. The Jesuits established Santa

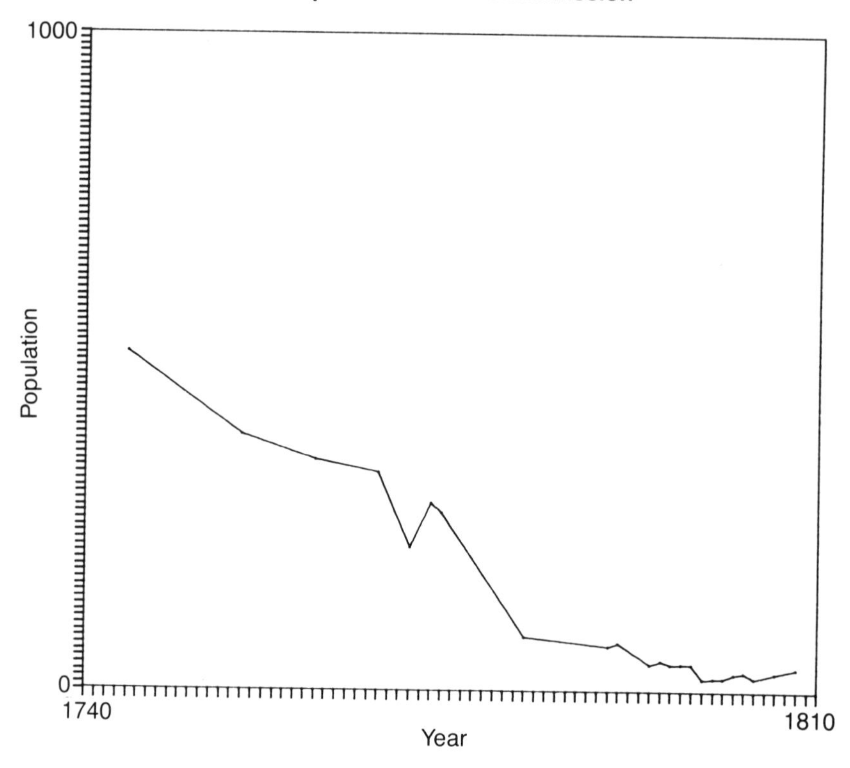

Gertrudis mission in 1752 near a spring in a dry wash with enough land to grow some grain. In preparation for the establishment of the new community, the missionary stationed at San Ignacio began baptizing Indians in the 1740s in the territory to be assigned to the future mission. This represented the implementation of a new method of acculturation, which entailed the conversion of a part of the Indian population in the territory of a new mission prior to the actual establishment of the new community. In this way, the missionaries could count on a source of labor, from the very beginning of their ministry, without having to expend scarce food resources to attract and feed converts.[19]

Missionary Fernando Konsag, S.J., assigned to establish Santa Gertrudis mission, congregated the bulk of the Indian population in the *cabecera* and satellite villages within the space of ten years, recording 1,009 more

Table 2.11 Comondú Mission Demographic Statistics, 1736–1805

Year	Population	CBR	CDR	GRR	NRR	Life Expectancy
1738	514*	62	54	3.80	1.21	20.1
1743	533*	55	64	3.39	.81	15.1
1744	513					
1748	474*	51	68	3.04	.56	11.9
1753	423*	65	70	3.74	.78	13.4
1755	387					
1758	368*	58	80	3.14	.47	9.7
1762	350					
1763	340*	58	78	3.05	.46	9.8
1768	245	70	157	3.32	.05	1.4
1773	165	72	196	2.78	.02	.9
1778	187*	36	142	1.28	.01	1.0
1782	80					
1783		33	227	.97	.00	.4
1788	56*	54	179	1.75	.01	.9
1793	56*	43	118	2.02	.04	1.5
1798	40	43	184	2.84	.02	1.0

*Population estimates generated by *Populate.*
Source: San José de Comondú Mission baptismal and burial registers, Asociación Historica Americanista, México, D.F., available on microfilm at the Bancroft Library, University of California, Berkeley; and Robert H. Jackson, "Demographic Patterns in the Missions of Central Baja California," *Journal of California and Great Basin Anthropology* 6 (1984), pp. 100–101.

baptisms than burials from 1752 to 1763. In 1755, the population of the new establishment stood at 1,586; there were 1,730 in 1762; and 1,360 in 1768, following the Jesuit expulsion from the peninsula. However, because of the ecological limitations of the Central Desert, the majority of the converts resided in satellite villages and visited the central mission on a rotating basis. The epidemics between 1768 and 1782, and the resettlement of Indians from the Santa Gertrudis region to other missions located in less arid parts of the peninsula, contributed to a rapid decline in the population after 1768. In 1774, there were 798 Indians at Santa Gertrudis, but only 317 remained following the severe smallpox epidemic of 1781–1782, 203 in 1800, and 137 in 1808. As the population declined, the missionaries resettled most of the survivors in the *cabecera.*[20]

The demographic collapse of 1768–1782 can be clearly seen at Santa Gertrudis mission. Mean life expectancy between 1757 and 1771 averaged

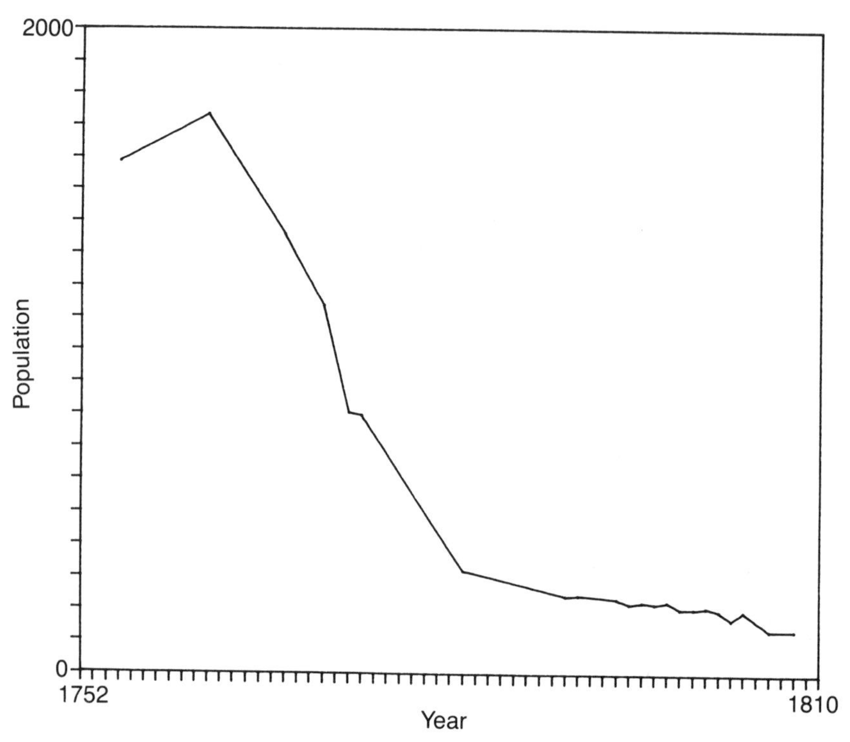

10.4 years, and the decline in the population was only about 1 percent each year. The data from the quinquennium 1752 to 1757 has been thrown out in order to avoid distortions inherent in the data during the first years of the operation of a mission and because of the difficulty in establishing the initial population with sufficient confidence. From 1772 to 1784, life expectancy dropped to an average of 1.9 years, and the population decline would have been around 94 percent over a generation had the same rates of mortality been sustained. The Indian population recovered between 1787 and 1801. Mean life expectancy at birth rose to 22.2, and the net reproduction ratios averaged 1.02, indicating a low rate of growth. The gross reproduction ratio averaged 2.84. Nevertheless, death rates continued to be higher than birthrates and the population declined, although at a slower rate than in the crisis years from 1768 to 1782 (see Table 2.12).

Following the expulsion of the Jesuits, the Franciscan and Dominican missionaries expanded the frontier, establishing ten additional missions in

Table 2.12 Santa Gertrudis Mission Demograhic Statistics, 1757–1811

Year	Population	CBR	CDR	GRR	NRR	Life Expectancy
1755	1,586					
1759	1,432*	42	63	1.87	.27	9.4
1762	1,730					
1764	1,642*	42	63	1.77	.32	11.5
1768	1,360					
1769	1,313*	52	74	2.39	.38	10.2
1774	798	43	106	2.34	.09	2.8
1779	555*	52	119	3.08	.06	1.6
1782	317					
1784	383*	40	121	2.19	.04	1.4
1789	280*	40	46	2.18	.72	20.8
1794	234	41	53	2.65	.84	20.1
1799	203	41	45	3.68	1.49	25.8
1804	198	44	106	4.77	.37	5.4
1808	137					
1809	124*	44	84	3.82	.48	8.3

*Population estimates generated by *Populate.*
Source: Santa Gertrudis Mission baptismal and burial registers, available on microfilm at the Bancroft Library, University of California, Berkeley; and Robert H. Jackson, "Demographic Patterns in the Missions of Central Baja California," *Journal of California and Great Basin Anthropology* 6 (1984), pp. 107–08.

the peninsula.[21] Franciscan missionary Junipero Serra, O.F.M., the spiritual leader of the Spanish colonization of Alta California, established San Fernando de Velicata mission in 1769 as a forward base for the Alta California–bound expedition in a small valley with a permanent stream located on the northern edge of the Central Desert. The existence of a large stretch of Indian territory not already controlled by the Spaniards was seen as a potential threat to the colony to be established in Alta California, and a conscious effort was made to expand the mission frontier toward San Diego in a relatively short period of time.[22] This accelerated the congregation of the Indians in the missions, and thus placed a larger number of people at risk to epidemic disease–related death in a shorter period of time. Increased traffic through the northern region also facilitated the spread of epidemics, and the presence of a permanent garrison of soldiers led to the spread of syphilis.

The population of San Fernando totaled 368 in 1771, but then increased to 1,406 in 1775 due to the resettlement of Indians. The rapid expansion

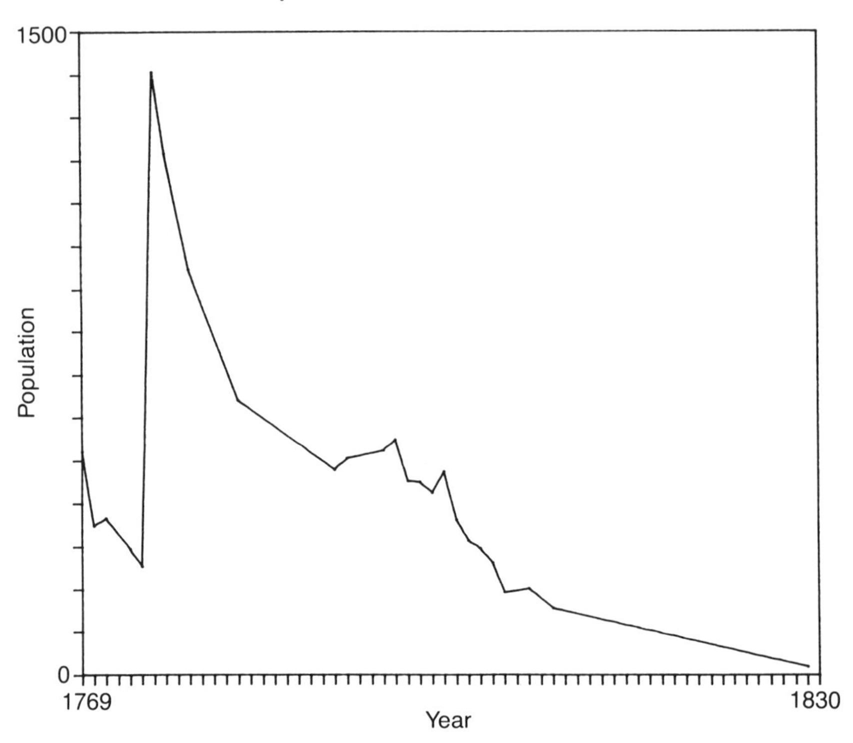

of the mission population resulted from the baptism and congregation of 937 pagans between 1771 and 1775, and from the closure of Santa María mission (established in 1767) and the transfer of the population of the former establishment to the jurisdiction of San Fernando.[23] The numbers declined in subsequent years. There were 1,216 in 1776; 642 in 1782, following the severe smallpox epidemic; 363 in 1800; 155 in 1808; and a mere 19 in 1829. The population dropped precipitously as a result of high mortality and a decline in the number of converts brought to the mission. Between 1777 and 1796, the Dominican missionaries stationed at San Fernando baptized 64 converts, an average of some 3 per year. In the previous eight years, the missionaries baptized an average of 171 converts each year.[24]

As in the other establishments, the epidemics between 1769 and 1782 occurred in the single most important period in the demographic history of San Fernando mission. Mean life expectancy averaged .9 years during the crisis, but then increased to 11.7 years over the next three quinquennium. The net reproduction ratio indicates a rate of population decline of more than 90 percent between 1774 and 1783, and would have exceeded a generation had the same mortality rates continued. The mean net reproduction ratio in the years from 1784 to 1798 was .27 or a 63 percent rate of decline, which was still very low but somewhat better than during the two previous quinquennium. Significantly, the gross reproduction ratio was low in relation to the missions further south, perhaps showing the effects of the spread of syphilis. Death rates rose again after 1799, and life expectancy and the net reproduction ratio dropped correspondingly (see Table 2.13).

After 1774 the Dominicans, who replaced the Franciscans in 1773, began establishing missions in northwestern Baja California, in a different ecological zone, the coastal desert that borders the Pacific Ocean. The climate of the coastal desert is more moderate than that of the Central Desert, and it grows more moist as one goes farther north. The Dominicans established six missions in as many coastal valleys with permanent streams, plus three more in the mountains in the interior.

Table 2.13 San Fernando Mission Demographic Statistics, 1774–1813

Year	Population	CBR	CDR	GRR	NRR	Life Expectancy
1775	1,406					
1776	1,216	69	301	2.79	.00	.5
1781	792*	39	110	1.37	.02	1.2
1786	559	50	76	1.67	.18	7.2
1791	506	39	52	1.60	.41	16.1
1796	452	20	55	1.18	.22	11.9
1801	313	15	116	1.19	.02	1.2
1806	201	14	115	1.07	.01	1.2
1811	128*	27	103	1.49	.03	1.6
1816	87*	5	90	.21	.00	1.6
1829	19					

*Population estimates generated by *Populate*.
Source: San Fernando Mission baptismal and burial registers, St. Albert's College, Oakland, California, available on Microfilm at the Bancroft Library, University of California, Berkeley; and Robert H. Jackson, "Demographic Patterns in the Missions of Northern Baja California," *Journal of California and Great Basin Anthropology* 5 (1983), pp. 132–33.

The Dominicans established the first mission in 1774, with the designation of Rosario, and relocated the mission to a second site after about 1800, when a spring at the first site went dry. However, despite the more favorable conditions for agriculture, the Dominicans adopted the system—at least in the case of Rosario mission—of leaving a part of the Indian population in satellite villages. When the spring dried up at the first site, the missionary stationed in the Rosario Valley relocated to a satellite village and directed the construction of a new and somewhat smaller building complex.

The record indicates that there were two phases of Indian conversion and incorporation: the first, in the 1770s, brought the Indians living in the valley proper into the mission and involved the baptism and congregation of 640 converts, including 412 in 1775; and a second phase in the 1780s and early 1790s following the severe smallpox epidemic of 1781–1782, involved the resettlement of Indians in the areas immediately surrounding the Rosario Valley and the baptism of another 263 converts in the years from 1782 to

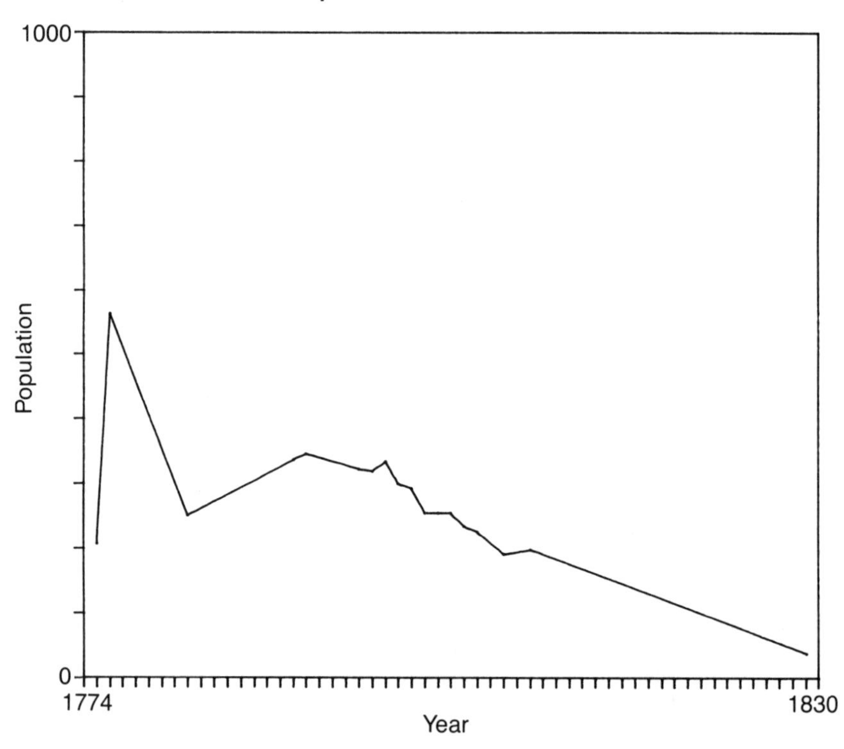

1795. In 1776, the population stood at 564, but then declined to 251 in 1782. By 1793 the population of the mission had grown again to 390, mainly through the recruitment of new converts. The numbers dropped, in subsequent years, to 256 in 1800, 199 in 1808, and a mere 38 in 1829.[25]

The baptismal and burial registers for Rosario mission are nearly complete. The first continuous record dates to the founding of the mission in 1774, and the records end in the 1820s, when the number of missionaries stationed in the peninsula dropped to the point that a resident priest could no longer be assigned to the Rosario Valley. However, the first quinquennium of data has been thrown out to avoid possible distortions due to the difficulty of establishing accurately the initial population of a community being organized and settled.

The smallpox epidemic from 1781 to 1782 elevated death rates at Rosario mission, while mean life expectancy and the net reproduction ratio were low. Between 1789 and 1803, however, death rates dropped somewhat, and life expectancy rose to an average of 7.9 years. A second severe epidemic in the quinquennium 1804–1808 lowered life expectancy again, but then conditions at Rosario improved after 1809. Life expectancy increased to an average of 10.7 years (see Table 2.14).

Table 2.14 Rosario Mission Demographic Statistics, 1779–1823

Year	Population	CBR	CDR	GRR	NRR	Life Expectancy
1781	376*	38	124	1.96	.03	1.4
1782	251					
1786	328	77	133	3.29	.06	1.6
1791	347	51	84	1.99	.17	5.9
1796	320	28	76	1.10	.09	5.5
1801	255	15	49	69	.13	12.4
1806	191	29	102	1.71	.04	1.7
1811	176*	26	76	1.88	.18	6.5
1816	143*	24	59	1.95	.42	13.7
1821	118*	29	71	2.64	.48	11.8
1829	38					

*Population estimates generated by *Populate*.
Source: Rosario Mission baptismal and burial registers, St. Albert's College, Oakland, California, available on microfilm at the Bancroft Library, University of California, Berkeley; and Robert H. Jackson, "Demographic Patterns in the Missions of Northern Baja California," *Journal of California and Great Basin Anthropology* 5 (1983), pp. 132–33.

The Indian population of Rosario did not evidence the same moderate to high birthrates observed in the missions farther south; and the gross reproduction ratio, the index of the ability of the population to produce children, averaged 1.91. In contrast, the mean gross reproduction ratio was 2.66 at Mulege, 2.70 for Comondú, and 2.84 at Santa Gertrudis, but only 1.40 at San Fernando and 1.84 at Santo Domingo. The evidence suggests that the Indians in the northern missions produced fewer children then in the missions farther south. This pattern can probably be explained by the impact of disease, and the harshness of the Franciscan and, especially, the Dominican regime, which placed more emphasis on agricultural production and thus more labor demands on the adult Indian population, both men and women. The conclusion that can be made would maintain that conditions in the northern missions decreased the ability of the Indian population to reproduce, while, at the same time, high rates of mortality killed the majorty of the Indians in the space of several generations.

The final mission examined here is Santo Domingo, established by the Dominicans in 1775 in a narrow valley with a permanent stream to the north of the Rosario Valley and near San Quintin Bay. Due to a number of factors, one of which was the distance of the mission from the bay and its rich marine-food resources, the process of the congregation of the Indians living in the territory surrounding the mission was slower, and the largest recorded population of 390 was recorded in 1799, more than twenty years after the establishment of the mission. The Dominicans baptized the largest number of converts in the 1780s and 1790s, performing a total of 370 baptisms of converts in the years from 1787 to 1796, or a mean of 41 per year. This compares to a total of 192 baptisms of converts and an average of 24 per year from 1777 to 1785, the second most intensive period of the congregation of converts. The population declined after 1800. There were 278 Indians living at the mission in 1801, 194 seven years later in 1808, and 73 in 1829. The relatively large population at such a late date can be attributed to the closure of San Pedro Mártir mission (established in 1794) at some point after 1808, and the relocation of the population from that mission to Santo Domingo.

Life expectancy fluctuated at Santo Domingo mission, and averaged .9 years in the 1780s, but it rose to a mean of 8.8 years after 1794. The net reproduction ratio was consistently low, and shows that the Indian population faced a rate of decline between 74 percent and 99 percent over the space of a generation. Low birthrates and high mortality, particularly high rates of infant and child mortality, destroyed the population of Santo

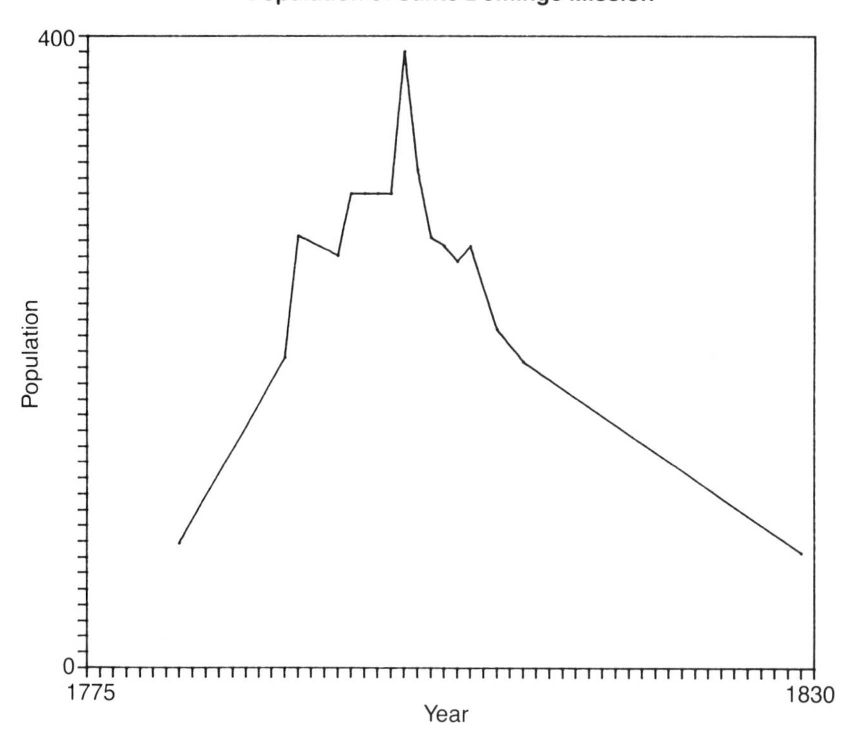

Domingo, as well as the populations of the other northern Baja California missions (see Table 2.15).

Demographic Collapse in Alta California

Regional variations occurred in the vital rates of the Alta California missions. The vital rates of the southern missions were less severe than the vital rates of the establishments in the northern part of the province. Case studies of demographic collapse in Alta California are organized into three geographic groups: three southern missions, namely, San Gabriel (established in 1771), San Juan Capistrano (established in 1777), and San Luis Rey (established in 1798); six missions in the central Alta California region: San Carlos (established in 1770), San Luis Obispo (established in 1772), Santa Cruz (established in 1791), Soledad (established in 1791), San Juan

Table 2.15 Santo Domingo Mission Demographic Statistics, 1780–1809

Year	Population	CBR	CDR	GRR	NRR	Life Expectancy
1782	79	73	199	3.55	.03	1.1
1787	83*	53	190	1.94	.01	.7
1792	145*	40	134	1.27	.01	1.0
1797	241*	30	62	1.00	.12	7.9
1802	267	20	54	.86	.15	11.2
1807	239*	38	82	2.42	.24	6.6
1829	73					

*Population estimates generated by *Populate*.
Source: San Domingo Mission baptismal and burial registers, St. Albert's College, Oakland, California, available on microfilm at the Bancroft Library, University of California, Berkeley; and Robert H. Jackson, "Demographic Patterns in the Missions of Northern Baja California," *Journal of California and Great Basin Anthropology* 5 (1983), pp. 132–33.

Bautista (established in 1797), and San Miguel (established in 1797); finally, the five missions in the San Francisco Bay region: San Francisco (established in 1776), San Rafael (established in 1817), Santa Clara (established in 1777), San Jose (established in 1797), and San Francisco Solano (established in 1823).

The Franciscans established San Gabriel mission in the Los Angeles Basin in 1771, and relocated the mission to its present site in the San Gabriel Valley in 1774, following problems with the development of agriculture and hostility from local Indians exacerbated by acts of brutality committed by the soldiers assigned to protect the missionaries.[26] The Franciscans stationed at San Gabriel followed a policy of congregating the bulk of the Indian converts at the *cabecera,* but they did establish *ranchos* at different places in the mission territory. For example, in the 1830s the missionaries began developing a large cattle ranch at San Bernardino, which also became a major population center for recent Cahuilla converts from the San Bernardino and surrounding areas.

Birthrates at San Gabriel mission ranged from moderate to high as measured by the crude birthrate and gross reproduction ratio, but they declined as the number of women in relation to the total population dropped. Death rates were chronically high, averaging 94 per thousand population, but the patterns of mortality also show episodes of extremely

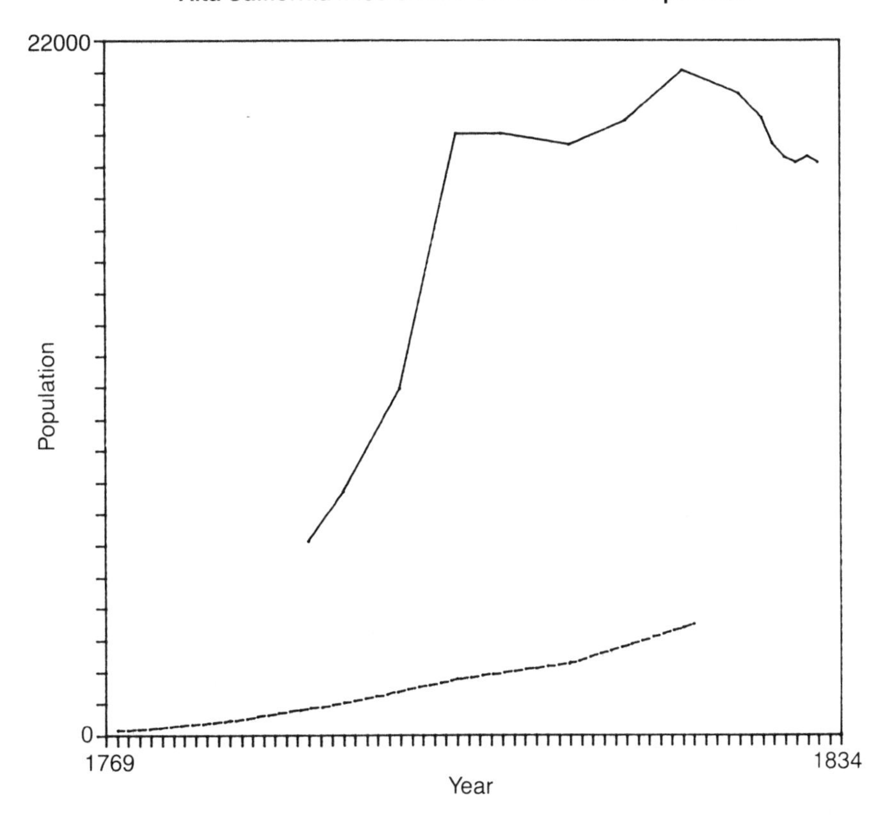

high mortality caused by epidemics in 1781 and in the first decade of the nineteenth century. The Indian population consistently declined, averaging a net reproduction ratio of 0.22, or a decline over a generation of 78 percent. The inviability of the Indian population was reflected in the low mean life expectancy at birth, which averaged 6.4 years. The most destructive period for the population occurred in the years after 1800, when several strong epidemics attacked the Indian population, and a rapid growth in the population of the mission exacerbated poor living conditions caused by overcrowding, poor sanitation, and polluted water supplies. In the 1780s, the population more than doubled, from 452 in 1780 to 1,078 in 1790. A second period of rapid population growth through recruitment of converts occurred in the first years of the nineteenth century, when the

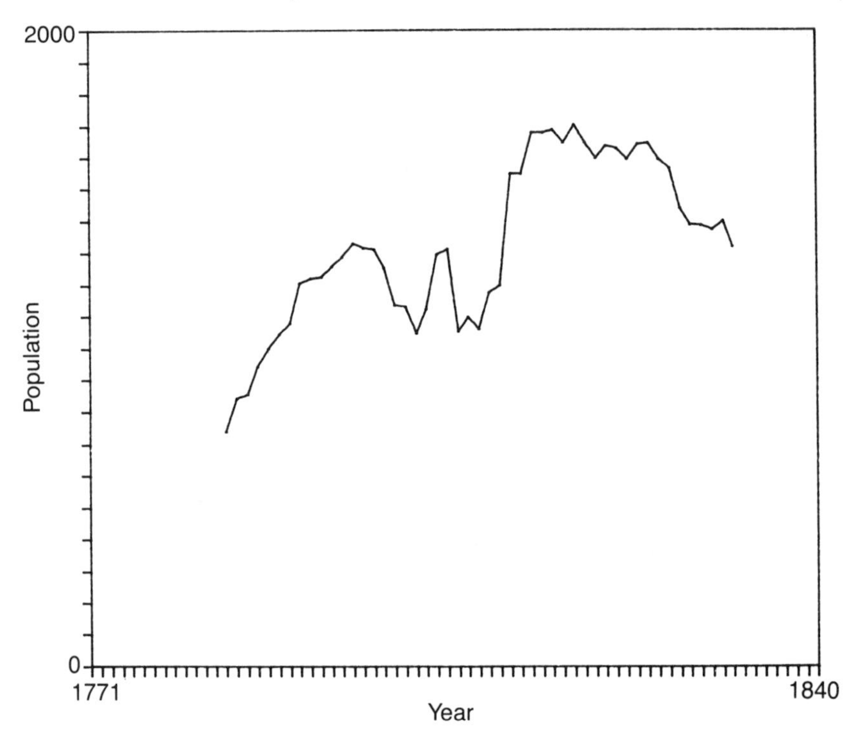

mission population jumped from 1,108 in 1806 to 1,550 in 1811, and 1,644 in 1816. Most, if not all, of the new converts lived at the *cabecera,* adding to the problems of overcrowding (see Table 2.16).

The second southern Alta California mission examined here is San Juan Capistrano, established by the Franciscans in 1776 and relocated several years later, in 1778, to a site with greater agricultural potential. The majority of the converts lived at the *cabecera,* but because the population was smaller than San Gabriel's the problem of overcrowding was not as great. Nevertheless, the population of the mission was not viable.

In contrast to the patterns observed for San Gabriel mission, the *congregación* program at San Juan Capistrano was more gradual, and there were no wild fluctuations in the numbers of converts brought into the mission over a short period of time. Moreover, the population of San Juan Capistrano was not as large, reaching a maximum size of 1,361 in 1812. The lower population densities contributed to vital rates that were not as

Table 2.16 San Gabriel Mission Demographic Statistics, 1779–1833

Year	Population	CBR	CDR	GRR	NRR	Life Expectancy
1781	570	69	114	3.82	.22	4.1
1786	857	65	92	3.25	.32	6.6
1791	1,202	70	111	3.20	.19	4.2
1796	1,331	49	69	2.24	.38	10.8
1801	1,129	43	122	1.99	.04	1.5
1806	1,108	38	127	1.71	.02	1.3
1811	1,550	40	118	1.83	.03	1.5
1816	1,644	29	91	1.33	.05	2.5
1821	1,626	35	78	1.85	.21	7.4
1826	1,565	28	78	2.00	.25	8.3
1831	1,398	18	43	1.93	.68	22.3

Source: San Gabriel Mission baptismal and burial registers and "Libro de Padrones," Mission San Gabriel, San Gabriel, California; Annual Reports, Archivo General de la Nación, México, D.F., and the Santa Barbara Mission Archive-Library, Santa Barbara, California.

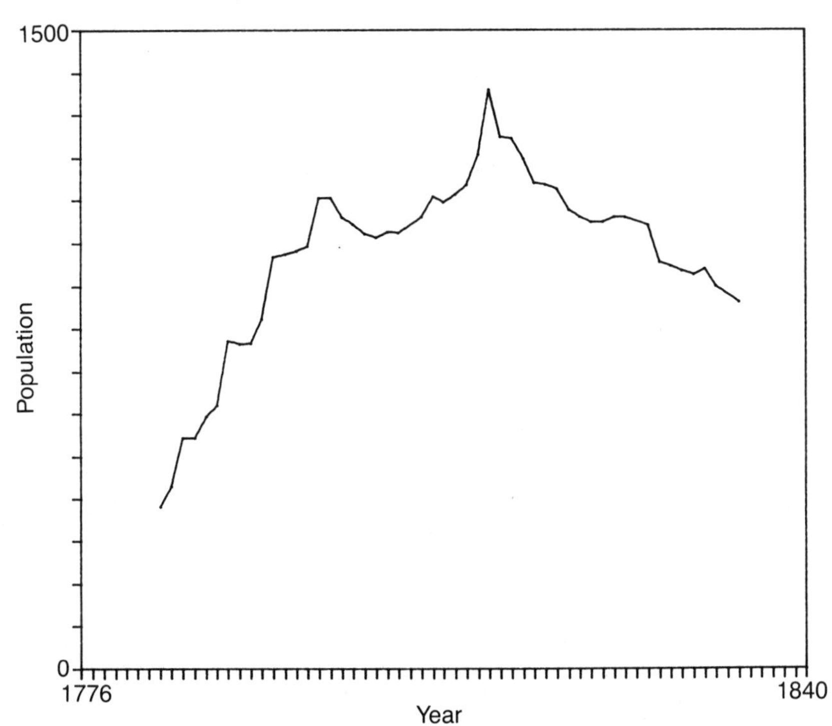

extreme as those at San Gabriel. Birthrates ranged from high to moderate, as shown by a mean crude birthrate of 47 per thousand population and a mean gross reproduction ratio of 2.62. Crude death rates averaged 67 per thousand population, and the rate of decline as measured by the net reproduction ratio indicates that a 49 percent decline over a generation was not as bad as the figure recorded for San Gabriel. Finally, mean life expectancy at birth fluctuated between a low of 7.9 to a high of 17.1 and averaged 12.3 years (see Table 2.17).

The final southern Alta California mission examined is San Luis Rey, established by the Franciscans in 1798. The baptismal and burial registers from San Luis Rey are not extant, but the vital rates for the years 1812–1832 and patterns of population growth and decline can be reconstructed from detailed annual and biennial reports. The population of San Luis Rey mission grew rapidly, with a total of 1,952 baptisms between 1798 and 1811 as against 512 burials. The population of the mission stood at 1,601 in 1811. The Franciscans achieved considerable success in their recruitment campaign over the next twenty years, with a total of 408 baptisms of converts in 1817, 387 in 1819, 138 in 1823, and 101 in 1826. In 1834, on the eve of the secularization of the mission, the population of the mission was 2,844, making it the most populous Alta California establishment.[27]

Table 2.17 San Juan Capistrano Mission Demographic Statistics, 1781–1835

Year	Population	CBR	CDR	GRR	NRR	Life Expectancy
1783	383	57	72	3.34	.62	11.9
1788	656	66	67	3.78	.90	15.1
1793	878	55	61	3.19	.80	15.9
1798	1,107	57	83	3.26	.43	8.7
1803	1,027	58	77	3.23	.48	9.7
1808	1,096	47	74	2.45	.35	9.3
1813	1,249	34	70	1.65	.20	7.9
1818	1,128	30	60	1.41	.22	10.2
1823	1,062	38	52	1.92	.49	16.2
1828	947	41	63	2.30	.49	13.7
1833	853	35	53	2.31	.62	17.1

Source: San Juan Capistrano Mission baptismal and burial registers, Mission San Juan Capistrano, San Juan Capistrano, California; Annual Reports, Archivo General de la Nación, México, D.F., and the Santa Barbara Mission Archive-Library, Santa Barbara, California.

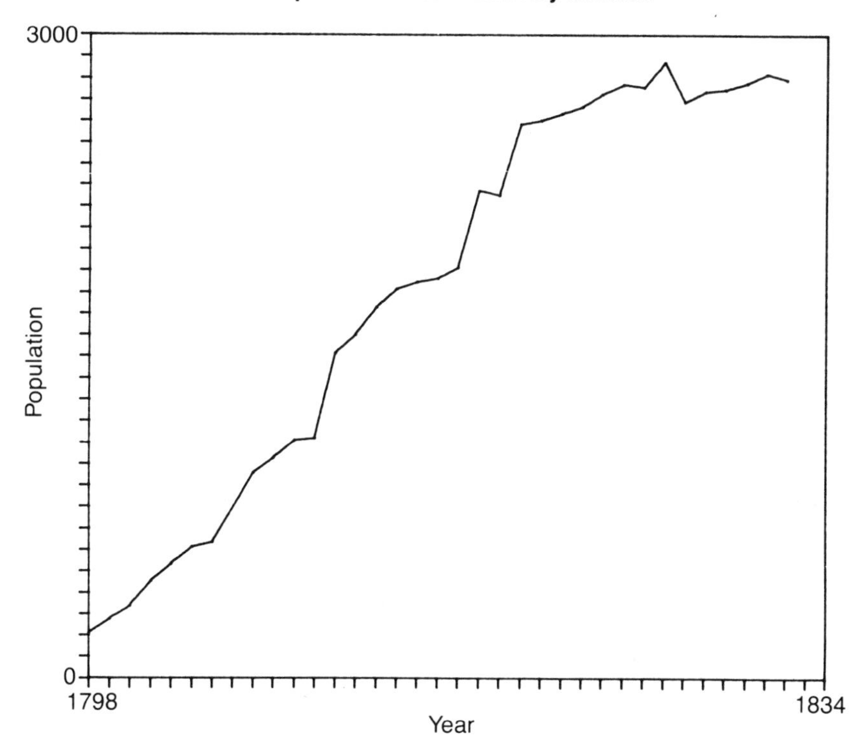

The dispersed population of the mission lived at the *cabecera* and several *ranchos,* including San Antonio de Pala and Los Flores. Although the population of San Luis Rey was inviable, the vital rates were not as bad as those at San Gabriel. Crude birthrates averaged 36 per thousand population, and the mean gross reproduction ratio was 1.96. Crude death rates were low at 47 per thousand population, and the mean net reproduction ratio of 0.58 indicates a rate of decline of 42 percent over a generation. Mean life expectancy at birth averaged 19.1 years, with a low of 12.6 years (see Table 2.18). The population of San Luis Rey mission declined gradually.

The Franciscan missionaries stationed at San Carlos mission, the first mission in the central Alta California region established in 1770, recruited converts from the Carmel River Basin, parts of the Salinas Valley, and nearby coastal areas, and this was accomplished from the 1770s through the first decade of the nineteenth century. The last phase of active recruitment occurred in the 1803–1807 quinquennium, with the missionaries

Table 2.18 San Luis Rey Mission Demographic Statistics, 1813–1832

Year	Population	CBR	CDR	GRR	NRR	Life Expectancy
1815	1,866	36	44	2.12	.68	20.4
1820	2,603	37	50	2.08	.55	16.9
1825	2,756	36	59	1.90	.37	12.6
1830	2,776	34	34	1.74	.73	26.6

Source: Annual Reports, the Santa Barbara Mission Archive-Library, Santa Barbara, California.

baptizing 108 converts, 71 converts in the year 1806 alone. After 1807, only 24 more converts came to the mission, and the population of the mission began a steady decline. The numbers reached a recorded maximum of 876 in 1795, then dropped to 747 in 1800, 550 in 1808, 381 in 1820, and a mere 165 in 1834, on the eve of the secularization of the mission.

Indian women at San Carlos mission bore children, and birthrates were moderate to high. The mean crude birthrate per thousand population was 51, and the gross reproduction ratio averaged 3.00. However, death rates were consistently higher than birthrates, averaging 90 per thousand population. The mission population experienced a net decline of 62 percent per generation, as indicated by a mean net reproduction ratio of 0.38. Finally, mean life expectancy was low, averaging 7.6 years at birth (see Table 2.19). The last quinquennium of data for San Carlos mission analyzed here shows a marked improvement in the vital rates of the mission population, with a lower crude death rate and higher gross reproduction ratio, net reproduction ratio, and life expectancy. The improvement can be attributed to a shift in the age and gender structure of the population, with some out-migration from the mission following the implementation of a program to emancipate more acculturated Indians, as outlined below.

The Franciscans established San Luis Obispo mission in 1772, in a well-watered valley located roughly halfway between San Gabriel and San Carlos mission and among the northern Chumash. The Franciscans also recruited Salina converts. Congregation of converts was almost continuous, from the foundation of the mission through the first years of the nineteenth century; and in the year 1803, 239 non-Christians received baptism, which was the single largest number of conversions in a given year. During the period of continuous active recruitment of converts, the population of the

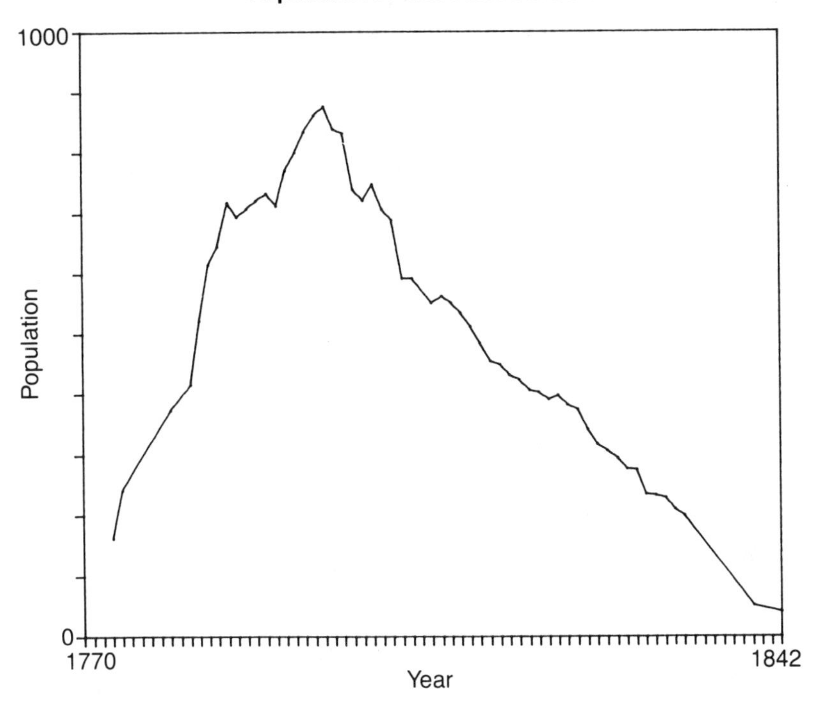

Table 2.19 San Carlos Mission Demographic Statistics, 1774–1833

Year	Population	CBR	CDR	GRR	NRR	Life Expectancy
1776	390	83	108	4.79	.48	6.7
1781	494	41	113	2.06	.04	1.6
1786	694	49	85	2.08	.14	4.8
1791	770	59	102	2.38	.14	4.0
1796	839	47	68	2.04	.35	11.0
1801	705	41	84	2.17	.21	6.6
1806	550	39	105	2.54	.08	2.3
1811	485	39	89	2.76	.20	5.0
1816	405	49	76	3.37	.57	11.0
1821	374	55	92	3.76	.52	9.0
1826	277	54	102	3.94	.41	6.9
1831	209	50	53	4.13	1.44	22.1

Source: San Carlos Mission baptismal and burial registers, Monterey Diocese Chancery Archive, Monterey, California; Annual Reports, Archivo General de la Nación, México, D.F.; and the Santa Barbara Mission Archive-Library, Santa Barbara, California.

mission fluctuated, but in 1804, it grew to 961, the largest recorded population. The numbers dropped after 1804, and stood at 203 in 1833. There was a last phase of the baptism of non-Christian Indians in 1834 and 1835. In two years 169 Yokuts from the San Joaquín Valley received baptism, although it is not clear if the Yokuts settled at the mission or went to work on nearby ranches.

Overcrowding appears not to have been as serious a problem at San Luis Obispo as at other missions, although the mission population was not viable. Birthrates ranged from high to moderate, but beginning in the first decade of the nineteenth century, they declined following a severe mortality crisis and a drop in the number of converts moving to the mission. The crude birthrate averaged 37 per thousand population, and the gross reproduction ratio 2.00. With the exception of the ten years between 1780 and 1789, death rates were consistently higher than birthrates, averaging 76 per thousand population. The population actually grew through natural

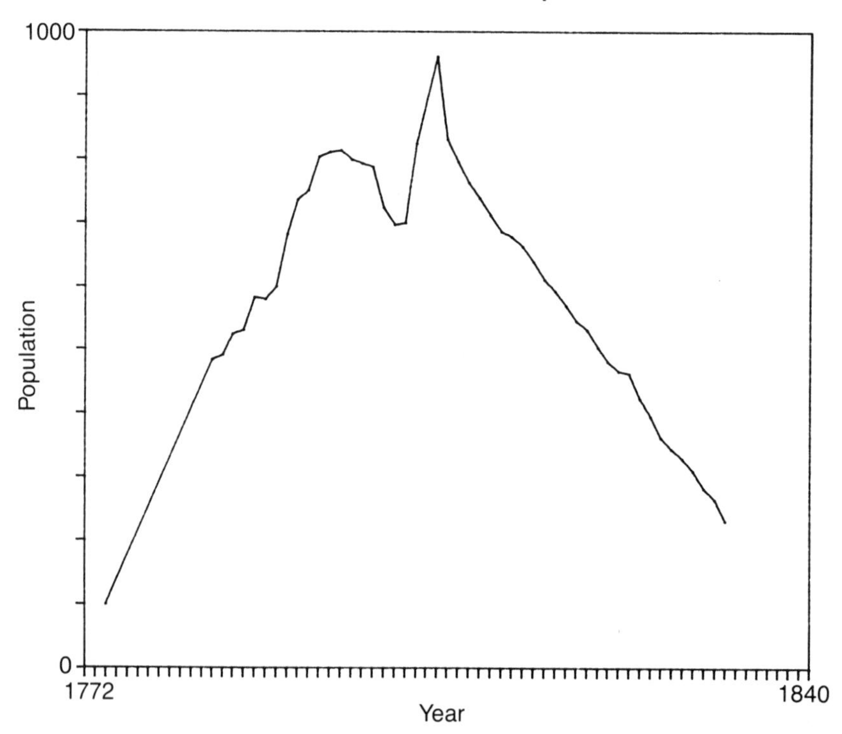

Table 2.20 San Luis Obispo Mission Demographic Statistics, 1780–1834

Year	Population	CBR	CDR	GRR	NRR	Life Expectancy
1782	464	58	51	3.53	1.17	21.0
1787	531	52	44	3.23	1.24	24.5
1792	736	42	64	2.61	.51	12.6
1797	799	35	82	1.86	.12	4.6
1802	699	43	104	1.86	.04	1.6
1807	795	33	66	1.23	.13	7.3
1812	677	38	76	1.46	.15	7.0
1817	570	38	73	1.79	.24	8.7
1822	467	28	75	1.76	.19	7.3
1827	344	14	86	1.14	.04	2.8
1832	231	20	114	1.50	.03	1.5

Source: San Luis Obispo Mission baptismal and burial registers, Monterey Diocese Chancery Archive, Monterey, California; Annual Reports, Archivo General de la Nación, México, D.F., and the Santa Barbara Mission Archive-Library, Santa Barbara, California.

reproduction until 1789, but then declined at a mean rate of 84 percent as indicated by an average net reproduction ratio of 0.16 between 1790 and 1834. Mean life expectancy at birth averaged 22.8 in the 1780s, but then dropped to an average of 5.9 over the following forty-four years. The rapid decline of the population was partially related to a severe epidemic in 1802 (see Table 2.20).

In the 1790s, the Franciscans expanded the number of missions in Alta California. In the summer of 1791, the missionaries established Santa Cruz mission on the northern shore of Monterey, at a site that proved to be among the deadliest for Indians congregated in the missions, and which was due, in part, to the cool and damp weather exacerbating the problems associated with higher population densities. The resettlement of Indian converts occurred in two phases: the conversion of the local Ohlone population, largely completed about 1810; and the recruitment of Yokuts from the San Joaqín Valley from 1815 to 1826. There were 523 Indians congregated at the mission in 1797, the largest recorded population. The numbers dropped to 358 in 1816, but then rapidly increased to 519 five years later, as a result of the recruitment of Yokuts. The population then declined after 1821, and totaled 238 in 1834, when the Mexican government began the process of the secularization of the missions.[28]

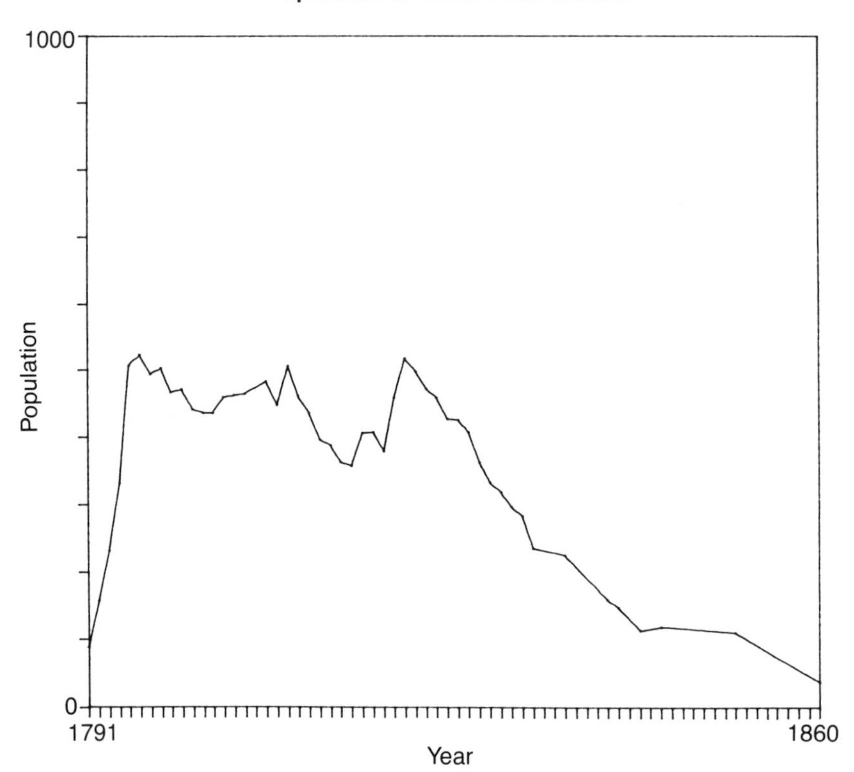

Crude birthrates at Santa Cruz mission were low when compared to other mission populations, averaging 29 per thousand population and a mean gross reproduction ratio of 1.20. The highest crude birthrates of 44 and 38 per thousand population occurred in years of active recruitment of Yokuts, which increased the number of women of child-bearing age in relation to the total population. Crude death rates were extremely high, averaging 109 per thousand population, and the net reproduction ratio was low, with a mean figure of 0.04. The average rate of decline was 96 percent over a generation, and mean life expectancy at birth averaged a mere 2.3 years (see Table 2.21).

In the same summer of 1791, the Franciscans established Soledad mission in the Salinas Valley. The records for Soledad mission are incomplete. The burial registers are missing, but patterns of mortality can be reconstructed, for most of the history of the mission, from extant annual and biennial reports that record totals of burials. Data for the years

Table 2.21 Santa Cruz Mission Demographic Statistics, 1796–1840

Year	Population	CBR	CDR	GRR	NRR	Life Expectancy
1798	504	28	139	1.05	.01	1.3
1803	437	27	105	.79	.01	1.5
1808	485	25	133	.70	.01	1.0
1813	398	21	97	.55	.02	2.3
1818	410	41	92	1.60	.07	3.1
1823	474	38	102	1.40	.07	3.6
1828	364	25	103	1.08	.03	1.8
1833	261	27	86	1.51	.09	4.4
1838	164*	32	121	2.62	.05	1.6

*Population estimate generated by *Populate.*
Source: Santa Cruz Mission baptismal and burial registers, Monterey Diocese Chancery Archive, Monterey, California; and Robert H. Jackson, "Patterns of Demographic Change in the Missions of Central Alta California," *Journal of California and Great Basin Anthropology* 9 (1987), pp. 263–65.

1793–1832 are used for the purposes of the analysis here. The Franciscans stationed at Soledad mission converted and congregated the local Esselen-Salina population in the 1790s and in the first two decades of the nineteenth century; and then they congregated nearly 200 Yokuts from the San Joaquín Valley. The population of the mission reached a recorded high of 688 in 1805, but it fluctuated and declined in subsequent years. There were 436 Indians living at the mission in 1820, and 350 in 1834, on the eve of secularization.[29]

Demographic patterns at Soledad mission closely paralleled patterns at Santa Cruz mission. The crude birthrate ranged from moderate to low, averaging 39 per thousand population, and declined in the early years of the nineteenth century. During the 1798–1802 quinquennium, the crude birthrate was 84 per thousand, but dropped to 22 per thousand during the next quinquennium, as a consequence of the impact of a severe epidemic in 1802. The gross reproduction ratio averaged 2.12, but also dropped following the 1802 epidemic. Mortality was chronically high, averaging 142 per thousand population, with a high of 326 per thousand during the 1798–1802 quinquennium, and the net reproduction ratio of 0.06 indicates a rate of decline of 94 percent over a generation. The high mortality was reflected in a low mean life expectancy at birth, which averaged 2.2 years (see Table 2.22).

San Juan Bautista mission, established in 1797 in the San Benito Valley, evidenced patterns that were similar to those of Santa Cruz and Soledad

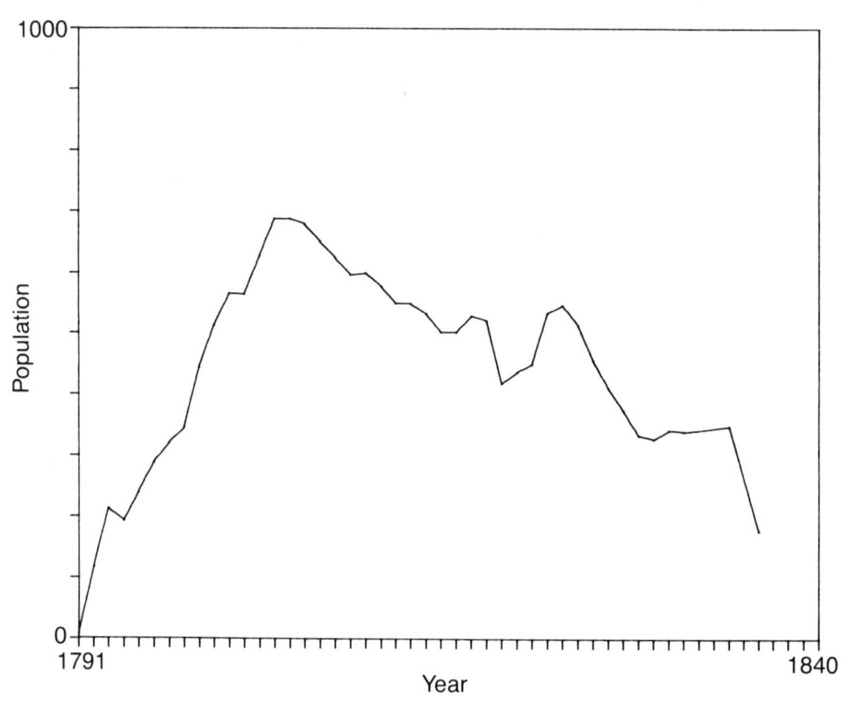

Table 2.22 Soledad Mission Demographic Statistics, 1793–1832

Year	Population	CBR	CDR	GRR	NRR	Life Expectancy
1795	240	96	190	4.92	.08	1.4
1800	512	84	326	2.64	.00	.5
1805	688	22	183	.63	.00	.4
1810	598	13	90	.35	.00	1.3
1815	500	26	76	.84	.04	3.1
1820	436	25	88	1.24	.04	2.5
1825	454	28	81	2.68	.23	5.8
1830	342	17	100	3.65	.11	2.3

Source: Soledad Mission baptismal register, Monterey Diocese Chancery Archive, Monterey, California; Annual and Biennial Reports, Archivo General de la Nación, México, D.F., and the Santa Barbara Mission Archive-Library, Santa Barbara, California.

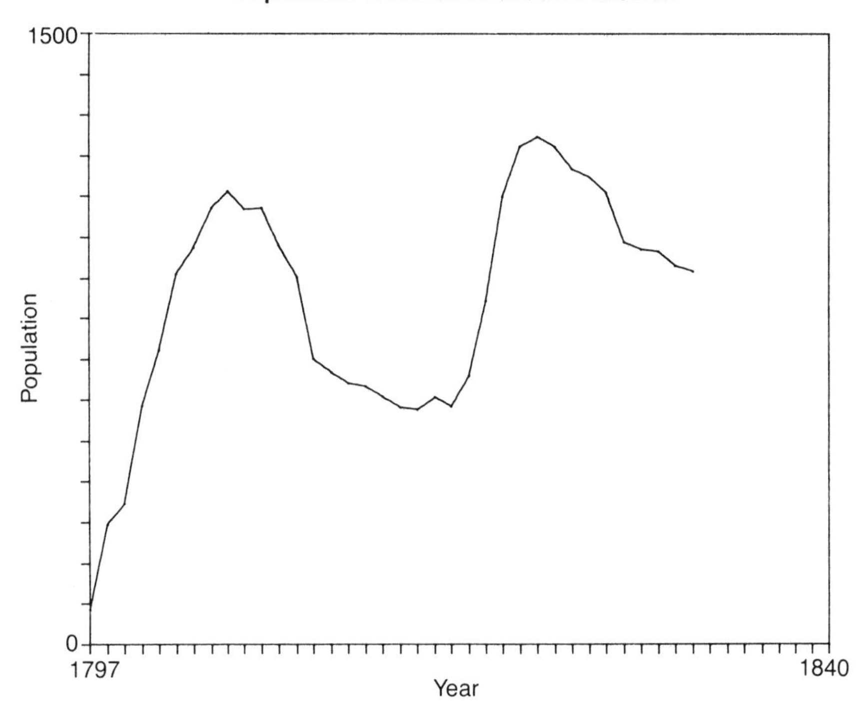

missions, but with some variations. There were two distinct phases of expansion in the size of the mission population related to recruitment: a first period between 1797 and 1807, when the Franciscans congregated the local Ohlone population; and a second period from 1819 to 1823, with the congregation of Yokuts from the San Joaquín Valley. During the first phase of expansion, the number of Indians living at the missions reached a high of 1,112 in 1805, and the population was 1,248 in 1823, following the congregation of Yokuts. The numbers dropped after 1823, and stood at 858 in 1834.[30]

Crude birthrates at San Juan Bautista were moderate to high, averaging 43 per thousand population, and the mean gross reproduction ratio was 1.63. Crude death rates were high, averaging 98 per thousand population, and the mean net reproduction ratio of 0.13 indicated a rate of decline of 87 percent. The average mean life expectancy at birth was 5.0 years (see Table 2.23).

Table 2.23 San Juan Bautista Mission Demographic Statistics, 1802–1831

Year	Population	CBR	CDR	GRR	NRR	Life Expectancy
1804	1,073	41	137	1.29	.03	1.6
1809	902	38	98	1.02	.07	5.1
1814	607	49	89	2.45	.11	3.3
1819	660	58	74	2.35	.40	11.1
1824	1,221	43	95	1.50	.14	6.3
1829	969	28	96	1.17	.04	2.8

Source: San Juan Bautista Mission baptismal and burial registers, Monterey Diocese Chancery Archive, Monterey, California; and Robert H. Jackson, "Patterns of Demographic Change in the Missions of Central Alta California," *Journal of California and Great Basin Anthropology* 9 (1987), pp. 267–68.

Later in the summer of 1797, the Franciscans established San Miguel in the southern reaches of the Salinas Valley. As was the case at San Juan Bautista mission, there were two periods of expansion of the mission population related to recruitment efforts: first, from the foundation of the mission until 1814, when the Franciscan congregated the Salina population; and second, in 1834 and 1835, when 254 San Joaquín Valley Yokuts received baptism. The numbers fluctuated, but reached a maximum recorded figure of 1,078 in 1814. The population then declined, reaching 599 in 1834, on the eve of the secularization of the mission.[31]

Birthrates at San Miguel mission ranged from moderate to high, but the population was not viable because of consistently high mortality. Mean crude birth and death rates, respectively, were 41 and 70 per thousand population, and the average gross and net reproduction ratios were 2.10 and 0.31. Although it was not as high as at several of the missions farther north, the mean rate of decline of 69 percent over a generation still spelled virtual extinction for the Indian population congregated at the mission. Mean life expectancy at birth was as high as 13.5 years and averaged 10.2 years, which indicates that levels of health were somewhat better than at the other establishments in the region (see Table 2.24).

The final region considered here is the San Francisco Bay area. The Spanish first colonized the San Francisco Bay region in 1776 and 1777, as part of the plan to occupy the Bay to prevent hostile foreign powers from taking the harbor. In 1776, the Franciscans established a mission at San

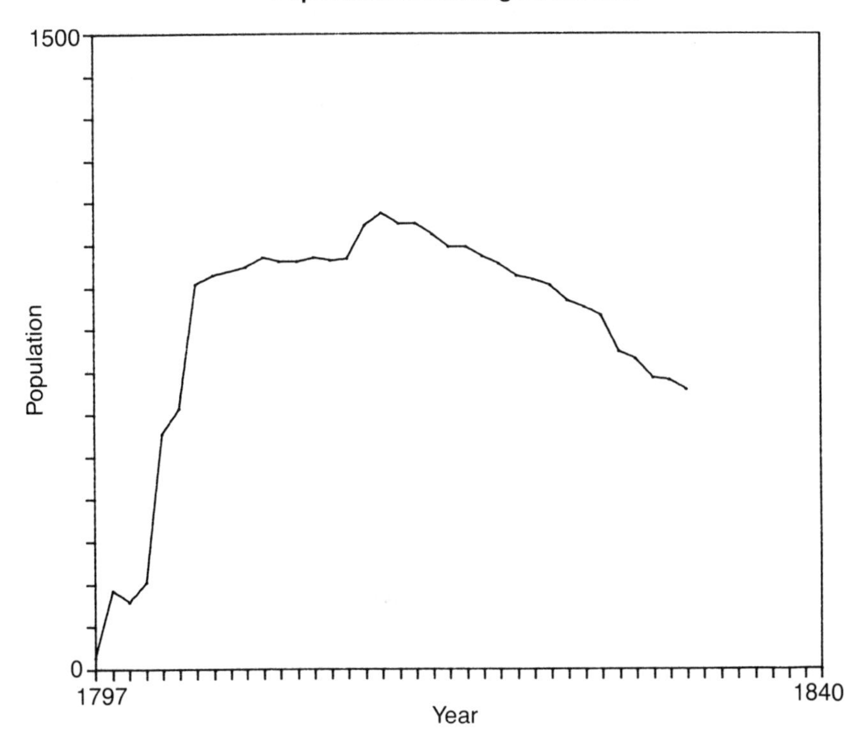

Francisco, and a second mission community at Santa Clara in the following year. The crown organized an overland expedition from Sonora, in 1775, which was led by Juan Bautista de Anza and brought colonists and soldiers who founded a military garrison at San Francisco in 1776, and a farming village at San José in 1777. From the nucleus of two missions, the Franciscans began to congregate the local Indian population. In the 1790s, the Franciscans, in concert with civil officials, expanded the number of missions in order to control a larger number of Indians. In the summer and fall of 1797, the missionaries founded four mission communities, including one at San José that was close to a pass in the southeastern bay area leading into interior valleys. The last two missions were founded in the early nineteenth century. The missionaries stationed at San Francisco organized a satellite village (*asistencia*) in 1817 at San Rafael, a site with a warmer climate, to enable the growing number of sick Indians at that mission to recover from the damp chill of San Francisco and the chronic ailments brought on by the climate and unhealthy living conditions in the mission. The Franciscans elevated San Rafael to full mission status in 1823. In 1823, the missionaries established San Francisco Solano mission at Sonoma as part of a colonization scheme in the northern part of Alta California, in an effort to prevent further Russian expansion inland from the trading post established at Ross in 1812.

The missionaries at San Francisco resettled converts from tribelets throughout the northern bay region, and the population of the mission community continued to grow as the Franciscans congregated more Indians to the *cabecera.* The population of the mission was 635 in 1800, but the greatest increase in the mission population came after 1800, as the missionaries turned their attention to the *rancherías* located across the bay and northeast of the mission. After 1817, the pace of resettlement increased as the missionaries congregated Indians from San Rafael and surrounding areas. In 1804, the population totaled 1,103; the numbers stood at 1,252 in 1820; and there were 1,801 in 1821, prior to the founding of San Francisco Solano mission and the elevation of San Rafael to mission status, and the resulting transfer of converts to the jurisdiction of the recently established mission. After 1823, the population fluctuated but declined, primarily because of the transfer of Indians to the jurisdiction of the two missions established farther north. There were 208 Indians living at the mission in 1823, and 204 in 1832.[32]

The population of San Francisco mission evidenced a pattern of moderate to high birthrates, but consistently high death rates averaged 127 per thousand and a mean rate of decline of 92 percent over a generation. The

Table 2.24 San Miguel Mission Demographic Statistics, 1800–1832

Year	Population	CBR	CDR	GRR	NRR	Life Expectancy
1805	1,000	63	101	3.55	.29	5.5
1810	971	39	56	2.03	.43	13.6
1815	1,050	38	64	1.82	.30	10.6
1820	973	40	63	1.90	.34	11.5
1825	867	35	57	1.76	.37	13.5
1830	684	28	76	1.51	.14	6.2

Source: San Miguel Mission baptismal and burial registers, Monterey Diocese Chancery Archive; Annual Reports, Archivo General de la Nación, México, D.F., and the Santa Barbara Mission Archive-Library, Santa Barbara, California.

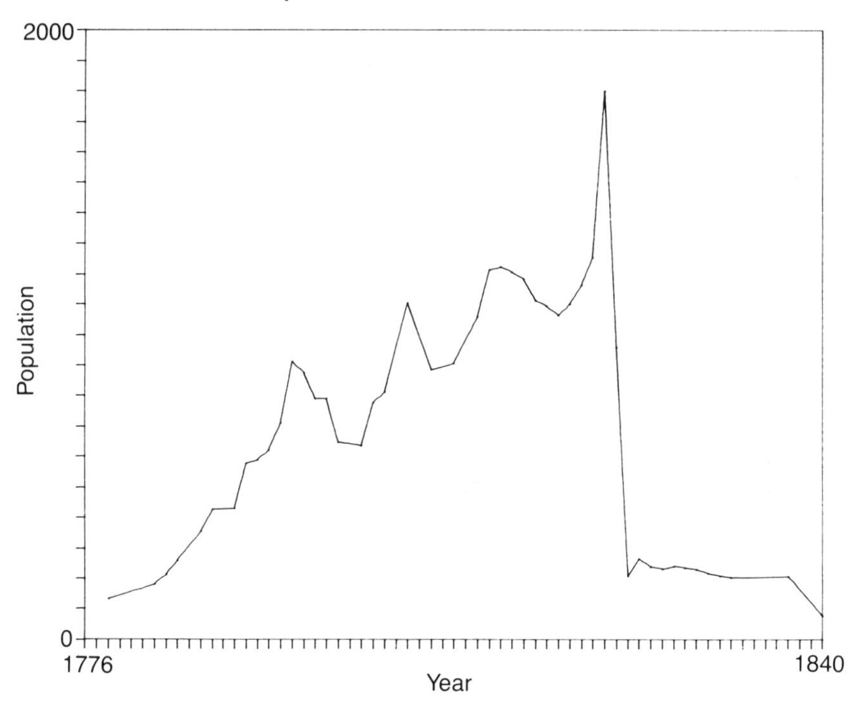

high mortality also translated into a low mean life expectancy that averaged 4.2 years at birth. The frightful mortality can be attributed to several factors: overcrowding and the related problem of poor sanitation in the adobe Indian housing; polluted water; dehydration among children, caused by diarrhea; syphilis; chronic respiratory ailments; and the practice of locking up women and girls at night in unhealthy dormitories. The stresses of cultural change also contributed. The cool and damp San Francisco climate exacerbated the unhealthy conditions in the mission, but it alone was not responsible for the high mortality. After 1823, death rates dropped and life expectancy somewhat improved, which highlights the role of overcrowding and poor living conditions in the destruction of the Indian population (see Table 2.25).

The bulk of the population at San Rafael mission was transferred there from San Francisco and from other nearby missions, which explains the low birthrates, which averaged 20 per thousand and dropped during the

Table 2.25 San Francisco Mission Demographic Statistics, 1781–1835

Year	Population	CBR	CDR	GRR	NRR	Life Expectancy
1783	215	63	100	1.98	.20	6.9
1788	426	54	96	1.58	.15	6.3
1793	711	35	176	.93	.00	.8
1798	645	35	120	.82	.02	2.0
1803	1,051	42	145	1.35	.01	1.1
1808	906	26	168	.63	.00	1.0
1813	1,205	45	185	1.23	.01	.9
1818	1,100	31	152	.84	.01	1.1
1823	208	31	131	.63	.04	4.9
1828	236	38	65	1.92	.30	10.1
1833	204*	18	56	1.11	.19	11.2

*Population estimate generated by *Populate*.
Source: San Francisco Mission baptismal and burial registers, San Francisco Archdiocese Chancery Archive, Colma, California; Annual Reports Archivo General de la Nación, México, D.F., and The Santa Barbara Mission Archive-Library, Santa Barbara, California.

1820s, and the gross reproduction ratio, which averaged only 0.60. The Indians sent there to recuperate from chronic ailments contracted at the other missions were physically weak because of their poor health, and the Indian women were less capable of bearing children. This especially would have been the case for women suffering from syphilis. On the other hand, the lower population density, warmer climate, and lesser emphasis placed on the use of permanent adobe housing for the Indian population accounts for death rates lower than those documented for San Francisco mission and a higher mean life expectancy. Nevertheless, the population was not viable, and it dropped rapidly once the source of recruits dried up. The population reached a recorded high of 1,073 in 1831, following a period of active congregation of new converts, but then it declined as fewer converts settled at San Rafael and converts were transferred to the jurisdiction of the newly established San Francisco Solano mission.[33] Mortality rates were moderate, averaging 50 per thousand population, and the population experienced an average rate of decline over a generation of 83 percent. The average mean life expectancy was 19.6 years (see Table 2.26).

The population of Santa Clara mission expanded rapidly between the 1770s and 1790s, as the missionaries resettled Indians from *rancherías* located throughout the south bay region. In the year 1794, the numbers

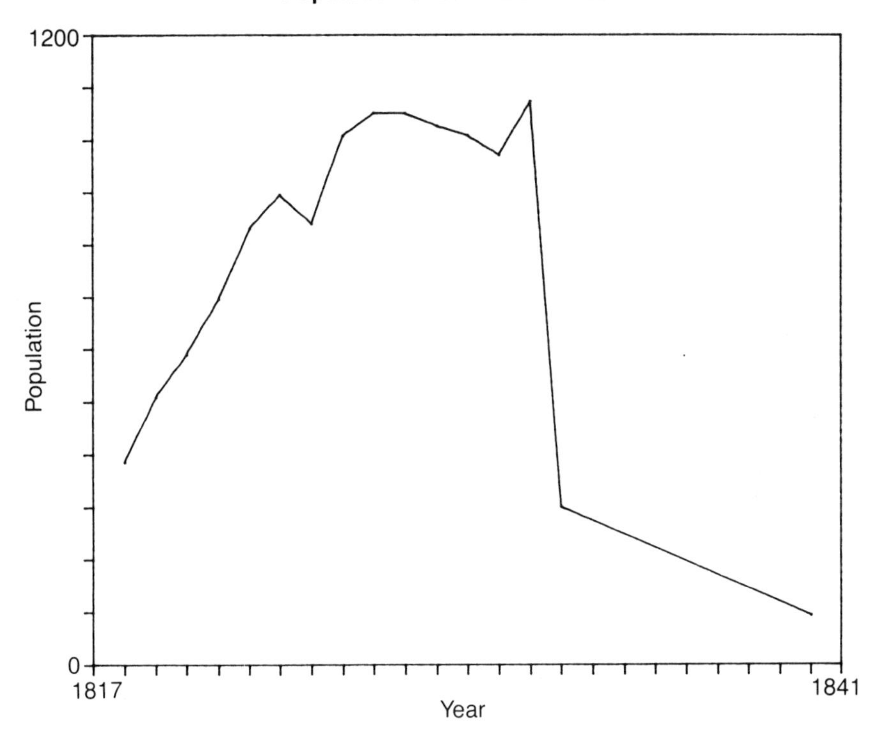

stood at 1,418. In subsequent years, the population fluctuated as the Franciscans congregated Indians from an increasing distance from the mission center, and, in the 1820s, Yokuts from the San Joaquín Valley. The population was 1,462 in 1827, following the last phase of congregation,

Table 2.26 San Rafael Mission Demographic Statistics, 1817–1836

Year	Population	CBR	CDR	GRR	NRR	Life Expectancy
1819	509	30	67	.68	.21	19.6
1824	839	24	69	.69	.09	9.0
1829	1,008	15	36	.48	.16	21.8
1834	262	12	27	.53	.23	27.8

Source: San Rafael Mission baptismal and burial registers, San Francisco Archdiocese Chancery Archive, Colma, California; and Annual Reports, the Santa Barbara Mission Archive-Library, Santa Barbara, California.

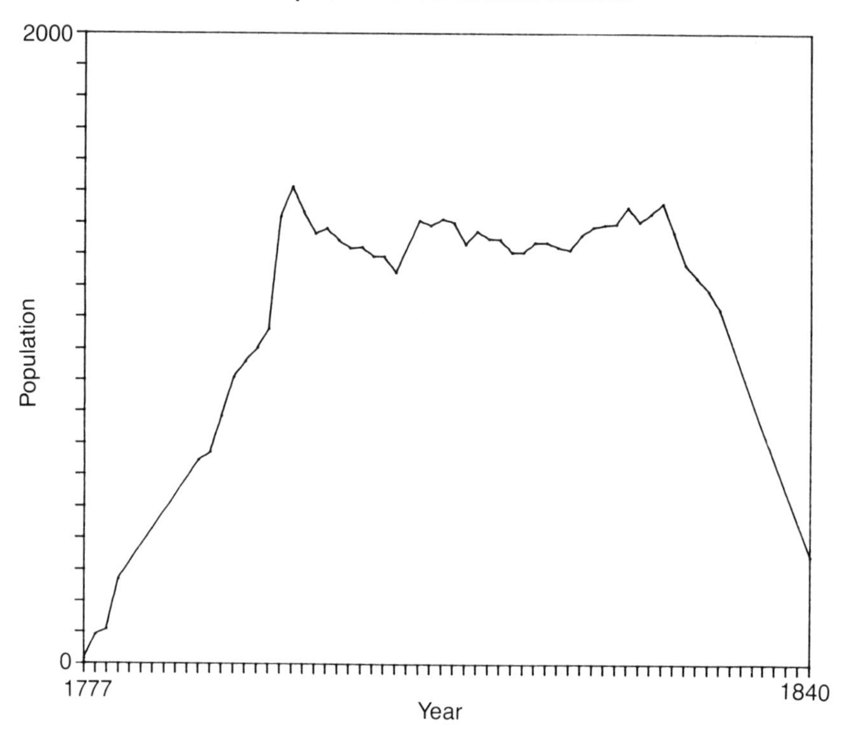

and stood at 1,125 in 1832.[34] Birthrates were high to moderate, but they declined in the early nineteenth century because of the declining number of women of child-bearing age, the physical debilitation of women surviving syphilis and other chronic ailments, and the practice of abortion commented upon by the missionaries. Crude birth and death rates averaged 35 and 114 per thousand population, respectively, and the gross and net reproduction ratios were 1.13 and 0.05. Mean life expectancy at birth averaged 3.2 years, and the mean rate of population decline over a generation averaged 95 percent. Conditions improved somewhat after 1810, with the congregation of Central Valley Yokuts, and the numbers grew to 1,450 in 1824. However, the mission population still was not viable (see Table 2.27).

The population of San José mission was the largest in northern Alta California, and high population density and a rapid expansion of the population contributed to poor living conditions. In the first phase of

Table 2.27 Santa Clara Mission Demographic Statistics, 1782–1832

Year	Total Population	CBR	CDR	GRR	NRR	Life Expectancy
1784	428*	61	145	1.82	.07	2.7
1789	787	52	163	1.36	.02	1.2
1794	1,418	40	140	.98	.01	1.3
1799	1,343	38	126	.98	.02	1.5
1804	1,240	31	134	.98	.01	1.2
1809	1,398	29	100	.90	.03	2.5
1814	1,306	28	78	1.07	.10	6.1
1819	1,313	25	76	1.11	.11	6.5
1824	1,450	27	88	1.22	.08	4.5
1829	1,269	19	87	.83	.05	4.1

*Population estimate generated by *Populate*.
Source: Santa Clara Mission baptismal and burial registers, Archives of the University of Santa Clara, Santa Clara, California; Annual Reports, Archivo General de la Nación, México, D.F., and the Santa Barbara Mission Archive-Library, Santa Barbara, California.

congregation of the local Ohlone population, between 1797 and 1805, the population grew to 779, but then dropped to 545 in 1810. After 1811, the Franciscans congregated several thousand Miwoks and Yokuts from the San Joaquín Valley and the Sacramento River delta area, and the numbers grew to 1,886 in 1831.[35] The crude death rate averaged 132 per thousand, and the net reproduction ratio was 0.01, which indicates a 99 percent rate of decline over a generation. Birthrates were moderate, averaging 29 per thousand population, and declined. The rate of natural reproduction, the gross reproduction ratio which averaged 0.79, shows that if infant-child mortality rates had not been so high, the population still would not have grown. The high rate of infant mortality also manifested itself in a low rate of mean life expectancy, which averaged a mere 1.7 years. The vital rates of San José mission, among the worst in the Alta California missions, again highlight the significance of population density and general living conditions and sanitation as factors contributing to demographic collapse (see Table 2.28).

The final case study examined here is San Francisco Solano mission, established in 1823. As at the other missions in the San Francisco Bay region, death rates were consistently higher than birthrates, and life expectancy was low. The average crude birth and death rates were 33 and

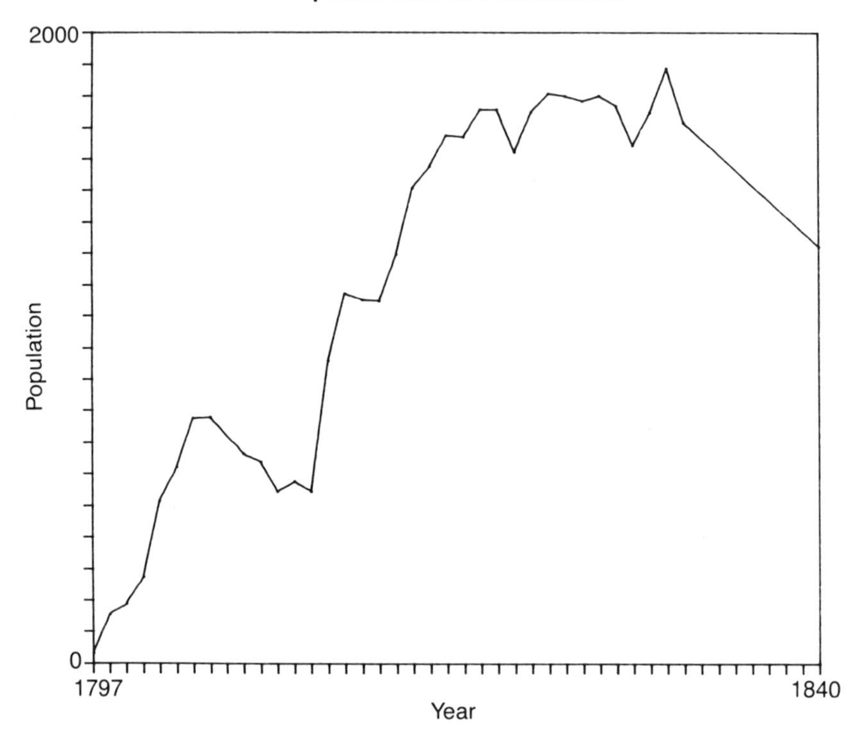

Table 2.28 San José Mission Demographic Statistics, 1802–1836

Year	Total Population	CBR	CDR	GRR	NRR	Life Expectancy
1804	779	42	280	.97	.00	.7
1809	578	25	100	.54	.02	2.8
1814	1,149	39	104	1.03	.03	2.2
1819	1,670	34	109	.96	.02	1.6
1824	1,806	22	113	.67	.01	1.4
1829	1,641	17	104	.56	.01	1.4
1834	1,229	25	113	.80	.01	1.5

Source: San José Mission baptismal and burial registers, San Francisco Archidocese Chancery Archive, Colma, California; Annual Reports, Archivo General de la Nación, México, D.F., and the Santa Barbara Mission Archive-Library, Santa Barbara, California.

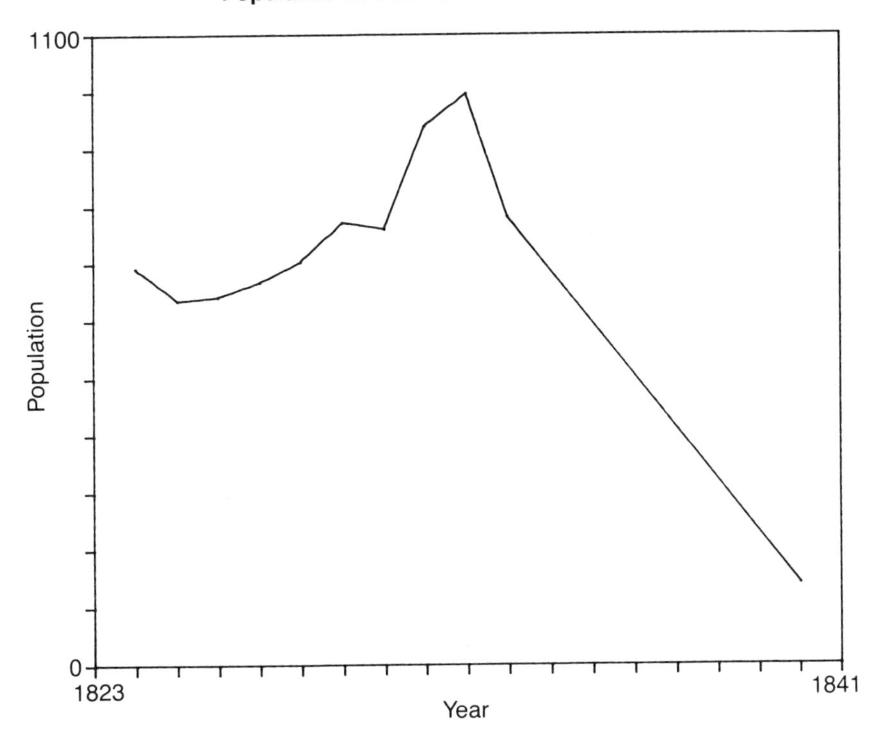

90 per thousand population, and the mean gross and net reproduction ratios were 1.68 and 0.07, or a 93 percent rate of decline over a generation. Mean life expectancy was low, averaging a mere 3 years (see Table 2.29). Following the establishment of the mission, the Franciscans transferred more than 600 converts from San José, San Francisco, and San Rafael to the jurisdiction of the new community. Over the next nine years, the mission population expanded, reaching a recorded high of 996 in 1832; but the numbers dropped in the last years of the operation of the mission, to 648 in 1834, despite the continued recruitment of converts, reflecting the exodus of converts to work on the cattle ranches being organized in the district or a complete escape from the area of effective Mexican control in California. Based upon the net difference between baptisms and burials in 1833 and 1834, the mission population should have been some 1,032, but, as noted above, the population recorded in 1834 was 648, indicating that some 384 Indians left the mission in two years.[36]

Table 2.29 San Francisco Solano Mission Demographic Statistics, 1823–1832

Year	Total Population	CBR	CDR	GRR	NRR	Life Expectancy
1825	634	24	73	1.60	.10	4.6
1830	760	41	106	1.76	.03	1.4

Source: San Francisco Solano Mission baptismal and burial registers, the Bancroft Library, University of California, Berkeley; Annual Reports, the Santa Barbara Mission Archive-Library, Santa Barbara, California.

Gender and Age Structure[37]

Two characteristics common to all three regions studied here were an unbalanced gender and age structure. Death rates were particularly high among women and young children, and progressively the mission populations experienced a deficit of women and children. The gender and age imbalance can be documented in several ways, depending on the type of documentation available.

Records for the Pimería Alta are relatively incomplete when compared with the records for the Baja California and Alta California missions. Family size, however, can be used to illustrate the imbalance in the population. Two sets of figures indicate the size of the Indian family at one point in time: the average nuclear-family size, based upon the calculation of the mean size of the family as related to the total population and the number of families; and the actual nuclear family size, which compares the frequency of families of different sizes ranging from sizes of two to five or six. However, there are methodological weaknesses in the use of these indicators. The average nuclear-family size produces a figures that may be slightly larger than the actual family size, especially in cases where families were broken up by the premature death of one spouse or of both spouses, and large numbers of orphans were cared for by family members or others. The inclusion of orphans and incomplete families tends to inflate the mean family size. Evidence also suggests that couples, in some cases, took in orphan relatives, also inflating the mean size of the family. Nevertheless, the average family size does indicate long-term trends (see Table 2.30).

For most of the eighteenth century, Indian families living in the missions were small. The pattern is consistent with the documented high rates of

Table 2.30 Average Nuclear Family Size (A.N.F.S.) at Selected Pimería Alta Missions

Year	Mission	Population	Families	A.N.F.S.
1729	San Ignacio	77	27	2.9
	Dolores	31	9	3.4
	Remedios	26	7	3.7
	Cocospera	75	21	3.6
1730	Dolores	29	9	3.2
	Remedios	30	10	3.0
	Caborca	223	74	3.0
	San Ignacio	94	32	2.9
1761	Cocospera	133	52	2.6
	Guevavi	101	31	3.3
	Ati	142	46	3.1
	Caborca	556	163	3.4
1768	Tubutama	167	41	4.1
	Caborca	564	132	4.3
	Ati	146	37	3.9
1797	Tumacacori	69	19	3.9
	Tubutama	34	8	4.3
	Bac	116	35	3.3

Source: Robert H. Jackson, "Causes of Indian Population Decline in the Pimería Alta Missions of Northern Sonora," *The Journal of Arizona History* 24 (1983), p. 416.

infant and child mortality. At any one point in time, the average Indian family had only one or two living children in the household, although over the entire period of fertility, a woman who survived in the mission community for more than a couple of years might bear as many as six or seven children.

The actual family size shows that small nuclear families with two or three members, and with no children or only one child, were most common. For example, detailed censuses of the population of San Francisco Xavier del Bac missions in 1766, 1768, and 1801 recorded a total of 96 percent, 94 percent, and 95 percent, respectively, of the nuclear families with a size of two to four individuals, and no, one, or two children. The pattern of small nuclear families was generalized throughout the Pimería Alta missions, and in the Baja and Alta California missions as well (see Table 2.31).

Evidence for the gender and age structure of the Baja California missions is limited to a series of reports prepared in 1786, in the middle and late 1790s, and in the first decade of the nineteenth century. The Indian

Table 2.31 Actual Nuclear Family Size of Selected Pimería Alta Missions

Year	Mission	Family Size of: 2	3	4	5	6	7
1766	Bac	17	17	11	1	1	0
	Tucson	10	5	11	8	0	0
1768	Bac	22	17	11	1	0	2
	Guevavi	9	2	2	0	0	0
	Tumacacori	10	8	2	1	0	0
	Sonoita	12	2	2	3	0	0
1796	Tubutama	12	3	0	1	0	0
	Cocospera	6	5	2	5	0	0
1801	Bac	18	11	7	2	0	0
	Saric	7	0	0	0	0	0

Source: Robert H. Jackson, "Causes of Indian Population Decline in the Pimería Alta Missions of Northern Sonora," *The Journal of Arizona History* 24 (1983), p. 416.

population of the Baja California missions had a surplus of males, and the gender imbalance was particularly marked at several of the older establishments. In the 1790s, for example, there were roughly three males for every female at Comondu mission, and more than two males for every female at Mulege, Purísima, and San Ignacio missions. On the other hand, the populations of several of the northern missions, where the missionaries continued to congregate substantial numbers of converts, evidenced a more balanced gender structure or a surplus of females. For example, the populations of San Pedro Mártir (established in 1794) and Santa Catalina (established in 1797) missions both had a surplus of females (see Table 2.32).

High rates of infant and child mortality were a second factor that reduced the ability of the mission populations to reproduce, let alone survive. The imbalanced age structure can be documented with the number of *parvulos* (children under age ten) as a percentage of the total population. *Parvulos* made up roughly a quarter of the total population of the Baja California missions at the end of the eighteenth century, although young children comprised a larger percentage of the population of the recently established missions still engaged in congregating converts (see Table 2.33).

An analysis of the gender and age structure of the Alta California missions is more complex. The mission populations had a nearly balanced age structure in the 1790s, during a period of active congregation of converts. However, the populations became unbalanced as a result of high rates of

Table 2.32 Sex Ratio (Males: Females) in the Baja California Missions

Mission	1786*	1798	1800	1802
Loreto	.72**	.57	.54	.61
San Francisco Xavier	.71	.38	.47	.52
Mulege	.70	.62	.63	.54
Comondú	.38	.38	.33	.53
La Purisima	.52	.49	.46	.47
San Ignacio	.94	.81	.75	.78
San Jose del Cabo	.53	.62	.66	.60
Todos Santos	.49	N/A	N/A	.80
Santa Gertrudis	.81	.74	.72	.72
San Francisco de Borja	.72	.77	.81	.69
San Fernando	.97	.89	.93	1.22
Rosario	1.12	.88	.92	.89
Santo Domingo	.84	.84	.91	.86
San Vicente	1.19	1.07	1.13	1.12
San Miguel	N/A	.76	1.07	.80
Santo Tomas	N/A	.82	.99	.84
San Pedro Martir	1.24	1.29	1.42	1.49
Santa Catalina	N/A	2.27	1.72	1.55

*Ratio of adults (over age 10?) men to women.
** Includes the population of Loreto Presidio.
Source: Annual Report, 1786, the Bancroft Library, University of California, Berkeley; Biennial Reports 1798, 1800, and 1802, Archivo General de la Nación, México, D.F.

mortality among young girls and women and the decline in the number of females in periods of limited congregation of converts. In 1832, the ratio showed a significant imbalance in a number of missions. For example, there were more than two males for every female at Santa Cruz and Soledad missions. In the long run, the deficit in the number of women limited the ability of the mission populations to reproduce, and manifested itself in the declining crude birthrates documented above (see Table 2.34).

The gender imbalance can be further illustrated by comparing the number of females as a percentage of the total population over time, and the population of females as related to the number of baptisms of girls and women over time. Santa Cruz mission, one of the missions with the greatest gender imbalance in the 1830s, is selected for the purposes of this analysis. In 1797, females made up 47 percent of the population of the mission. The percentage of females dropped in subsequent years, and reached a low of 31 percent in 1832. It should be pointed out that increases in the percentage

Table 2.33 ***Parvulos* (Children under Age 9) as a Percentage of the Total Population of the Baja California Missions in Selected Years***

Mission	1795	1796	1797	1798
Loreto	20	18	20	22
San Francisco Xavier	17	22	19	16
Mulege	25	30	27	24
Comondú	9	5	7	5
La Purísima	25	25	25	16
San José del Cabo	29	27	27	15
Todos Santos	29	27	30	48
Santa Gertrudis	41	22	40	38
San Francisco de Borja	10	22	13	9
San Fernando	18	22	24	24
Rosario	28	26	23	N/A
Santo Domingo	30	31	30	30
San Vicente	45	43	39	41
San Miguel	42	15	25	23
Santo Tomás	32	34	37	41
San Pedro Mártir	7	55	36	33
Santa Catalina	N/A	N/A	42	66
Total	25	26	27	27
Total Population**	3,143	3,139	3,010	2,673

*Does not include San Ignacio, for which the data is incomplete.
**Does not include missions for which data is incomplete.
Source: Annual Reports; Archivo General de la Nación, México, D.F.

after 1797 occurred during periods of active recruitment of large numbers of converts, and dropped during periods of less active congregation. Between 1791 and 1832, the Franciscans stationed at Santa Cruz baptized 1,133 females. In that same year, only 87 women and girls lived at the mission, a mere 8 percent of the total of female baptisms accumulated from the date of the establishment of the mission. In a period that roughly corresponds to two generations, the relative and actual number of women brought into the mission declined (see Table 2.35).

High rates of infant and child mortality were a second factor that substantially reduced the viability of the mission populations. As shown in the individual case studies presented above, women bore children, but young children died in frightful numbers. By the 1830s the adult males made up the single largest group in the mission populations; and ironically,

Table 2.34 Sex Ratio (Men: Women—Above Age 9) in the Alta California Missions in Selected Years*

Mission	1796	1798	1810	1832
San Diego	1.20	1.15	.89	.59
San Carlos	.98	.96	.94	.85
San Antonio	.89	.85	.69	.53
San Gabriel	1.01	1.00	.63	.90
San Luis Obispo	1.15	1.06	.74	.42
San Francisco	.94	.87	.74	.46
Santa Clara	.77	.75	.68	.61
San Buenaventura	N/A	.95	1.13	.65
Santa Barbara	1.01	.98	1.00	.73
La Purísima	1.05	1.06	1.01	.62
Santa Cruz	N/A	.87	.59	.43
Soledad	.81	.97	.64	.37
San José	N/A	.93	.61	.69
San Juan Bautista	N/A	.73	.82	.69
San Miguel	N/A	.78	.90	.84
San Fernando	N/A	.95	.97	.84
San Luis Rey	N/A	.98	.99	.85
Santa Ines	N/A	N/A	1.16	.81
San Rafael	N/A	N/A	N/A	1.16
San Francisco Solano	N/A	N/A	N/A	.99

*Excludes San Juan Capistrano, for which no reports are available after 1798. Adults are defined in the missions as being nine years of age and above.
Source: Annual Reports: Archivo General de la Nación, México, D.F.; and the Santa Barbara Mission Archive-Library, Santa Barbara, California.

Table 2.35 Female Population at Santa Cruz Mission as Related to Total Population and the Total Number of Baptisms of Females

Year	Population	Female Population	% of Total Population	Female Baptisms to Date
1797	509	238	47	378
1813	398	139	35	789
1814	404	139	34	796
1820	401	175	44	950
1823	474	182	38	1,039
1824	457	184	40	1,060
1825	429	161	38	1,067
1826	428	167	39	1,087
1828	364	114	31	1,102
1832	284	87	31	1,133

Source: Robert H. Jackson, "Disease and Demographic Patterns at Santa Cruz Mission, Alta California," *Journal of California and Great Basin Anthropology* 5 (1983), p. 42.

Table 2.36 ***Parvulos*** **(Children under Age 9) as a Percentage of the Total Population of the Alta California Missions in elected Years***

Mission	1789	1796	1798	1810	1832	1839
San Diego	33	20	21	28	19	33
San Carlos	27	21	18	12	22	26
San Antonio	31	42	22	13	15	7
San Gabriel	N/A	26	24	22	30	36
San Luis Obispo	26	14	15	11	6	21
San Francisco	N/A	14	12	14	13	19
Santa Clara	56	18	21	12	7	3
San Buenaventura	35	12	14	10	14	13
Santa Barbara	29	14	14	22	15	45
La Purísima	N/A	23	18	11	9	28
Santa Cruz	N/A	30	24	8	11	29
Soledad	N/A	41	38	16	17	12
San José	N/A	N/A	47	15	18	18
San Juan Bautista	N/A	N/A	28	12	15	12
San Miguel	N/A	N/A	50	19	13	34
San Fernando	N/A	N/A	44	24	51	55
San Luis Rey	N/A	N/A	43	37	29	32
Santa Ines	N/A	N/A	N/A	19	11	34
San Rafael	N/A	N/A	N/A	N/A	17	39
San Francisco Solano	N/A	N/A	N/A	N/A	22	30
Total	N/A	21	21	18	21	29
Total Population	N/ A	11,216	11,811	17,632	15,964	7,246

*Does not incude San Juan Capistrano Mission for which no reports are available after 1798.

Source: Annual Reports: Archivo General de la Nación, México, D.F.; Santa Barbara Mission Archivo Library, Santa Barbara, California; and Mission Statistics, the Bancroft Library, University of California, Berkeley.

the age and gender imbalance contributed to the ability of the Franciscans to control a sufficiently large labor force in order to produce the surpluses that supported the military garrisons in the province during the difficult years of the Mexican independence wars (1810–1821), as well as to construct the impressive building complexes most associated with the missions. The age structure tended to be more balanced during periods of active congregation, when the missionaries resettled entire families and large numbers of children. The number of children dropped when the missions approached the condition of being closed communities. *Parvulos* made up 18 percent of the population of twenty missions in 1810,

Table 2.37 Average Family Size and the Population of Children at Santa Cruz Mission in Selected Years

Year	Population	Families	Average Family Size	Children	Children as % of the Total Pop.
1792	158			74	47
1798	504			121	24
1806	466			56	12
1813	398	83	4.8	32	8
1814	404	83	4.9	34	8
1820	461			77	17
1823	474	102	4.6	90	19
1824	457	103	4.4	73	16
1825	429	83	5.2	67	16
1826	428	85	5.0	56	13
1828	364	70	5.2	50	14

Source: Robert H. Jackson, "Disease and Demographic Patterns at Santa Cruz Mission, Alta California," *Journal of California and Great Basin Anthropology* 5 (1983), p. 41.

following the first phase of congregation in most of the missions. It increased to 21 percent in 1832, after a second period of congregation in the late 1810s and early 1820s. The increase in the percentage to 29 percent in 1839 can be attributed to the exodus of adult males from the missions following secularization (see Table 2.36).

A detailed examination of changes in the age structure of Santa Cruz mission further illustrates the problem of the imbalance in the age structure. Table 2.37 includes data on the total and relative number of young children at Santa Cruz mission, the number of families, and the average family size. In 1798, children under age ten numbered 121, making up 24 percent of the total population. The number of children dropped until the large-scale congregation of Yokuts in the late 1810s and early 1820s increased to 90 and 19 percent of the population in 1823, and then declined in the late 1820s and early 1830s. There was always a large number of families, primarily because of the Franciscan policy of remarrying widows and widowers as quickly as possible. Family size was small, but the average family size (total population divided by the number of families) is somewhat misleading in this case. Because of the high mortality rates, there was also a large number of orphans and a proportionally large number of adult men, which inflates the average family size (see Table 2.37).

Conclusions

The detailed case studies presented here show that while variation occurred between and within the three regions studied here, the Indian populations congregated into the missions were universally inviable, incapable of growing through natural reproduction. Death rates were chronically higher than birthrates, and took a particularly heavy toll among women of child-bearing age and young children. With the exception of the period of recruitment of converts, the missions increasingly revealed imbalanced age and gender structures. The mission populations experienced periods of growth in the total number of converts, but with several limited exceptions, this growth resulted from the congregation of converts that masked the continued collapse of the mission populations.

What factors contributed to the demographic collapse of the Indian populations? Most scholars agree that periodic epidemics of Euroasiatic diseases such as smallpox and measles, to which the Indian populations initially had no immunity, were important factors. Certainly, epidemics were traumatic episodes that drastically raised mortality rates over the short term. However, epidemics do not adequately explain the chronically high mortality rates in the Alta California missions, which were geographically isolated from the rest of New Spain until the early nineteenth centuy. Epidemics, which rapidly spread along established trade and transportation routes, did not reach Alta California with the same frequency as they reached the Pimería Alta missions in northern Sonora and Baja California. Other factors, both biological and nonbiological, were also crucial.

The following chapter outlines the biological and non-biological factors that caused the demographic collapse of the mission populations of northwestern New Spain. Special attention is given to the case of the Alta California missions, which present patterns similar yet distinct from patterns documented for the Pimería Alta and Baja California missions. Topics considered include the impact of epidemic and chronic endemic disease, living conditions in the missions and Indian diet, and warfare.

3

Causes of Demographic Collapse

As documented in the previous chapter, increased mortality, and not the inability of women to bear children, was the primary cause for the demographic collapse of the Indian populations congregated in the mission communities of northern Sonora and the Californias. What factors contributed to high rates of mortality? This chapter examines different biological and non-biological factors contributing to the demographic collapse of the Indian populations, including contagious epidemic and chronic endemic disease; the stresses of cultural change; and changed living conditions, including housing. Special emphasis is placed on the Alta California missions. In contrast to the pattern observed in Sonora and Baja California, few epidemics reached Alta California between 1769 and 1834. Yet mortality rates were as high or greater than those in Baja California and the Pimería Alta. This chapter explores the impact of epidemics on the Indian populations living in the missions, and the specific conditions in the Alta California missions that caused consistently high mortality in the absence of a large number of epidemics.

The Impact of Epidemic Disease

Until the development of modern medicine and programs of public sanitation, disease in endemic and epidemic forms claimed the lives of many people. Table 3.1 records the number of disease-related deaths at Aconchi (Sonora) in the 1840s as a percentage of total deaths. Disease was responsible for at least half of all deaths. Old age, accidents, homicides, and raids by hostile Indians accounted for the bulk of nondisease-related mortality.

The northwestern frontier of New Spain was tied into a system of regional trade. Epidemics spread along established trade routes throughout

Table 3.1 Disease as a Cause of Death in Aconchi, Sonora, 1846–1851

Year	Deaths Due to Disease (Percentage)
1846	50
1847	81
1848	78
1849	58
1850	56
1851	96 "Asian Cholera"

Source: Aconchi burial register, Banamichi Parish Archive, Banamichi, Sonora.

the larger region, and major outbreaks reached the northern frontier at least once every generation (see Appendix 1). In order to understand the impact of epidemic disease on native populations, it is necessary to outline epidemic mortality within the context of patterns of mortality during nonepidemic years. Table 3.2 summarizes an analysis of epidemic mortality during three epidemics in Baja and Alta California, using *Populate* and a five-year sample of mortality organized so that the midpoint of the quinquennium corresponds to an epidemic outbreak. The 1769 measles and 1781–1782 smallpox epidemics in Baja California raised mortality rates in excess of 100 per thousand population, which means that more than 10 percent of the population died. As shown in Chapter 2, mortality in nonepidemic years in the Baja California missions was generally higher than birthrates, but substantially lower than the rates in excess of 100 per thousand population during major epidemic outbreaks. On the other hand, the 1827–1828 measles outbreak in Alta California did not raise mortality rates much above the rates already documented for nonepidemic years. Epidemics in Baja California and in northern Sonora were traumatic events that more than doubled or tripled normal death rates, but with no recovery or rebound through natural reproduction following the epidemic. In contrast, with the exception of the severe outbreaks in 1802 and 1806, epidemics in the Alta California missions did not substantially raise rates above the chronically high mortality documented for the missions.

It is necessary to document morbidity and mortality and age-specific mortality during epidemics in order to evaluate the impact of epidemic outbreaks on native populations. I analyze the severe 1806 measles epi-

Table 3.2 Vital Statistics during Selected Epidemic Outbreaks in Baja and Alta California

Year	Mission Group	Number of Missions	Pathogen	CBR	CDR	Life Expectancy
1769	Baja California	4	Measles	44	106	2.1
1781–1782	Baja California	9	Smallpox	49	138	1.4
1827–1828	Alta California	20	Measles	28	74	6.2

demic at San Francisco de Asis mission in northern Alta California, and the 1827–1828 measles epidemic in the Alta California missions, using data abstracted from extant annual reports.

Data from San Francisco mission gives an indication of the severity of the 1806 measles epidemic, which was one of several severe epidemics in the Alta alifornia missions during the 1800–1809 decade. At the end of 1805, the population of San Francisco mission was 1,163. There was a total of 471 recorded burials at the mission during 1806, which indicates a crude death rate per thousand population of 405. At the end of 1806, 886 converts remained at the mission. Several letters written by the missionaries stationed at San Francisco provide additional information on the impact of the measles outbreak. The epidemic began at San Francisco in March or at the beginning of April. At the end of April, 400 converts reportedly were already sick. By the end of May the number of sick Indians increased to 800, and more than 200 had already died. This indicates a morbidity rate of 69 percent by the end of May, and a mortality rate of about 25 percent. Subsequent epidemics, such as the 1827–1828 outbreak, were not as severe. Burial figures analyzed in Table 3.3 reflect total deaths during the year of the outbreak at specific missions, either 1827 or 1828. Mortality is divided into two cohorts: children under age nine, and older children and adults over age nine (see Table 3.3). In nonepidemic years, infant and child mortality rates in the missions were high, and the same pattern is observed during the measles epidemic. A proportionally high number of children died. Children under age nine made up 21 percent of the population of fifteen missions, yet they accounted for 44 percent of all deaths. On the other hand, 56 percent of the deaths were those of adults and of children over age nine, the cohort that made up 79 percent of the total

Table 3.3 Patterns of Mortality during the 1827–1828 Measles Epidemic in Selected Alta California Missions*

Mission	Total Deaths				Population in 1826	Children as % of Pop.
	Adults	%	Children	%		
San Diego	67	52	61	48	1,704	20
San Carlos	22	43	29	57	279	30
San Gabriel	104	63	61	37	1,565	30
San Francisco	15	75	5	25	232	16
Santa Clara	122	65	67	35	1,428	12
San Buenaventura	33	51	32	49	852	16
Santa Barbara	47	46	56	54	867	17
Santa Cruz	42	68	20	32	428	13
Soledad	33	67	16	33	409	19
San José	180	71	74	29	1,783	13
San Miguel	59	57	45	43	852	17
San Fernando	42	46	49	54	911	41
San Luis Rey	94	35	178	65	2,869	24
San Rafael	36	59	25	41	1,051	22
Solano	55	63	33	37	641	26
Total	951	56	751	44	15,871	21

*26 percent of children under age nine died at San Luis Rey, and 13 percent at San Gabriel.
Source: Annual Reports, Santa Barbara Mission Archive-Library, Santa Barbara, California.

population of the fifteen missions. The 1827–1828 measles epidemic carried off a larger number of adults than in nonepidemic years, which was a common pattern observed for most Indian populations living in the missions in northwestern New Spain.[1]

The evidence suggests that patterns of epidemic mortality differed between the Indian populations living in the mission communities and the largely non-Indian settler population; whereas the majority of deaths recorded among the settler population were young children and teenagers who most likely had not been previously exposed to a given contagion. Table 3.4 records the pattern of mortality at Pitic, in southern Sonora, during the 1826 measles epidemic, one of the few cases in which parish priests or missionaries recorded the specific age of epidemic victims in northwestern New Spain. Of a total of 606 deaths attributed to measles, 78.6 percent were children under age ten. Adults over the age of twenty-one accounted for a mere 2.3 percent of measles deaths (see Table 3.4).

Table 3.4 Pattern of Age-Specific Mortality during the 1826 Measles Epidemic at Pitic, Sonora

Age Cohort	Number of Deaths	Percentage
0–9	476	78.6
10–21	116	19.1
21+	14	2.3
Total	606	100.0

Source: Pitic Burial Register; Hermosillo Parish Archive, Hermosillo, Sonora.

Contagious diseases, such as measles, took the form of childhood ailments among the settler population, although, at times, intense episodes, when accompanied by adverse ecological conditions or when introduced from outside a community during a general epidemic, did kill adults. An individual surviving a disease outbreak built up immunities, and generally survived subsequent epidemics of the same disease. Moreover, morbidity, the rate of infection, was probably lower, and the percentage of the infected dying most likely was not as high. In contrast, morbidity among the Indians living in the missions most likely was higher since a larger number of adults and teenagers contracted the different diseases. The ratio of infection to death was also higher than it was for the settler population. Moreover, the total number of deaths would have been higher since a larger percentage of the total population would be infected. Finally, mortality rates also were high as a consequence of the lack of effective medical care for the sick in the missions, which was a consequence of the state of medical knowledge in the seventeenth and eighteenth centuries.[2]

The general belief held by missionaries that epidemics were a punishment sent by God probably limited their responses to outbreaks. The fatalistic acceptance of the inevitability of disease and God's role in sending contagions led many missionaries to practice passivity in the face of epidemics. Why alter God's will? Moreover, there was a certain millenarian fundamentalism shared by many missionaries. Suffering on earth merely prepared Indian converts for a better life in heaven in God's grace. These attitudes contributed to a rejection of innovations in medicine that saved lives. In 1781, for example, only three missionaries in Baja California used inoculation by variolation, a technique recently introduced into Mexico that substantially reduced smallpox mortality. Death rates at the three missions were low, whereas hundreds of Indians died from smallpox in the missions where the missionaries refused to inoculate.[3]

Seasonal Mortality

Studies of northern Europe have shown distinct patterns of seasonal mortality associated with a greater number of deaths due to the colder and damp weather in the winter and spring, as well as with related respiratory ailments that claimed the lives of the old and the infirm.[4] Was there a similar pattern of seasonal mortality in the mission communities of northwestern New Spain? Tables 3.5–3.7 summarize samples and the distribution of frequencies by the percentage of recorded burials in Sonora, Baja California, and Alta California by season: fall (September–November), winter (December–February), spring (March–May), and summer (June–August).

Table 3.5 summarizes a sample of 17,291 burials from parishes throughout Sonora. It should be noted that the run of sacramental registers is incomplete for most Sonora parishes; and a number of the samples recorded below are very small, which can skew the results. Nevertheless, taken as a whole the sample does document the frequency of mortality by season. On the other hand, the sample is unevenly weighted by the parishes for which the record is larger and more complete. Despite these caveats, valid general conclusions can be made, and the sample indicates that there was no substantial increase in mortality during the winter. Only 22.3 percent of all burials were recorded during this season. On the contrary, mortality was greatest in the two seasons of greatest change in temperatures, a total of 27 percent in the fall and 26.9 percent in the winter. Moreover, there was no great seasonal variation as observed in Europe, with a difference of only 4 percent separating the seasons with the lowest and highest frequency of deaths.

Two possible explanations account for the pattern of seasonal mortality observed in Sonora. First, there is no dramatic temperature variation between the warm and cold seasons, as in northern Europe, and the climate in Sonora is drier. Warm temperatures are conducive to the spread of contagion, but winter weather in Sonora does not cause or exacerbate the same type of chronic cold-damp weather respiratory ailments characteristic of northern Europe. Second, and perhaps less important, epidemics spawned in the cool highlands of central Mexico took some time to reach the northwestern frontier, and may have reached northern Sonora more frequently in the fall and spring.

Table 3.5 Seasonal Mortality in Selected Sonora Parishes, by Percentage

Parish	Fall Sept.–Nov.	Winter Dec.–Feb.	Spring Mar.–May	Summer June–Aug.	Total Burials
Caborca	36.1	25.7	19.4	18.8	2,928
Magdalena*	35.2	24.7	17.7	22.4	847
Magdalena**	30.2	21.1	14.1	34.6	361
Soamca	33.2	24.7	23.0	19.1	178
Guevavi	23.2	36.9	22.5	17.3	444
Cocospera	41.5	13.9	26.2	18.5	65
Arispe***	24.4	32.7	18.9	24.1	544
Caborca†	24.0	22.5	33.5	20.0	686
Caborca††	44.7	25.5	21.3	29.8	57
Ati	31.9	19.9	27.3	20.9	326
Pitiquito	25.3	24.3	25.3	25.1	371
Tumacacori	27.3	24.9	25.2	22.5	626
Ures	29.7	21.2	23.1	26.0	3,041
Arispe†††	23.9	20.2	34.0	21.9	2,822
Bacoachi	23.4	22.7	22.0	32.0	419
Aconchi‡	31.3	19.4	20.9	28.4	268
Aconchi‡‡	17.3	33.5	23.7	25.5	600
Pitic de Seris	27.1	19.1	26.1	27.7	1,062
Pitic Presidio	16.1	17.4	32.7	23.4	2,282
Total of Sample	27.0	22.3	26.9	23.4	17,291

*1702–1816
**1814–1832
***1764–1796
†1790–1803
††1762–1783
†††1780–1843
‡1796–1814
‡‡1840–1853

A slightly different pattern is observed in the sample of 14,123 burials from nine Baja California missions, although the degree of variation between the frequency of mortality by season is still small, with a difference of 6 percent between the seasons with the lowest and highest percentage in the sample of deaths. The greatest concentration of deaths was in the winter (26.3 percent) and spring (28.1 percent), the period of the coldest temperatures (see Table 3.6). With the exception of the coastal desert in the northern part of the peninsula, the climate is similar to Sonora with

Table 3.6 Sesonal Mortality in Selected Baja California Missions, by Percentage

Mission	Fall Sept.–Nov.	Winter Dec.–Feb.	Spring Mar.–May	Summer June–Aug.	Total Burials
Mulege	25.5	25.8	27.1	21.6	1,320
Comondú	27.1	21.9	29.3	21.7	1,766
Purísima	14.8	19.6	28.2	37.4	358
Sta Gertrudis	22.9	24.1	32.1	20.9	3,537
San Borja	21.2	29.1	25.9	23.8	2,749
San Fernando	21.8	27.1	27.5	23.6	1,947
Rosario	24.0	31.4	23.8	20.9	1,198
Sto Domingo	26.8	30.1	22.4	20.8	684
San Vicente	24.1	27.8	29.4	18.6	564
Total of Sample	23.3	26.3	28.1	22.4	14,123

dry winters, so cold weather did not have the same impact as in northern Europe.

The final sample of 16,552 burials from five Alta California missions gives slightly different results, with the frequency of deaths spread more evenly by season. The difference between the seasons with the highest and lowest numbers of deaths was a mere 3 percent. However, there was some variation between missions located in warmer and cooler, as well as foggier, coastal climates. For example, Santa Clara and San Rafael missions, located in warm parts of the greater San Francisco Bay region, evidenced a more even distribution of the frequency of deaths. On the other hand, San Francisco and Santa Cruz, both located in cooler and damp micoclimates influenced by the cold Pacific Ocean, had a larger percentage of deaths concentrated in the winter and spring. The greatest variation was at Santa Cruz characterized by a cool and damp winter and spring, with 57.9 percent of all burials taking place in these seasons. There was a difference of 12 percent between the seasons of least and greatest mortality (see Table 3.7).

Although there was some seasonal variation in the distribution of the frequency of deaths in Sonora and the Californias, respiratory ailments of the types associated with the cold and damp winter weather of northern Europe were not a major factor in Indian demographic collapse. However, there were a few exceptions, such as San Francisco and Santa Cruz missions in northern Alta California, where cold and damp weather contributed to

Table 3.7 Seasonal Mortality in Five Alta California Missions, by Percentage

Mission	Fall Sept.–Nov.	Winter Dec.–Feb.	Spring Mar.–May	Summer June–Aug.	Total Burials
San Fran.*	23.9	26.5	27.7	22.0	5,374
Sta Clara	25.1	25.9	23.6	25.4	7,404
Santa Cruz	21.9	32.2	25.7	20.3	2,109
San Rafael	27.2	23.7	26.8	22.3	839
Solano	34.0	23.6	18.3	24.1	826
Total of Sample	24.9	26.7	25.1	23.5	16,552

*Includes burials of 167 non-Indians, plus 18 burials for which no date was given.

higher rates of mortality in the winter and spring. Cold, damp, and unsanitary housing may have been an important factor in higher rates of mortality in northern Alta California. Adobe housing can be damp in the winter, which would have exacerbated debilitation due to syphilis and other chronic ailments. These illnesses were more related to the living conditions that existed in the missions, and they were only made worse in some mission communities by the weather.

Nonepidemic Causes of Demographic Collapse

In studying the demographic collapse of Native Americans following sustained contact with Europeans in the fifteenth and sixteenth centuries, scholars have identified the obvious cause as epidemics that in a short period of time carried off large numbers of people in dramatic and frequently well-documented episodes. In northern Sonora and Baja California, periodic epidemics of contagious disease significantly increased death rates, and clearly accelerated the process of demographic collapse by carrying off adults of child-bearing age, thus reducing the ability of the populations to reproduce. Moreover, epidemics exacerbated the frightfully high infant and child mortality rates, and virtually destroyed the populations of Indians congregated in the missions in a short period of time.

Few epidemics broke out in the Alta California missions, and the three most serious outbreaks occurred after 1800. How does the scholar explain the chronically high rates of mortality in the Alta California missions, and particularly, the high mortality among infants, children, and women? The explanation can be found in a reconstruction of the quality of life in the missions. This is not to deemphasize the importance of disease as a cause of high mortality. Syphilis was a debilitating disease introduced into Alta California by Spanish soldiers and colonists, and it spread through the Indian populations with devastating affect, as did the mercury often used as a treatment for the disease.[5] Respiratory ailments and illnesses caused by poor sanitation were also factors. However, these diseases were also common in Europe and in other parts of Spanish America; and they did not elevate mortality rates to the same level on a chronic basis, as was the case in the Alta California mission communities.

Women and young children were the most vulnerable segment of the mission populations, and they suffered exceptionally high death rates out of proportion to their numbers in the total population. Women of child-bearing age were perhaps most at risk. There appears to have been little or no prenatal care; and evidence suggests that the missionaries included women in the mission work force, which would have made pregnancies more dangerous. Moreover, the attempt by the missionaries to wipe out many of the native cultures may have denied young women access to traditional child-care knowledge. Children were born stillborn, or died shortly after birth due to the complications of birth or due to congenital illness such as syphilis. Dehydration also claimed many lives in the first year or two of life. Finally, qualitative evidence also suggests that abortion was commonly practiced in the mission communities; and the response by missionaries to apparent or real instances of provoked abortion contributed to the humiliation of Indian women, raised levels of stress, and only exacerbated the social conditions that had led women to abort in the first place.[6]

The climate of coercive social control that existed in the missions engendered a negative psychological response among Indian converts, and contributed to stress which reduced the efficiency of the body's immunological system. One element of the Franciscan agenda in Alta California was to contribute to the costs of the colonization of the region by providing the military garrisons in the region with cheap foodstuffs and clothing. The Franciscans required a large and stable labor force, but they had to deal with a rapidly declining Indian population and active resistance which frequently took the form of mass flight.[7] The Franciscans responded to active and passive resistance, especially to flight, by imposing different forms of social control in an attempt to limit mobility, and they used corporal punishment to enforce discipline. The public use of corporal punishment humiliated and physically injured the individual punished, and it did not always control the behavior that the missionaries found objectionable. The response prepared by the missionaries stationed at Santa Cruz mission to a questionnaire sent to California in 1813 by the Spanish Cortes provides a chilling glimpse of the use of corporal punishment as a means of social control. The Franciscans wrote that

> the Indians of this Mission [Santa Cruz] . . . profess . . . the virtue of obedience. . . . It is certain that the gardener, [even] if he knew his job very well, would put the plants in the ground with the roots up, if the Father [the missionary] so ordered. And when he wants to punish them, he need do no more than to order them to undress in order to execute it, and they receive their lashes.[8]

It should be noted that the Indians at Santa Cruz and other missions did not accept corporal punishment and other forms of social control as passively as the Franciscans believed. In 1812, for example, a group of converts at Santa Cruz mission murdered missionary Andrés Quintana, O.F.M., because of his plans to punish Indians in an especially sadistic form, with a cat-o'-nine-tails with barbed metal on the ends of the leather strips.[9] Despite efforts made by apologists for the Franciscans to trivialize the impact of the use of corporal punishment on the psychological and physical state of the converts, the evidence overwhelmingly substantiates the interpretation that coercive social control contributed in a large way to high levels of stress among the Indians living in the missions.

A report, written in 1797 by California governor Diego de Borica, outlined several causes for the high mortality rates in the California missions.[10] Borica identified four causes: (1) the heavy work load and the poor diet of the Indians living in the missions; (2) the practice of locking women and girls, particularly the wives of Indians who had fled from the missions, in unsanitary and damp dormitories at night; (3) poor sanitation in the missions; and (4) the loss of liberty and mobility that the Indians experienced following congregation in the missions. The following sections examine, in more detail, the factors that Borica outlined in his report, beginning with a discussion of diet.

Diet, Recruitment, and Depopulation

One of the most controversial and most difficult aspects of mission life to document is the quantity-and-quality balance of the Indian diet in the missions. Sources for the discussion of the mission diet include contemporary accounts prepared by the missionaries and foreign visitors to the missions, and figures on total grain production, which are found in extant annual reports. There are several deficiencies and biases in both sources. Most accounts written about the missions, particularly by late eighteenth-century European visitors to the missions and the missionaries themselves, reflect the attitudes of a privileged elite group from stratified hierarchical and race-based *ancien-régime* societies with preconceived notions about the proper rural social order in Europe and/or central Mexico, and about what peasants and the urban poor should and could live on, no matter how abundant and balanced or unbalanced the diet of the poor might be. From this perspective, the amount of food provided to Indian converts, when compared to what these observers might think appropriate for a population of similarly low social status in their native country, could appear to be abundant. This perception also had a basis in societies with little understanding of human nutritional requirements. Second, the figures on total grain production have little meaning when attempting to quantify the mean food consumption of the Indians living in the missions. The missionaries provided a considerable amount of food to the military garrisons in the province and to settlers, to promote the further colonization of the region, and they stored grain against future need, so the grain production listed in the annual reports does not reflect the amount of food actually consumed by converts.[11]

Scholarly opinion about the quantity and quality of the Indian diet in the missions varies. Sherburne Cook noted reports of the inclusion of quantities of meat in the Indian diet, but he concluded that the mission diet was still deficient, and was below the optimum in calories and balance necessary to provide the body with sufficient resistance to disease.[12] In a recent study, Ann Stodder concluded that malnutrition was an important factor in demographic collapse in the missions and, in conjunction with syphilis, caused lowered birthrates among women.[13] However, Stodder did not provide empirical evidence to substantiate her arguments. In some missions, Indians supplemented the food distributed by the missionaries with wild foods obtained through hunting or gathering, and in periods of poor crops or crop failure they were sent by the missionaries to collect wild foods. Anthropologist David Huelsbeck argued that wild foods were not a necessary element in the Indian diet, and were, in fact, a luxury item.[14]

The amount and quality of the Indian diet in the missions cannot be quantified. Rough calculations can be made on the basis of grain production, but only by keeping in mind that production levels were greater than

Table 3.8 Mean Grain Consumption in *Fanegas* in Selected Alta California Missions, 1820–1824

Mission	Wheat	Corn	Barley	Total
San Diego	1.8	.5	.95	3.25
San Gabriel	2.2	1.9	0	4.1
Santa Inés	2.6	1.5	.4	4.5
San Miguel	1.5	.03	.07	1.6
San Carlos	1.4	.08	1.1	2.58
Santa Clara	1.7	.4	.4	2.5
San Rafael	1.5	.3	.95	2.75

Source: Annual Reports, Santa Barbara Mission Archive-Library, Santa Barbara, California.

the actual amount of grain and produce supplied to the converts. Indians living in the missions consumed a maximum of between 1.6 and 4.5 *fanegas* of grain per person per year, based upon a calculation for a five-year sample (1820–1824) of the mean amount of grain per convert in seven missions. The amounts recorded in Table 3.8 are high, because the estimates have not been adjusted to take into account the grain and produce supplied to the military and settlers and the amount of seed reserved for the next year's planting.

In a recent study of rural Spain in the eighteenth century, historian Richard Herr estimated the mean consumption by Spanish peasants of wheat per individual per year, which places the data on mean grain consumption in the Alta California missions in context. According to previously published figures, annual wheat consumption in Spanish cities in the early modern period (sixteenth to eighteenth centuries) ranged from 4.0 to 4.7 *fanegas* per person, with some variation on the actual quantity consumed between the urban poor, the middle class, and the wealthy. The Spanish figures are close to estimates for other parts of Europe during the same period; from 5.0 in England, a figure which may have to be adjusted downward to 3.7 *fanegas,* to a low of 2.3 *fanegas* in the Netherlands. Wheat consumption depended on supply, price, and the relative importance of bread in the diet. However, wheat consumption alone does not account for the quantity of different foods in the diet, although the grain certainly was a very important component. On the basis of a detailed analysis of the rural economy of parts of Spain, Herr estimated that a rural family required an income equivalent to 6.0 to 12.0 *fanegas* of wheat per individual per year for basic levels of subsistence.[15]

How do Herr's figures compare to grain consumption in the Alta California missions? Herr's calculations attempt to establish a figure upon which to base income and status in rural villages, and he uses wheat as the standard with which to compare income generated from the sale of agricultural produce and other related economic activities. On average, each rural family had to dispose of an income equivalent to the value of 6.0 to 12.0 *fanegas* of wheat when sold on the market to ensure a minimum level of subsistence. This would include goods produced within the peasant household, goods and services purchased outside the peasant household, and the different taxes and feudal dues paid to the state, to the church, and to local elites. These figures do not reflect actual consumption of food, which may have been closer to the estimates for Madrid and for other Spanish cities.

The Indians living in the mission communities exchanged labor for food, clothing, and housing in a nonmarket economy; and mission labor can be conceptualized as a form of tribute paid to the state and administered by the missionaries. The missionaries determined the distribution of food and other surpluses produced by the labor of the Indians, using their own criteria as to what amount of food was sufficient to guarantee a basic level of subsistence for the Indians, but, at the same time, also providing for the needs of the military garrisons in the province. Any estimates of mean consumption based upon production figures more closely approximate actual consumption than do Herr's figures, keeping in mind that a considerable surplus from the mission economies went to support the military. Although not conclusive, the figures in Table 3.8 strongly suggest that in terms of staple grains, mean consumption in the missions was lower than consumption in contemporary Spanish cities and in the Spanish countryside. However, as suggested above, there was variation in patterns of consumption in the cities based upon wealth, so conceivably Indians living in the missions may have consumed similar quantities of, or perhaps even slightly more, food than the urban poor.

A second question related to production and consumption in the mission communities is the possible relationship between the resettlement of recruits to the missions and the use of food as an inducement to attract converts. This question, in turn, is significant within the context of the debate over voluntary or forced resettlement to the missions. If food, a steady diet without seasonal variation, was an important way of attracting Indians living outside the missions, then the forced relocation of Indians to the missions would have been unnecessary. I have subjected fifteen-year samples of grain production and the baptism of recruits from San José and Santa Inés missions, both taken during periods of heavy resettlement of

Table 3.9 Grain Supply as a Factor in the Relocation of Converts to Santa Inés and San José Missions, 1810–1819

Mission	Correlation of Grain Supply to Recruits	Regression Analysis		
		DF*	Adjusted R-Sqd.	t
Santa Inés	−.38	14	.0747	−1.460
San José	−.0278	14	.0761	−.100

*Degrees of Freedom.
Source: Annual Reports, Santa Barbara Mission Archive-Library, Santa Barbara, California.

converts to both mission communities, to two statistical tests to show the significance or lack of significance between grain production (food supply) and the number of recruits brought into the missions. The assumption being tested contends that factors other than food supply dictated the success of the missionaries in relocating converts, including the size of the non-Christian population in the region from which the missionaries drew recruits; the number of military expeditions sent to return fugitives and punish or forcibly relocate hostile non-Christians; and levels of resistance by non-Christians, among others. Correlation and regression statistical analysis are used to test the significance of the relationship between the two variables, with the results reported in Table 3.9. The results show a low level of correlation between the two variables, and little statistical significance as measured by a low adjusted r^2 and t statistics. Food supply was not a major determinant in the ability of the Franciscans to relocate Indians to the missions.

Sanitation, Housing, and Overcrowding

Until the nineteenth century, European doctors and scientists did not understand the relationship between sanitation, contaminated water supplies, and the spread of disease. Premodern cities, particularly in the poorer neighborhoods, were characteristically overcrowded, had poor or nonexistent sanitation, and were populated by residents frequently debilitated by chronic ailments caused by the conditions in which they lived. Infant and child mortality rates were high, although they did not reach the levels doumented for the mission communities of northwestern New Spain.

Housing directly contributed to high rates of infant mortality. The greatest danger for newborns in the first year or two of life was dehydration caused by diarrhea associated with a number of ailments. A second threshold in the life of a young child was reached when a toddler was placed on the floor for the first time, where it could catch a different series of illnesses, especially if exposed to unsanitary conditions in houses and dormitories. In the 1797 report, Diego de Borica identified poor sanitation as an important factor in the high death rates observed in the missions, as well as the practice of locking girls, single women, and the wives of absent or fugitive men, in dormitories at night. Borica described how he entered one such dormitory at an unidentified mission and was forced to leave the building because of the stench of human feces. Moreover, other accounts describe the dampness in the dormitories and the inadequate cover provided to the Indians, generally consisting of a single blanket. As Borica alluded to in his report, locking up females in dormitories at night was an important form of social control. The missionaries, who felt that the Indians were promiscuous, used the dormitories to protect and control the virtue and virginity of single girls and women. However, incarceration in dormitories disrupted normal social relations between the sexes and, in some instances, family life as well.

Although incomplete, the chronologies of building construction recorded in the annual reports prepared by the Franciscans document the building of dormitories and the importance of said structures as a form of social control. Table 3.10 lists the date of the construction of dormitories at selected missions for which there is a record of building construction from the date of the organization of the mission community. The missionaries directed the construction of dormitories for girls and single or widowed women at the beginning of the development of the complex of mission buildings, generally within a year or two of the establishment of the missions. Other types of buildings with priority included temporary chapels and residences for the missionaries. In a number of cases, larger dormitories were built at a later date to accommodate the growing population of women and girls as the mission populations expanded.

In 1798, the missionaries stationed at San Luis Rey mission directed the construction of a dormitory for girls and women. They later organized an agricultural station at San Antonio de Pala in an interior valley, and settled a substantial Indian population at the new settlement. In 1819, the Franciscans had a dormitory built at Pala for single men and women, although they did separate the sexes (see Table 3.10). Dormitories for single men were less common, since the missionaries were less concerned about male

Table 3.10 The Chronology of Dormitory Construction at Selected Alta California Missions

Mission	Year Mission Established	Year Built	Description
Sta Barbara	1786	1787	For girls and women
		1789	For girls and women
San Juan Bautista	1797	1797	For girls and women
		1815	For single men and widowers
San Luis Rey	1798	1798	For girls and women
San Antonio de Pala (Rancho of San Luis Rey Mission)	c. 1815	1819	For single men and women
San Rafael	1817	1817	For women and girls
		1825	For single men

Source: Annual Reports, Archivo General de la Nación, México, D.F., and the Santa Barbara Mission Archive-Library, Santa Barbara, California.

virtue and promiscuity. Moreover, since they already controlled the population of single women, it was not necessary to duplicate the effort by having dormitories built for single men, thus taking labor away from other projects deemed by the Franciscans to be more important. However, as large flight from the missions increasingly became a problem, dormitories were built to house single men as well. For example, a dormitory for men was built at San Juan Bautista in 1815, in response to a growing problem of flight. The construction of the dormitory for men became urgent as the Franciscans stationed at San Juan Bautista resettled Yokuts from the San Joaquín Valley, a group more inclined to resist the mission regime through flight since they lived at some distance from their native territory.

How did Indians forced to sleep in the dormitories react to this form of social control? The account of Lorenzo Asisara, an Indian born at Santa Cruz mission in 1820 and interviewed in 1877 by Thomas Savage while living near Watsonville, California, gives some indication of Indian responses to incarceration in dormitories. In 1812, Lorenzo's father participated in the murder of Santa Cruz missionary Fr. Andres Quintana, O.F.M. According to the account, the Indians attacked Quintana at night while the Franciscan went to the mission orchard to attend to a sick Indian, and left the Franciscan unconscious in his bed. The ring-leaders then released the single men and women from the dormitories, and the Indians went down to the orchard and "had their pleasure." The elimination of the authority of the missionary allowed the Indians greater sexual freedom. A second episode gives a fuller understanding of the functioning of the dormitory system at Santa Cruz mission. The missionary kept a master list of the converts who were to spend the night in each dormitory, and accompanied by the soldiers stationed at the mission, he took a count of the Indians already in the structure to ensure that none had escaped. Asisara relates how one inmate of the dormitory for single men arrived late, and was ordered whipped on the stomach by missionary Ramón Olbes, O.F.M., as punishment. The Indians in the dormitory rioted in support of the Indian convert, throwing rocks and tiles at the Franciscan and the soldiers. The priest and his escort had to escape from the dormitory, and the Indians expected a strong punishment from the missionary who had a reputation for the frequency and severity of the lashes given to the converts. However, perhaps as a consequence of the united response of the Indians in the dormitory, Olbes merely reprimanded the participants in the incident, in a sermon delivered the next day.[16]

Dormitories were not the only form of permanent adobe housing that posed a health problem when combined with poor sanitation and overcrowding. California Indians generally occupied several semipermanent village sites, on a seasonal basis and in a specific territory, and exploited different food sources. Moreover, the Indians built their dwellings of tule grass or other nonpermanent materials, and periodically burned the dwellings when they became infested with vermin. Finally, population densities in individual villages were low, and sanitation was not a significant problem.

The program of congregation brought large populations together in spatially compact communities, contributing to a major problem of sanitation and the pollution of water from the communal sources located in the Indian villages. Moreover, the concentration of a large number of people living together in a small space facilitated the spread of disease. Finally, although not given a high priority during the initial stage of the development of the complex of mission buildings, the missionaries had permanent adobe housing built for Indian families, partially as a means of social control once the Franciscans began to resettle converts from greater distances from the mission community.

In the early stage of mission development, Indian families lived in traditional style housing, generally tule grass structures. Once the missionaries had constructed the basic complex of buildings, which included a church, a residence for the missionaries, granaries, workshops, housing for the soldiers stationed at the mission and their families, and mills, they directed the construction of adobe houses for Indian families. This housing took several forms: either long barrackslike structures with small apartments for individual families, or rows of smaller buildings that housed several families. The record, both annual reports and plat maps prepared following secularization, indicates that a hundred or more of such housing units were built in some missions.[17]

The missionaries also changed the style of dress of the converts living in the missions, substituting cotton, and particularly, woolen cloth for the traditional materials used by the Indians. The common practice was for the Franciscans to distribute a single set of clothing and blankets that the Indians wore until a new set was issued. Communal laundries were built at the missions, and Indian women made efforts to keep clothing and blankets clean. However, the new-style clothing easily harbored potentially dangerous parasites, and it could not be discarded with the same frequency as could traditional clothing. Finally, the missionaries attempted to establish new standards of dress, which required Indians to frequently wear the new garments. Although not necessarily an important factor in the elevation of death rates, change in clothing styles and materials exemplified the way in which the social engineering practiced by the missionaries damaged the health of Indian converts.

Labor and Social Disruption

The functioning of the mission economies depended upon an abundant labor supply, and the mission economies, in turn, produced surpluses that subsidized the cost of colonizing of the region. The Franciscans, backed by the small number of soldiers stationed at the missions, imposed a rigid system of coerced disciplined labor that was enforced by the use of corporal punishment and by other forms of control. Moreover, the mission labor regime instituted a gender reversal in the household economy, and forced converts into sustained field labor; building construction; and artisan industry, such as textile production. Prior to the arrival of the Spaniards, men hunted and engaged in periodic warfare, and women collected and prepared food. The Franciscans put men into sustained agricultural labor, which resembled the mundane work of women, generated disaffection, and contributed to a general psychological disorientation caused by the acculturation program in the missions.[18]

Although not the exclusive objective, the recruitment of new converts throughout the period of the history of the missions served to replenish an unstable, yet vital, labor supply. The search for new converts took the missionaries to greater distances from the mission communities, and the use of different degrees of force in relocating converts to the missions generated passive and active forms of resistance, including large-scale flight.[19] The missionaries responded to flight by imposing tighter social controls, including locking up single men and widowers in dormitories at night.

Contemporary sources document individual examples of flight from the missions, and the way in which the Franciscans classified fugitives and Indians returned to the missions on the basis of their ability to work. Two letters written in 1798 by Santa Cruz missionary Manuel Fernández, O.F.M., show the tendency to categorize Indians on their ability to work. Sections of the two letters are translated below.

> I tell you that the Neophytes that are presently fugitives are 46 adult males, 34 adult [females], 27 boy children 8 years [of age and] below, and 35 girl children, that together are 138 [people]. *Those that daily unite for the labors are something more than 30 to 40 men.* [emphasis added][20]
>
> Joaquín Mesa arrived with 52 of the recent fugitive Neophytes: 30 are 15 years [of age] and above, and so above [advanced age] *that only 14 of them barely serve for work* [emphasis added] and 22 are *parvulos* [young children].[21]

The military in California participated in expeditions to recapture fugitives from the missions and to relocate Indians to the mission communities. The threat of attack from the military expeditions mounted in Spanish-Mexican territory contributed to the social and political reorganization of groups living outside the area of Spanish-Mexican control, particularly in the Sacramento and San Joaquín valleys. There was also an intensification of a cycle of violence, as some tribelets adapted their economies to raiding missions and ranches to obtain horses for riding and consumption, and the Spanish-Mexican military responded with further punitive expeditions.[22]

Diego de Borica recognized, in the 1790s, the impact on the Indian population of the imposition of an alien labor regime, but a relationship cannot be established between heavy labor, inadequate diet, and malnutrition without a scientific examination of a large sample of skeletal remains from mission cemeteries. The pressure on the labor force intensified after 1810, with the beginning of the independence war in central Mexico and the collapse of the system that provided essential supplies to the missions and to military garrisons. The Franciscans harnessed the mission economies to support the entire colonial system in Alta California, and labor became increasingly important as they expanded production levels to meet the new demands of the military.[23]

The reorganization of the mission economies coincided with the last phase of recruitment, which, in the northern and central missions, resulted in the organization of expeditions to the Central Valley, as well as in the escalating violence noted above. The resettlement, often by force, of recruits from a greater distance from the mission communities led to increased flight and to the imposition of tighter social controls. Converts brought to the missions from a greater distance were more inclined to flee the missions, and the greater demands placed on the mission economies made it imperative for the missionaries to maintain the size of the labor force. Labor demands in the missions may have been heavy in the 1790s, but they became particularly disruptive after 1810.

Acculturation, Changes in the Indian Worldview, and Psychological Dislocation

One of the principal objectives of the missionaries was to transform the Indians' worldview and remake the Indian populations over in the image of the central Mexican peasantry, which supported the colonial order with their labor and surplus production siphoned off through tribute and other taxes. The missionaries attempted to destroy all traditional Indian religious beliefs. However, the missionaries did not always have a complete knowledge of these beliefs and practices, and the Indians may have consciously attempted to keep the Franciscans in the dark about their religion.[24]

A process of syncretism, similar to that described by Nancy Farriss in the Yucatán Peninsula, may also have occurred in the California missions, although the evidence is contradictory.[25] Some of the converts were either brought into the missions as young children, or they were the sons and daughters of converts born in the mission communities. If they survived for a reasonable period of time, the young children would be heavily indoctrinated, whereas adults may have acquired a veneer of Christianity and possibly have incorporated some Christian beliefs and practices into their worldview. Moreover, with the high rates of mortality and the resettlement of large numbers of recruits to the mission communities, all converts were exposed to a large number of people who continued to practice their traditional religion. This is not to say that the missionaries did not try to stamp out the more open or visible Indian religious practices, such as dances. The missionaries stationed at Santa Clara mission identified dancing as one of the principal vices of the Indians, and they probably made efforts to eliminate the practice.[26] The personality of the missionary also determined the willingness of the individual Franciscan to go forward with the effort to wipe out Indian religion. In 1816, for example, the missionaries stationed at San Francisco mission staged a traditional Indian dance for the leaders of a visiting Russian expedition, which seems to indicate that they did not view traditional dance in the same light as their colleagues stationed at Santa Clara mission.[27]

The personality of the individual missionary was an important factor in the rigor of the campaign to wipe out traditional Indian beliefs, as was the ability of the converts to prevent the Franciscans from learning about their worldview and about any covert practice of their religion, especially dances. The use of corporal punishment was a key element used in the effort to convince converts to abandon their religious practices. The Franciscans probably experienced mixed results in their witch hunts (the missionaries identified shamans as *hechizeros,* or witches), but the result was one additional forced change that contributed to the violent wrenching of the Indians from one culture to another, with little thought given to the psychological consequences.

Dances and other communal religious practices cemented social relations, and provided a distraction from repeated daily activities. Iberian Catholicism contained outward signs of pomp that attracted Indians, such as passion plays. The socializing benefits of Catholic practice were balanced by the stark reality of the brutality of the mission regime, which depended on the use of corporal punishment to maintain order, exacerbated by the impact on the converts of seeing friends and family members dying by the hundreds from painful diseases they did not understand and the physical deterioration of many from syphilis and other chronic ailments.

Contemporary accounts talk of a melancholy attitude among many converts, which was symptomatic of the general psychological dislocation caused by life, the living conditions, and high rates of morbidity and mortality in the mission. The general depression among the Indian population manifested itself in several forms. Stress, which must have been high in the mission communities, weakens the immunological system, contributing to the phenomenon described by some observers as natives giving up the ghost and lying down to die.[28] Induced abortion was a second response. Social disruption and psychological dislocation, functions of the extreme paternalism practiced in the missions, left the Indians ill prepared to deal with the new conditions that existed in California following the closing of the missions in the mid-1830s, and explain what Anglo-American settlers in the region interpreted as the shiftlessness of the Indians.[29]

Warfare, Indian Raiding, and Demographic Collapse

Disease, social disruption, and psychological dislocation were the primary causes for Indian demographic collapse in northwestern New Spain. Although generalized throughout the region, the factors outlined above varied between the three mission groupings studied here. Epidemics substantially elevated mortality rates in the Pimería Alta and Baja California missions, and constituted the single most important factor. High rates of infant and child mortality only exacerbated the situation. In the Alta California missions, on the other hand, chronic ailments frequently associated with the living conditions that existed in the missions proved to be especially deadly for Indian converts. At the same time, a significant outside factor must be considered, mortality due to warfare: revolts, or raids launched by hostile Indians from outside the Spanish sphere of influence. This section briefly examines the role of warfare in demographic collapse.

Warfare assumed two forms in northwestern New Spain: revolts, and raids by hostile Indians. Warfare did not necessarily cause a large number of deaths, but it did disrupt mission life and expose vanquished Indians to mistreatment at the hands of soldiers. Revolts took two forms: primary resistance, which generally occurred within a short period of time following initial contact with colonists and missionaries, and was an initial reaction to depredations on traditional food resources and the social changes being introduced; and secondary resistance, frequently revitalization movements, which took place a generation or two after the arrival of colonists and missionaries, and frequently attempted to redress grievances or restore conditions to what they had been prior to the arrival of Europeans. There are instances of primary resistance in northwestern New Spain in the 1690s in the Pimería Alta, in the 1730s and 1740s in Baja California, and in the 1770s in Alta California. Secondary resistance occurred in the Pimería Alta in the 1750s, and in Alta California in the 1820s.

Raids by hostile Indians, particularly by the Apaches, were a serious problem in northern Sonora in the eighteenth century. The structure of Apache raiding precluded a mass slaughter of Indians living in the mission communities. The Apaches generally lived and waged war in small bands, and they had no large-scale political organization, which would have allowed for a more sustained form of warfare. Bands might cooperate on specific raids, but only on a short-term basis. Most raiding parties in Sonora probably numbered between ten and forty warriors. In February of 1769, for example, some thirty Apaches attacked San Francisco Xavier del Bac mission. Within a matter of minutes, the marauders ran off most of the mission livestock, but they wounded only one Pima.[30]

There were instances of attacks by large bands against both the missions and the military. In most cases, these raids resulted in few deaths, but there are several examples of attacks that left a signifiant number of people dead. Apache bands scored major victories in raids against the missions and non-Indian settlements. One of the bloodiest took place in 1757. An Apache war band, with rebel Pima allies, attacked and killed thirty-two people at San Lorenzo, a farming village located near Magdalena *visita* of San Ignacio mission.[31] Thirteen years later, in 1770, the marauders killed nineteen people at Sonoita *visita* of Guevavi mission. Shortly after the attack, the Franciscans moved the survivors to the villages located on the Santa Cruz River.[32]

One document records, in detail, patterns of Apache, Seri, and rebel Pima raids on Sonora between 1755 and 1760. Although there were some raids against the missions, the non-Indian settlements apparently were the favorite targets of the Apaches and their allies. Deaths in the region totaled some forty-nine settlers, nine Pimas, and four Yaquis and Nijoras. As previously noted, the most successful attack occurred at San Lorenzo in 1757, and the attack accounts for the majority of the fatalities among the settlers. Herds of livestock were the primary goal, and few people died. In 1759 and 1760, Apache bands raided San Luis, Buenaventura, and Santa Barbara, cattle ranches located south of Guevavi mission, and killed one Tubac resident in November of 1758. Similarly, the marauders stole eighty horses from Cocospera mission, and one hundred horses and mules from Soamca in 1758. In 1758 and 1759, settlers living at Terrenate presidio lost livestock to the raiders. Aside from the one attack on San Lorenzo, most victims were travelers caught on the roads, between the relative safety of the settlements. In November of 1758, "*un Yndio Zimaron*" [fugitive Indian] killed a Yaqui woman near Santa Ana. In 1759 and 1760, five more people died near the village. In February of 1759, hostile Indians killed a

Spaniard near Tubac presidio. Indian hostilities modified settlement patterns in the region. According to the 1760 report, settlers had abandoned Tucubavia ranch, Ocuca, and Arituaba between 1751 and 1760, as a consequence of raids by hostile Indians.[33]

Spanish military forces were not entirely impotent in the face of Indian raiding, although the Apaches and their allies skillfully practiced hit-and-run tactics. One Spanish victory appears in the 1760 report. Sixteen rebel Pimas died during a 1756 attack on Pitiquito *visita* of Caborca mission, but at a cost of one soldier killed.[34]

The missionaries generally identified in the burial registers the people killed by the Apaches and by other hostile Indians. An examination of the registers of Guevavi-Tumacacori missions, one of the most exposed sections of the frontier, shows that deaths attributed to hostile Indians formed only a small percentage of total deaths. Between 1743 and 1766, Jesuits stationed at Guevavi buried a total of 439 people, but only 5 killed by hostile Indians, or 1 percent of the total sample.[35] In the Franciscan period following the Jesuit expulsion, the missionaries stationed at Guevavi-Tumacacori buried 653 people and 41 victims of hostile Indians, including the 19 killed at Sonoita in 1770, or 6 percent of the total sample.[36] A casual survey of extant burial registers from the Pimería Alta missions substantiates the pattern outlined above.

Conclusions

The previous chapters outlined a pattern of high mortality and rapid demographic collapse in the mission communities of northwestern New Spain. A variety of factors contributed to the collapse of the Indian populations living in the mission communities, although there was variation between the three regions studied. Epidemics raised mortality rates in the missions in northern Sonora and Baja California, killing both adults and children and exacerbating a pattern of chronically high rates of infant and child mortality. In the long run, the populations in the two regions would have aged as fewer children survived, and would have gradually declined over a number of generations. Periodic epidemics were traumatic episodes that accelerated the process of demographic collapse, and in many mission communities, the net population loss during epidemic years accounted for at last 50 percent of the decline in total numbers. Epidemics, more than any other single factor, were responsible for population losses in northern Sonora and Baja California.[37]

The case of the Alta California missions was distinct. The record shows that few epidemics reached the region, yet death rates were chronically high, and generally higher than death rates in Sonora and Baja California mission communities in non-epidemic years. Chronic ailments such as syphilis and other diseases caused high rates of infant and child mortality. High mortality rates were related to the living conditions in the missions, the degree of sociocultural dislocation caused by the program of acculturation directed by the Franciscan missionaries, and the psychological impact of rapid social change and the high mortality rates. The Alta California missions present the worst-case scenario of the three mission groupings studied.

The evidence suggests that the Franciscans in Alta California disposed of relatively more coercive force in the form of the four military garrisons in the province, which enabled them to initiate more drastic change in the lives of the Indian converts. Moreover, the climate of most of Alta California is cooler and damper than that of Baja California and Sonora, and mission agriculture supported a larger population in the mission centers and thus higher population densities. The missionaries in Baja California had access to relatively little land suitable for agriculture, and maintained a more dispersed pattern of settlement until the Indian populations were substantially reduced in size. In the Californias, the missionaries congregated Indians in newly organized settlements, whereas the Jesuits in the Pimería Alta settled at existing *rancherías* and merely had to siphon off a surplus from the existing subsistence economy. Finally, the level of sociocultural organization varied between the regions, as did the degree of social dislocation. The Indians living in the Alta California missions experienced the most rapid changes in life-styles and in socioeconomic organization. The Franciscans made greater demands on the converts, and they had the resources available to bring large numbers of people to the mission communities to repopulate the missions. Agriculture in Baja California supported smaller populations, and in some instances, large segments of the converted population had experienced only slight changes in their life-styles. Northern Pimas experienced the least amount of change and social dislocation, and they were able to escape the control of the missionaries by selling their labor in the local economy. Indians living in the missions in the Californias—regions in which the missionaries had relatively more influence in the formulation of government Indian policy—had less of an opportunity to escape mission life, and they might be dragged back to the mission communities by the soldiers, a possibility that reinforced the authority of the missionary.

How unique or common were the demographic patterns documented for the mission communities of northwestern New Spain? What comparisons can be made with other contemporary populations? The following chapter compares demographic patterns in the mission communities with other populations in the Americas and elsewhere.

4

Demographic Collapse in a Comparative Context

The previous chapter outlined the causes of the demographic collapse of the Indian populations congregated in the mission communities of northwestern New Spain. Although they were drastic throughout the larger region, the rates of decline varied between the three regions studied here. An examination of these variations sheds further light on the process of Native American demographic collapse. Was the collapse of the Indian populations in the missions a unique phenomenon, or a common occurrence in colonial situations similar to the northern frontier of New Spain? How do the vital rates documented for the mission communities compare with the vital rates of contemporary non-Indian populations in the Americas and in Europe?

This chapter offers a comparative analysis of the vital rates observed in the missions of northern Sonora and the Californias. The first section outlines similarities and differences in the formation of the mission communities through the resettlement of converts in Baja and Alta California. The second section compares the collapse of the Indian populations of Sonora and the Californias with Indian populations in other parts of Spanish America. The final section documents the demographic collapse of the Indian populations within the context of the vital rates of contemporary non-Indian populations, including the population of the settlers and soldiers living in the four military garrisons established in Alta California at the end of the eighteenth century and preindustrial peasant populations in Europe and Asia.

The Formation of the Mission Communities

The Indian populations of the mission communities of northwestern New Spain were unstable, and the Jesuit, Dominican, and Franciscan missionaries attempted to resettle converts and thus repopulate the missions. The ability of the missionaries to congregate converts, either voluntarily or through force, was a major determinant of the size of the mission populations. Aggregate data abstracted from mission parish registers is presented to document the recruitment and resettlement of converts to mission communities, as well as the net growth and decline of populations.

Chapter 1 outlined the process of the conversion and congregation of the Indian populations of northwestern New Spain in spatially compact villages, and the continuing efforts of the missionaries to attract Indians from the surrounding desert region to resettle in the missions. The availability and willingness of non-Christian Indians to live at the missions determined the rate of change in population levels. High death rates generally wiped out any growth through natural reproduction in the missions, and the mission populations would have declined had the missionaries not been able to tap a pool of potential converts living outside the missions and at greater distances from the mission communities. This is not to say that the populations of some mission communities did not experience short periods of growth through natural reproduction, but the long-term pattern was one of unstable populations dependent on the influx of recruits to replace individuals who died.[1]

Missionaries in the Pimería Alta and Alta California had greater apparent success in relocating converts, partially because of the relatively larger size of the Indian populations still living outside the missions. As noted in Chapter 1, the missionaries in northern Sonora took advantage of an existing pattern of seasonal migration to exploit food resources in convincing or pressuring Papagos who had come to the mission communities on a seasonal basis to remain there. However, the evidence suggests that the missionaries stationed in strategic locations on the edge of the *Papagueria* had the greatest success in resettling Papagos and in repopulating the mission communities. The case of the Alta California missions is similar, but the Francisans stationed there had a larger potential pool of converts to draw upon.

Tables 4.1 and 4.2 summarize data on decade totals of baptisms and burials from selected Baja and Alta California missions, and they document the relationship between the baptism of converts, births, burials, and the growth and decline of the mission populations. Distinct patterns emerge in a comparison of the Baja and Alta California mission communities. In many of the Baja California missions, the Jesuit, Franciscan, and Dominican missionaries incorporated the bulk of the local Indian population into the mission communities in a short period of time. At San Francisco de Borja and San Fernando missions, for example, the bulk of the baptisms of converts and the expansion of the mission population through the congregation of converts occurred in a period of about ten years. At San Fernando, the missionaries baptized 1,220 converts in a decade, and then baptized only 70 more converts over the next thirty-eight years. As the number of recruits dropped and birthrates failed to match the high rates of mortality, the population dropped. The process of congregation was more gradual in the northern Dominican missions of Rosario and Santo Domingo. Finally, Mulege and Comondú were older establishments founded in the first decade of the eighteenth century, and the extant sacramental registers summarized here document declining populations.

The populations of the Baja and Alta California missions grew during periods of active recruitment of converts, but the periods of growth were longer in the Alta California establishments because of the ability of the Franciscan missionaries at many establishments to relocate converts from increasing distances from the mission communities. For example, the population of San Juan Bautista grew during two distinct periods, as the Franciscans stationed there congregated the local population and then relocated Yokuts converts from the neighboring San Joaquín (Central Valley). The populations of other missions, such as San José, grew as the Franciscans continued to resettle converts. The pattern of population growth in some Alta California establishments more closely resembled patterns in the Baja California missions, with a prolonged growth of the numbers during periods of active recruitment and resettlement, but declining when the pace of recruitment slowed.

Demographic Collapse in a Comparative Context

How does the collapse of the Indian populations congregated in the mission communities of northwestern New Spain compare to the vital rates and trajectory of change of other *ancien-régime* populations? This section outlines secular trends in preindustrial European and postconquest Latin American populations, and specific examples of vital rates of individual communities in northwestern New Spain, Europe, and the Philippines in Asia. The vital rates of these communities are compared to patterns observed for the mission communities studied here. The first case study is of the population of San Antonio de Valero mission in Texas.

During the period from 1727 to 1781, there were five major mortality crises at San Antonio de Valero mission: measles epidemics in 1728, in

Table 4.1 Net Population Growth and Decline in Five Selected Baja and Alta California Missions

Years	Baptisms of Converts	Births	Burials	Net Gain +/–
		(San Fernando de Velicata)		
1770–1779	1,220	233	N.A.	N.A.
1780–1789	29	298	623	–296
1790–1799	29	117	216	–70
1800–1809	0	37	308	–271
1810–1818	12	14	85	–59
		(Nuestra Señora del Rosario)		
1774–1779	617	66	314	369
1780–1789	172	151	362	–39
1790–1799	135	123	233	25
1800–1809	5	50	182	–127
1809–1819	3	31	87	–53
		(San Carlos)		
1790–1799	324	380	619	85
1800–1809	131	214	525	–180
1810–1819	12	209	339	–118
1820–1829	1	158	312	–153
1830–1832	0	32	38	–6
		(Santa Cruz)		
1791–1799	809	89	404	494
1800–1809	410	122	554	–22
1810–1819	246	114	405	–45
1820–1829	249	137	418	–32
1830–1834	23	46	128	–59
		(San Juan Bautista)		
1797–1799	315	31	296	50
1800–1809	1,178	325	917	586
1810–1819	180	310	579	–89
1820–1829	902	457	1,039	320
1830–1834	56	174	355	–125

Source: Robert H. Jackson, "Gentile Recruitment and Population Movements in the San Francisco Bay Area Missions," *Journal of California and Great Basin Anthropology* 6:2 (1984), pp. 225–39; Robert H. Jackson, "Disease and Demographic Patterns at Santa Cruz Mission, Alta California," *Journal of California and Great Basin Anthropology* 5:1 and 2 (1983), pp. 33–57; and Robert H. Jackson, "Patterns of Demographic Change in the Missions of Central Alta California," *Journal of California and Great Basin Anthropology* 9:2 (1987), pp. 251–72.

Table 4.2 Net Population Growth and Decline in Twelve Selected Baja and Alta California Missions

Years	Baptisms	Burials	Net Gain +|-
	(Santa Rosalia de Mulege)		
1722–1729		279	
1730–1739		80	
1740–1749		250	
1750–1759		144	
1760–1769		220	
1770–1779	83	70	10
1780–1789	46	137	−91
1790–1799	44	66	−22
1800–1809	18	55	−37
1810–1819	16	18	−2
	(San José de Comondú)		
1736–1739	80	70	10
1740–1749	280	323	−43
1750–1759	272	274	−2
1760–1769	214	336	−122
1770–1779	119	319	−200
1780–1789	41	185	−144
1790–1799	24	64	−40
	(Santa Gertrudis)		
1751–1759	1,777	909	868
1760–1769	1,052	1,021	31
1770–1779	431	789	−358
1780–1789	170	514	−344
1790–1799	99	118	−19
1800–1809	73	131	−58
	(San Francisco de Borja)		
1762–1769	2,151	828	1,323
1770–1779	486	1,229	−743
1780–1789	266	378	−112
1790–1799	113	201	−88
1800–1809	103	154	−51
	(Santo Domingo)		
1775–1779	112	25	87
1780–1789	256	168	88
1790–1799	336	176	160
1800–1809	112	191	−79
1810–1819	50	107	−57
1820–1829	18	35	−17
	(San Antonio de Padua)		
1771–1779	601	189	412
1780–1789	1,066	456	610
1790–1799	746	624	122
1800–1809	1,030	968	62
1810–1819	510	728	−218
1820–1829	351	553	−202
1830–1839	230	445	−215

(continued)

Table 4.2 *(Continued)*

Years	Baptisms	Burials	Net Gain +|-
	(San Luis Obispo)		
1772–1779	396	62	334
1780–1789	452	197	255
1790–1799	652	467	185
1800–1809	699	658	41
1810–1819	269	468	−199
1820–1829	104	328	−224
1830–1839	255	268	−13
	(San Francisco de Asis)		
1777–1779	111	14	97
1780–1789	584	244	340
1790–1799	1,171	989	182
1800–1809	1,795	1,521	274
1810–1819	1,815	1,966	−151
1820–1829	647	467	180
1830–1839	49	111	−62
	(Santa Clara de Asis)		
1777–1779	159	31	128
1780–1789	1,285	619	666
1790–1799	2,272	1,697	575
1800–1809	1,617	1,576	41
1810–1819	986	1,153	−167
1820–1829	1,211	1,227	−16
1830–1839	505	720	−215
	(San José)		
1797–1799	238	40	198
1800–1809	1,471	1,087	384
1810–1819	2,377	1,277	1,100
1820–1829	1,989	1,924	65
1830–1839	2,205	1,824	381
	(San Rafael)		
1817–1819	351	53	298
1820–1829	1,249	504	745
1830–1839	288	284	4
	(San Francisco Solano)		
1823–1829	626	337	289
1830–1839	865	519	346

Source: Robert H. Jackson, "Demographic Patterns in the Missions of Central Baja California," *Journal of California and Great Basin Anthropology* 6:1 (1984), pp. 91–112; Robert H. Jackson, "Disease and Demographic Patterns at Santa Cruz Mission, Alta California," *Journal of California and Great Basin Anthropology* 5:1 and 2 (1983), pp. 33–57; Robert H. Jackson, "Gentile Recruitment and Population Movements in the San Francisco Bay Area Missions," *Journal of California and Great Basin Anthropology* 6:2 (1984), pp. 225–39; and Robert H. Jackson, "Patterns of Demographic Change in the Missions of Central Alta California," *Journal of California and Great Basin Anthropology* 9:2 (1987), pp. 251–72.

1749, and again in 1768; and smallpox in 1762 and again in 1781. Moreover, there was elevated mortality during the 1757–1761 quinquennium. Crude death rates per thousand population fluctuated during the epidemic and nonepidemic years, but the impact of the epidemics can be seen clearly in elevated mortality rates and substantially lowered net reproduction ratios. In five quinquenniums during which no major epidemics attacked the population of San Antonio de Valero, the crude death rate averaged 52 per thousand population, and a net reproduction ratio of 0.42, which signifies a rate of decline over a generation of 48 percent. In the quinquennium during which there were epidemic outbreaks, the mean death rate was 95 per thousand population, 1.8 times the death rate in nonepidemic years, and it was as high as 121 per thousand population during the 1762–1766 quinquennium, or 2.3 times the mean crude death rate in nonepidemic years. The mean net reproduction ratio was 0.12, which signfies a rate of decline of 88 percent over a generation, 72 percent lower than in nonepidemic years. Finally, mean life expectancy at birth dropped dramatically from 15.5 years in nonepidemic periods to 3.9 during the six quinquenniums, with elevated mortality caused by epidemics.

Epidemics of contagious diseases were traumatic episodes that increased the overall death rates, substantially lowered life expectancy, and accelerated the process of demographic collapse. However, there were more nonepidemic than epidemic years, and the Indian population was not viable (or able to grow through natural increase), even in nonepidemic years.

The gross reproduction ratio, an index of the population's production of children, shows that in nonepidemic years birthrates ranged from moderate to high, although birthrates did dip in epidemic years, and especially in the late 1750s and the 1760s. The gross reproduction ratio averaged 1.70 in nonepidemic periods, 1.42 in epidemic years (the *grr* for the 1777–1781 quinquennium has been excluded because the data on births has been adjusted downward), and a mere 0.81 between 1757 and 1771. The consistently low net reproduction ratios in nonepidemic years were caused by the chronically high levels of infant and child mortality. According to the results of Schuetz's family reconstitution, more than 80 percent of the children born at the mission died before reaching age ten, which does not take into account young children brought into the missions with adult converts. Birthrates also dropped from the 1720s to the 1780s, reflecting a pattern of higher mortality among females than males, especially young mothers, and a declining number of women of child-bearing age in relation to the total population (see Table 4.3).

The population of San Antonio de Valero mission fluctuated in the first decades following the establishment of the mission, but slowly grew from the 1730s to the early 1740s. The Franciscan missionaries were able to recruit converts from outside the mission community to replace individuals who died and to expand the size of the mission population. Despite high levels of mortality, the population of the mission experienced a net increase of 161 from 1727 to 1746; the number of baptisms of converts reached 273, and births totaled 230. In 1746, the population of the mission was some 390. Over the following thirty-four years, the net decline in the population was some 293, which can be attributed to a decline in the number of converts entering the mission, down to some 131, and to falling numbers of births, down to some 183. The mean number of baptisms of converts was 14 during the earlier period of population growth, but fell to some 4 after 1747. The mean number of births dropped from 12 to some 5 in the years after 1747. In the late 1770s, a mere 77 Indians continued to live at San Antonio de Valero.

The greatest net decline in the mission population occurred during the 1762–1766 quinquennium, with a severe smallpox epidemic and the highest crude death rates for the period studied. The number of baptisms

Table 4.3 Quinquennium Totals of Baptisms and Burials Recorded at San Antonio de Valero Mission, 1722–1781

Quin.	Population Begin Quin.	Births	Baptisms of Converts	Burials	Net Gain +\-
1722–26	290	19	67	N.A.	
1727–31	229*	53	102	95	60
1732–36	289*	39	34	74	–1
1737–41	288*	64	86	76	74
1742–46	362*	74	51	97	28
1747–51	390*	57	58	163	–48
1752–56	342*	43	26	83	–14
1757–61	328	21	20	119	–78
1762–66	275	17	7	129	–105
1767–71	170*	15	10	54**	–29
1772–76	125	15	1	25*	–9
1777–81	77	23	1	34	–10

*Estimated figure
**Adjusted figure
Source: Mardith Scheutz, "The Indians of the San Antonio Missions 1718–1821" (Ph.D. dissertation, University of Texas at Austin), 1980, pp. 128, 131, 136–38, 142–44.

Table 4.4 Demographic Statistics of San Antonio de Valero Mission, 1727–1781

Year	Estimated Population	Crude Rates		Reproduction Ratio		Mean Life Expectancy
		Birth	Death	Gross	Net	
1729	207	51	92	2.88	.25	5.9
1734	271	29	55	1.44	.26	11.5
1739	282	45	54	2.16	.54	15.9
1744	350	42	55	2.09	.54	16.2
1749	333	34	98	1.79	.07	2.9
1754	321	27	52	1.49	.30	12.9
1759	275	15	87	.81	.02	2.0
1764	212	16	121	.72	.01	1.2
1769	149	20	72	.89	.06	4.9
1774	120	25	42	1.33	.45	21.2
1779*	71	45	101	3.24	.30	6.2

*Adjusted figures.
Source: Table 4.3.

of recruits and births dropped to 24, and the net population decline over five years was 105. Put in other terms, smallpox in the early 1760s was largely responsible for some 36 percent of the net population loss at San Antonio de Valero after 1747.

The Indian populations in much of North America experienced dramatic declines following sustained contact with Europeans and newly introduced diseases, such as smallpox and measles. Rates of decline varied from place to place as a function of climate, population distribution and the compactness of settlement, levels of nutrition, and the form and level of exploitation by the colonizers. Patterns documented for San Antonio de Valero, another mission community in northern Mexico, paralleled patterns documented for the Pimería Alta and Baja California, characterized by severe periodic mortality crises and not by the chronically high mortality seen in Alta California. In Peru, on the other hand, the Indian population dropped from as much as nine million prior to the first great epidemic of the 1620s to less than a million a century later.[2] Censuses and tribute counts from the end of the sixteenth century document the process of decline in Peru. The greatest rate of decline occurred on the Peruvian coast, with lower rates in the cooler highlands. There were an estimated 1,264,000 Indians in Peru in 1570 prior to the implementation of the policy of *reducción* under

Viceroy Francisco de Toledo, and 589,000 in 1620.[3] The Indian populations of the central areas of Spanish America, central Mexico and the Andean region, recovered following a prolonged period of decline.[4]

A detailed examination of the population of one Andean community in the late sixteenth century sheds light on patterns of Indian demographic collapse in other parts of Spanish America. In 1573, Spanish officials congregated the population of thirty separate settlements in the Valle Bajo of Cochabamba (Alto Peru), 2,573 people, in a single *reducción* named Tiquipaya, and they prepared a detailed census of the new community. The Quechua-Aymara population of the Valle Bajo had already declined as a consequence of the impact of epidemic disease, including a major outbreak in the years 1558–1561, which was reflected in the relatively small number of people in the age 10 to 29 cohorts. However, despite the impact of epidemics, the population of Tiquipaya did not manifest the same imbalances in the age and gender structure observed in the Baja California and, especially, Alta California missions. The population recovered somewhat from the impact of epidemics, as evidenced by the large number of children born following the 1558–1561 epidemic. Moreover, epidemics probably did not attack the population of the Valle Bajo as frequently or with as devastating an impact as in northwestern New Spain. Children under age ten made up 33 percent of the total population, although the age structure was distorted somewhat by the deficit in the age 10 to 29 cohorts. Finally, the population had a balanced gender structure, with girls and women making up 52 percent of the total population. A small number of men may have been away from the community because of migration or short-term labor drafts, but the gender structure was still more balanced than for the Baja and Alta California missions. Tiquipaya was a multiethnic community made up of fifteen *ayllu*. The gender structure was most imbalanced for those ethnic groups that originally came to the Valle Bajo from a considerable distance.[5]

The population of Tiquipaya had been exposed to epidemics and it declined in numbers prior to and following the preparation of the 1573 *padrón*. However, the impact of disease appears to have been more uniform throughout the population of Tiquipaya, and as a consequence there was no significant imbalance in the age and gender structure, as observed in the Baja and Alta California missions. This suggests that autonomous communities, such as the populations congregated to form Tiquipaya, did not experience the same sociocultural pressures and forms of social control as did the converts living in the Baja and, especially, Alta California missions.

Not all American populations experienced the same elevated mortality rates and population decline. Non-Indian populations living on the northwestern frontier of New Spain revealed patterns distinct from those documented for the mission communities. For example, the populations of the four military garrisons established in Alta California—San Diego (1769), Monterey (1770), San Francisco (1776), and Santa Barbara (1782)—proved to be fecund and grew at moderate rates, and mean life expectancy at birth was considerably higher than in the neighboring mission communities. The mean rate of growth for the garrison population was 12 per thousand population, whereas the Indians populations living in the missions declined. Mean life expectancy at birth for the population of the four garrisons was 31.4 years, which was substantially higher than life expectancy for the missions communities. The people living in the military garrisons in Alta California produced large numbers of children, as shown by a mean gross reproduction ratio of 2.95; and many children survived (see Table 4.5).

The second comparison is made between the mission populations and two rural villages in Western Europe. The population of Western Europe experienced a severe mortality crisis in the mid-fourteenth century known as the Black Death, which killed as many as a third of the population of the region; recurring plague epidemics extending into the early eighteenth century; the scourge of war; and other contagious epidemics, including

Table 4.5 Demographic Statistics of the Four Alta California Presidios, 1790–1834

Year	Population*	CBR	CDR	GRR	NRR	Life Expectancy
1792	788	48	32	3.07	1.54	33.5
1797	920	46	30	3.09	1.62	34.9
1802	1,038	43	39	2.92	1.18	26.4
1807	1,160	39	36	2.52	1.05	27.3
1812	1,306	54	44	3.28	1.24	24.7
1817	1,544	40	24	2.41	1.42	39.9
1822	1,753	40	28	2.47	1.29	34.9
1827	1,827	51	36	3.31	1.52	30.2
1832	2,360	53	36	3.51	1.62	30.6

*Population estimate generated by *Populate.*
Source: San Diego Mission, San Carlos Mission, San Francisco, and Santa Barbara Mission annual reports: Archivo General de la Nación, México, D.F., and the Santa Barbara Mission Archive-Library, Santa Barbara, California; and Ms. Mission Statistics, the Bancroft Library, University of California, Berkeley.

smallpox. Nevertheless, the populations of Europe gradually recovered and reached an equilibrium with available food resources that only changed with the industrialization of the nineteenth century; improvements in agriculture; and the development of faster forms of communications, which allowed the industrializing nations to draw upon larger parts of the world for the supply of foodstuffs.[6] Two Western European agricultural communities are studied here: Tourouvre-au-Perche in France, and Colyton in England. Historical demographers studied both villages, using family reconstitution, and the data for both are reanalyzed, using inverse projection.

The population of the French village Tourouvre-au-Perche experienced a mean rate of growth of only 2 per thousand during the eighteenth century, which highlights the precariousness of rural life in early modern Europe. The variability of agricultural production brought a degree of insecurity to rural life, and periodic famines and epidemic took their toll. Twelve quinquenniums in the sample examined here showed low to moderate rates of decline, although the worst mortality crisis lowered the net reproduction ratio only to .57, which was still substantially higher than the net reproduction ratios of the mission communities. However, during the course of the eighteenth century, death rates declined somewhat and life expectancy improved. On average, death rates in Tourouvre-au-Perche were substantially lower than those in the mission communities, and life expectancy was 35.9 years at birth, but the gross reproduction ratio was low at 2.05, which perhaps reflects the economic limitations on family formation (see Table 4.6).

The second European case study deals with Colyton in England, in the years 1545–1834, with the data reported at twenty-year intervals. The population of Colyton grew slowly at a mean rate of 2 per thousand population, but it also experienced severe mortality crises. For example, the plague outbreak of the late 1640s lowered the net reproduction ratio to .11 and mean life expectancy at birth to 10.3 years. However, in contrast to the mission populations of northwestern New Spain, the population of Colyton gradually recovered, although the recovery was interrupted by several mortality crises which were moderate when compared to the epidemics in northern Mexico. With the exception of the plague outbreak of the 1640s, mentioned above, the mean net reproduction ratio in periods of crisis in Colyton was .84, which indicates a rate of decline of only 16 percent had the same mortality rates been maintained over a generation. Moreover, mortality crises did not occur with the same frequency as in the mission communities. Finally, population growth through natural reproduction and migration in noncrisis years was sufficient enough to generate a rebound effect, a recovery of the population to precrisis levels. As already

Table 4.6 Demographic Statistics of Tourouvre-au-Perche (France), 1675–1799

Year	Total Population	CBR	CDR	GRR	NRR	Life Expectancy
1677	1,752	35	42	2.65	.86	23.0
1682	1,737	36	33	2.61	1.14	30.8
1687	1,759	34	32	2.34	1.04	31.4
1692	1,721	32	43	2.04	.60	20.9
1697	1,679	27	26	1.69	.86	35.9
1702	1,720	36	28	2.28	1.16	36.2
1707	1,744	36	39	2.38	.86	25.2
1712	1,686	26	37	1.72	.57	23.6
1717	1,683	34	24	2.35	1.38	42.0
1722	1,739	34	31	2.40	1.15	33.8
1727	1,757	32	31	2.30	1.07	32.8
1732	1,787	31	26	2.21	1.21	39.0
1737	1,812	28	28	2.02	1.01	35.4
1742	1,790	22	27	1.52	.72	33.7
1747	1,780	27	24	1.72	.97	40.0
1752	1,803	25	23	1.58	.92	41.3
1757	1,840	28	22	1.77	1.08	43.7
1762	1,889	31	26	2.07	1.13	38.6
1767	1,911	25	25	1.76	.94	38.1
1772	1,903	28	29	2.03	.96	33.6
1777	1,937	29	21	2.12	1.39	47.5
1782	1,963	29	32	2.05	.92	31.8
1787	1,977	29	23	2.00	1.22	43.8
1792	2,056	29	19	2.01	1.39	50.1
1797	2,113	21	20	1.51	.96	45.8

Source: Hubert Charbonneau, *Tourouvre-au-Perche aux xvii et xviii siècles* (Paris, 1970).

noted, mortality rates in the missions were chronically high, even in noncrisis years, so there was no recovery following epidemics (see Table 4.7).

The gross reproduction ratio of Colyton was low, with an average of 1.89, which highlights one of the fundamental differences between the populations of Europe and the mission communities studied here. European peasants made conscious economic decisions that affected family formation and the period of child-bearing. Although it varied from time and place, the mean age at first marriage of European women was in the low to mid-twenties, and the mean age at the birth of the last child was around age forty.[7] Moreover, the rate of survival of children was higher

Table 4.7 Demographic Statistics of Colyton (England), 1545–1834

Year	Total Population	CBR	CDR	GRR	NRR	Life Expectancy
1547	879	40	26	2.79	1.57	39.2
1567	1,000	29	19	1.93	1.26	46.0
1587	1,340	33	25	2.52	1.41	38.8
1607	1,554	36	23	2.24	1.31	40.9
1627	2,093	34	20	2.51	1.61	45.1
1647	2,162	13	54	.78	.11	10.3
1667	2,049	20	23	1.22	.70	39.8
1687	1,794	19	24	1.35	.84	43.8
1707	1,596	21	24	1.57	1.03	46.5
1727	1,364	25	32	1.62	.80	34.3
1747	1,303	24	23	1.91	1.20	44.2
1767	1,369	26	24	1.73	1.05	42.6
1787	1,353	26	27	1.73	.93	37.2
1807	1,596	31	19	2.40	1.68	49.7
1827	2,148	28	16	2.11	1.55	52.6
1832	2,268	26	18	1.87	1.28	48.5

Source: Ron Lee, "Estimating Series of Vital Rates and Age Structures from Baptisms and Burials: A New Technique with Applications to Pre-industrial England," *Population Studies* 28 (1974), pp. 495–512.

than that for the mission communities.[8] The number of women actually bearing children in Colyton and in other rural villages in Western Europe was considerably lower than the pool of potential mothers, because families were being formed well into the period of female fecundity. Economic factors, such as the access to land, delayed family formation, thus reducing the number of births among the number of women capable of bearing children. Men and women generally practiced abstinence until they had the financial resources to marry and begin a family. The European example stands in marked contrast to patterns observed in the mission communities. Although limited, the available data indicates that Indian women living in the missions began bearing children at about age fifteen, and the period of fertility ended with premature death around age twenty. Moreover, the high death rates among women meant the frequent formation of new families, often under pressure from the missionaries. Finally, more than 90 percent of the children born in the missions died before reaching age ten.[9]

The converts living in the missions did not feel the same economic and social pressures that delayed family formation. The mission economies generally were organized on the basis of paternalistic communalism, with food produced on mission lands distributed among converts. Paternalism reached its greatest expression in the Alta California missions, where the missionaries directed the development of large-scale mixed economies based on agriculture, ranching, and artisan production of textiles and leather goods, which supplied the minimal needs of most converts—which is not to say that the mission diet was or was not adequate. Ecological limitations in Baja California forced converts to forage for wild foods to supplement the items provided in the diet by mission agriculture. The northern Pima converts frequently retained control over plots of land exploited on their own behalf. Evidence cited in the previous chapter even indicates that at least in the case of the Alta California missions, the missionaries put pressure on Indian women to bear children. The practice of punishing women who were sterile, the concern over the practice of abortion and infanticide in the missions, and the rapid remarriage of widows and widowers suggests that the Franciscans were concerned about the declining population and consciously followed a policy of promoting family formation within the sacraments of marriage as well as unrestrained child-bearing.

The final case study concerns the rural village of Nagcarlan in the colonial Philippines. An analysis of Nagcarlan allows a comparison of the vital rates of communities in different colonial situations, and an evaluation of the impact of colonial policy on indigenous populations. Nagcarlan presents demographic patterns and a social context very distinct from the policy of *congregación* implemented in northwestern New Spain. The inhabitants of Nagcarlan were village-dwelling agriculturalists tied into an expanding pattern of incorporation in the international market economy through the production of raw materials for consumption in the Western industrialized nations. The structure of the local economy and the distribution of land changed as more production was geared to the international market, and the standard of living in Nagcarlan and other rural communities in the Philippines declined. The population of Nagcarlan grew during the course of the nineteenth century, but the decline in the standard of living can be measured in a drop in mean life expectancy.[10] Nevertheless, the degree of social disruption caused by the growing weight of colonialism and economic dependence in Nagcarlan did not create conditions of chronically high mortality comparable to the patterns observed in the mission communities (see Table 4.8).

Table 4.8 Demographic Statistics of Nagcarlan (Philippines), 1805–1897

Year	Total Population	CBR	CDR	GRR	NRR	Life Expectancy
1807	4,122	39	21	2.38	1.42	41.8
1812	4,698	33	21	1.97	1.24	41.4
1817	5,158	31	20	1.80	1.19	43.3
1822	5,400	40	23	2.40	1.54	41.3
1827	5,754	42	26	2.73	1.67	38.7
1832	5,555	40	27	2.74	1.55	36.2
1837	7,148	40	21	2.43	1.60	45.1
1842	7,394	39	26	2.75	1.51	36.6
1847	8,426	34	30	2.26	1.05	31.3
1852	9,031	38	26	2.29	1.26	37.3
1857	9,592	41	32	2.54	1.19	31.4
1862	10,057	44	37	2.71	1.14	28.0
1867	10,495	43	37	2.69	1.11	27.3
1872	10,746	43	32	2.80	1.33	31.5
1877	11,478	44	29	2.88	1.55	35.8
1882	12,654	45	47	2.97	.95	21.2
1887	12,411	44	33	2.92	1.36	30.9
1892	12,943	44	38	3.01	1.24	27.2
1897	12,433	55	51	4.01	1.23	20.2

Source: Peter Smith and Shui-Meng Ng, "The Components of Population Change in Nineteenth-Century Southeast Asia: Village Data From the Philippines," *Population Studies* 36:2 (1982), pp. 237–55.

Conclusions

The history of the demographic collapse of the Indian populations of the mission communities of northwestern New Spain represents a worst-case scenario of the impact of colonialism on indigenous populations related to social disruption with the implementation of colonial social and economic policies. The mission populations were not viable as a consequence of chronically high rates of mortality, and they experienced a real decline in numbers despite the efforts of the missionaries in many of the missions to repopulate the communities by the relocation of converts.

A comparison of the vital rates of mission and nonmission populations shows that the mission populations were indeed unique. World populations from the seventeenth to the early nineteenth centuries were exposed to disease. However, there was no long-term recovery or "rebound" in northwestern New Spain from the impact of periodic epidemics, as occurred even in other parts of Spanish America. In contrast, the settler populations living along the northern frontier of New Spain, such as the soldiers and settlers living in the four military garrisons in Alta California, reproduced vigorously and experienced moderate to high rates of growth. Even the peasant populations of Europe, exposed to epidemic and endemic disease and variable harvests, experienced low growth rates, and mean life expectancy was at least three times greater than in the mission communities.

Can vital rates be correlated with colonial situations? An analysis of the vital rates of the mission communities suggests that the program of social engineering carried out in the missions directly contributed to the high mortality rates that undermined the viability of the Indian populations. The program of congregating converts in spatially compact communities facilitated the spread of epidemic disease, and created large population centers characterized by overcrowding and unsanitary living conditions. Moreover, the forms of social control implemented by the missionaries combined with changes in the labor regime, and the modification of indigenous social and cultural patterns contributed to heightened levels of stress, and, especially in the Alta California missions, a form of psychological dislocation directly associated with the extreme paternalism of the mission regime. The degree of sociocultural disruption clearly was greatest in the Alta California missions, which, as the evidence presented here suggests, also experienced the highest rate of decline as measured by crude death rates and the net reproduction ratio.

The demographic collapse of the Indian populations congregated in the missions of northwestern New Spain represented an extreme example of the impact of unequal colonial or economically dependent relations on indigenous populations. The native peoples of the Americas, brought under varying levels of colonial control in the period following the discovery by Europeans of the New World, experienced drastic population losses and, in large measure, the destruction of their cultures and way of life, all in the name of progress justified by cultural chauvinism. In other colonial or dependent societies, the superficial benefits of material progress brought by Europeans, which were tied to the development of export-oriented economies, did not outweigh the erosion in the standard of living of indigenous populations, which followed economic reorganizations to produce raw materials for the international economy. The decline in mean life expectancy of the residents of Nagcarlan, for example, represented another demographic consequence of colonialism similar in many respects in its origins to the conditions that existed in the mission communities of northwestern New Spain. An examination of demographic patterns provides tangible evidence of the unequal relationship that evolved after 1500 between the dynamic North Atlantic economies and many non-Western societies.

The missions established in the frontier regions of northern New Spain paved the way for the creation of colonial societies modeled on the society that evolved in central New Spain. In many instances, settlers occupied mission communities and marginalized the converts in the villages that had been created for them. Indian converts also worked for settlers. The following chapter outlines the growth of the non-Indian, soldier-settler population in northern Sonora and the Californias.

Conclusions

Anthropologist Daniel Reff recently suggested that the Indians of Sonora accepted the Jesuit missionaries, in the years after 1620, as a response to the social collapse of Indian societies following the high mortality caused by the great sixteenth century epidemics that swept throughout Mesoamerica and its fringes.[1] The virulent epidemics of the sixteenth century undermined the existing social structure, and the survivors viewed the Jesuits as useful in providing a model for social and economic reorganization. Reff's hypothesis, both provocative and controversial, highlights the fact that the program of social and cultural reorganization undertaken by the missionaries in northwestern New Spain was not static, and followed a century of dramatic change in most Indian societies in the Americas. The process of demographic collapse and social reorganization under the direction of the Jesuit, Franciscan, and Dominican missionaries continued after 1620, and thousands of Indians died in the region prior to the establishment of the first mission in the Pimería Alta. Between 1591 and 1678, for example, Jesuit missionaries baptized some 500,000 Indians in Sinaloa and Sonora, yet in 1678 only about 63,000 Indians still lived in the missions, indicating a rate of depopulation of 70 to 80 percent.[2] Integration into the economy of colonial New Spain and the development of long-distance trade between central and northwestern Mexico tied the frontier into a single large disease pool, which periodically erupted into virulent epidemics that swept north from central Mexico with devastating consequences for the Indian populations congregated in the missions. However, the process of demographic collapse was not strictly biological, a result of elevated mortality rates caused by recurring epidemics.

The missionaries may have brought a new form of social organization to the Indians of northwestern New Spain, but the congregation programs brought other problems clearly manifested in the last phase of mission expansion to the Pimería Alta and the Californias, beginning in the late seventeenth and eighteenth centuries. The imposition of social controls, particularly in the Californias, coupled with the systematic effort to destroy the surviving elements of the Indians' culture, worldview, and social organization, caused psychological disorientation and extreme stresses that contributed to high death rates.[3] The degree of sociocultural disruption and stresses varied between the three mission groupings studied here, as well as from mission to mission. However, of the three areas examined here, the missionaries in Alta California exercised the greatest degree of social control over the converts, and thus modified their culture and social structure more than in the other missions in northwestern New Spain. Of the three jurisdictions, Alta California was the most isolated, and as a consequence, few epidemics reached the region. Nonbiological factors there were equally or more important than strictly biological factors in raising death rates and in causing the demographic collapse of the Indian populations congregated in the missions.

Conditions in the missions, particularly in the Alta California establishments, proved to be deadly for small children and, to a lesser degree, for women. Other historical populations frequently rebounded from the impact of epidemics through increased birthrates, and losses from epidemics were generally replaced within a generation. In the mission communities, on the other hand, epidemic mortality was coupled with frightfully high rates of infant and child mortality, so that there was no sustained recovery. Moreover, the frequency of major epidemics was such that the children who survived the first difficult years of childhood faced premature death either from dehydration, congenital syphilis, or a contagious malady during a major epidemic outbreak.

The history of San Francisco Xavier mission in Baja California is illustrative of the relationship between epidemics, infant and child mortality, and rates of population growth or decline. After 1699, when the Jesuits began the process of congregating the Indians in new settlements, the population experienced rapid decline. However, by the late 1730s enough people had survived the first wave of epidemics to begin a short period of growth through natural reproduction. Moreover, the Jesuits had completed the process of congregation, so that there was not a continuing movement into the missions of Indians with no previous, or with limited, exposure to contagious diseases, which in other circumstances contributed to the high mortality rates and placed all converts at greater risk by the mere presence of sick people in the spatially compact communities. The period of growth in the mission population ended with the expulsion of the Jesuits in 1768, the increased movement of soldiers and colonists between Baja California and the mainland, and a particularly devastating series of epidemics between 1769 and 1782 that doomed the Indian populations to extinction.[4]

A similar pattern can be observed in both the Pimería Alta and Baja California missions, but the Alta California missions presented a different scenario. First colonized at the beginning of the implementation of the fiscal reforms in the Spanish colonial system known as the "Bourbon reforms," the Alta California missions found that their missionaries placed more of an emphasis on economic development than did the Jesuits, Franciscans, and Dominicans stationed in northern Sonora and Baja California. The Franciscan-directed mission economies were organized to produce surpluses to help defray the costs of the colonization of Alta California, and imposed a correspondingly higher degree of social control over the converts to ensure sufficient labor. Many converts responded to the demands of the mission economy by running away from the missions, which prompted the Franciscans to impose even greater social control and to mount expeditions into the unpacified interior hinterland to bring back fugitives and forcibly relocate non-Christians to the missions.[5] The living and working conditions and the stresses of sociocultural change in the Alta California missions, coupled with chronic ailments yet with no pattern of recurring epidemics, were the principal factors in the demographic collapse and cultural-biological extinction of the Indian populations. The missionaries and colonial officials justified the perpetuation of a system that destroyed the Indian populations brought into the missions because of the needs of colonial policy and the apocalyptic vision of the missionaries. Their ultimate objective was to ensure the Indians' eternal salvation by their conversion, so there was no moral dilemma as long as the deaths of thousands of converts contributed toward populating heaven. Suffering on earth and receiving the sacraments were necessary for salvation.

The mission program in northwestern New Spain proved to be a critical element in the pattern of Spanish colonization of the region. The missionaries paved the way for settlement and the development of mines and farms by controlling the Indian populations and relocating populations to new communities thus opening lands for settlement. Moreover, where market-oriented economies developed, as in northern Sonora, the Indians living in the missions served as a labor pool, to be organized through labor drafts. The missionaries, elite members of a stratified hierarchical and racially based colonial society, saw their role as representatives of both church and state, and, specifically, a church that played an important role in cementing the colonial order through preaching an Iberian Catholicism oriented toward the construction of a hierarchical colonial society. The policy of congregation and enculturation was an integral part of frontier colonial policy, and it proved to be a success from the point of view of colonial officials concerned with the occupation of geopolitically sensitive frontier regions.

The demographic collapse and cultural and biological extinction of the Indian populations of northwestern New Spain was not intended, but it was intentional. Policymakers hoped to reproduce the structure of the colonial society and economy of central Mexico on the northern frontier. Indian labor was critical for the functioning of the economy, and tribute paid by Indian peasants was an important source of government revenue. The development of the frontier societies ideally required a stable tribute-paying Indian population and labor force, but the means of achieving the ends of frontier colonial policy destroyed the populations congregated in the missions. Colonial officials and the missionaries realized that the Indian populations were disappearing, but they made little adjustment in a program that in the short run fulfilled the objectives of the colonial state. In the 1790s, the proposal of Alta California governor Diego de Borica to loosen somewhat the social controls in the Alta California missions fell on deaf ears, because the intensification of the demands on the mission economies to support continuing colonization of the region and growing Indian resistance in the form of flight dictated the imposition of even tighter controls. Compromises were made in order to promote colonization policies, and the Indian converts were vital elements in those policies.

The missionaries themselves understood epidemics and the high mortality rates in the missions as God's punishment for the resistance of Indians to the mission program, or as punishment of Spanish colonists for their sins by depriving them of Indian laborers and tribute payers.[6] The missionaries also came with a clearly defined Eurocentric cultural and religious chauvinism, as well as with the conviction that their ideas and way of life were inherently superior to that of the Indians.

It was on the basis of the sense of the superiority of the Iberian culture, worldview, society, and economy that the missionaries and colonial bureaucrats pushed forward with the mission programs in northwestern New Spain, regardless of the fact that they knew from past experience that Indian populations brought into the missions most likely would experience a drastic decline in numbers. The government in Mexico City and the representatives of the regular orders working in the frontier missions intentionally expanded their activities, thus initiating the process of the cultural and biological destruction of the Indian converts brought into the missions. The consequences were far reaching for the natives living in northern Sonora and the Californias.

Appendix 1

Chronology of Major Epidemic Outbreaks in Northwestern New Spain, 1690–1851

Year(s)	Disease(s)
1697–1698	Smallpox
1709–1710	Smallpox
1718	Smallpox
1721	Influenza?
1723	Smallpox
1725	?
1728–1732	Measles, Dysentery
1737	?
1742	?
1744–1745	?
1746	?
1748–1749	Measles, Dysentery
1762–1763	Smallpox
1764	Smallpox
1766	"Peste"
1768–1770	Smallpox, Measles
1772–1773	Typhus?
1781–1782	Smallpox
1796–1797	Smallpox
1800–1801	Typhus or Typhoid?
1805–1806	Measles
1808	Smallpox
1816–1817	Smallpox
1826–1828	Measles
1831	Smallpox
1833–1834	Asian Cholera
1838	Smallpox
1843	Smallpox
1851	Asian Cholera

Source: Robert H. Jackson, "Causes of Indian Population Decline in the Pimería Alta Missions of Northern Sonora," *The Journal of Arizona History* 24 (1983), p. 409.

Appendix 2

Population of the Pimería Alta Missions

Village	1723	1730	1761	1766	1768	1772	1774	1784	1795	1796
Dolores	116	29								
Remedios		26								
Cocospera		75	133	147			133	78	43	85
San Ignacio	300	94	322	204	149		128	183	15	
Imuris		83	150	98	53	40	30	17	36	
Magdalena		77	107	97	92		57			
Soamca			114	135						
Caborca	1,000	223	556	302	564		211	115	215	
Pitiqui		313	269	132	310		202	192		
Bisani		178	235	117	271		122	230		
Ati		65	142	118	146	90	96	77	103	
Oquitoa		118	131	114	127	90	105	45		
Tubutama	1,000	131	368	173	167	52	93	33	66	98
Santa Teresa		81	152	90	61		49	56		
Saric			212	136	141		157	82	46	
Aguimuri			67	82	58					
Busanic			253	38	24					
Arizona			17							
Guevavi			101	82	53					
Sonoita			91	139	110					
Tumacacori			199	122	70		98	95	119	98
Calabazas			116	145	77		138			
Bac			309	188	208	160	160	169	119	
Tucson			311	138		300	239	142	78	

Pueblo	1797	1801	1802	1804	1806	1813	1818	1819	1820
Cocospera	70	82	86	76	69	89	87	103	94
San Ignacio	40	62	108	113	108	92	36	49	47
Magdalena	76	66							
Caborca	207	236	417	424	422	348	393	362	366
Pitiqui	100	94							
Bisani	154	92							
Ati	47	66	113	111	106	116			
Oquitoa	67	58					126	144	134
Tubutama	34	47	41	36	66	25		28	37
Santa Teresa	22	17							
Saric	32	27	25	33	25	21	25	19	18
Tumacacori	69	78	76	82	83	119	105	123	121
Bac	116	127	363	494	414	505	287	318	310
Tucson	278	246							

Source: Robert H. Jackson, "Demographic and Social Change in Northwestern New Spain: A Comparative Analysis of the Pimeria Alta and Baja California Missions" (Master's thesis, University of Arizona, 1982), pp. 176–78.

Appendix 3

Population of the Baja California Missions

Mission	1744	1755	1762	1768	1771	1773	1774	1782	1790	1791
Loreto	150	91	109	99	160	187	162	70		
San Francisco Xavier	352	380	448	482	212	279	264	169	115	142
Mulege	326	294	281	245	180	165	158	75	72	58
Comondu	513	387	350	330	216	284	269	80	67	73
Purísima	535	320	295	152	168	160	175	81	79	81
Guadalupe	701	472	524	544	140	169	176	105	84	73
Dolores	1,000	624	573	458						
Santiago	449	232	198	178	70	75	72	43	32	23
S. Ignacio		1,012	838	710	558	314	305	241	216	210
S. José del Cabo		73	63	71	50	51	50	28	62	51
Todos Santos		151	93	83	170	180	155	135	90	80
San Luis Gonzaga	516	352	300	288						
Sta. Gertrudis		1,586	1,730	1,360	1,138	808	798	317	241	244
San Borja			498	1,640	1,479	1,000	987	657	614	623
Sta. María				509	523	317	485			
San Fernando					368	296	256	642	479	506
Rosario								251	338	347
Sto. Domingo								79	196	273
San Vicente								83	251	181
San Miguel									117	
Sto. Tomás										92

(Continued)

Population of the Baja California Missions *(Continued)*

Mission	1794	1795	1796	1797	1798	1799	1800	1801	1802	1803
Loreto	48	49	49	45	37	31	34	23		
San Francisco Javier	107	108	105	104	103	99	103	98	98	98
Mulege	55	88	88	84	76	71	72	64	66	63
Comondú	40	46	40	41	40	19	21	20	26	30
Purísima	91	77	68	69	63		61	67	51	54
Guadalupe	74									
Santiago	70									
S. Ignacio	190	168	152	139	133	137	130	120	113	125
S. José del Cabo	102	84	70	77	81	78	78	77	83	88
Todos Santos	78	80	75	80	81	74	88	81	79	87
Sta. Gertrudis	234	217	224	218	226	203	203	208	198	171
San Borja	539	500	452	450	443	351	400	395	359	344
San Fernando	525	550	452	450	425	476	363	313	295	263
Rosario		323	320	334	300	293	256	255	255	234
Sto. Domingo	261	300	300	300	300	390	315	272	267	257
San Vicente	210	232	242	204	207	268	239	259	293	255
San Miguel	203	178	198	256	207	229	224	206	213	179
Sto. Tomás	151	211	209	196	202	245	253	256	267	264
S. Pedro Mártir	58	108	100	99	90	94	92	89	92	91
Sta. Catalina				44	100	184	193	223	260	256

Mission	1804	1806	1808	1813	1829
Loreto		14			
San Francisco Javier	98	86	83		
Mulege	66	51	39		
Comondú	20	28	36		
Purísima	51	55	61		
S. Ignacio	113	102	81		
San José del Cabo	83	92	109		
Todos Santos	79		82		
Sta. Gertrudis	198	137	137		
San Borja	359	270	192		
S. Fernando	193	201	155		19
Rosario	225	191	199		38
Sto. Domingo	267	214	194		73
San Vicente	239	231	211	183	80
San Miguel	189			314	154
Sto. Tomás	267	244	252		121
San Pedro Mártir	92	92	91		
Sta. Catalina	260	278	261		151

Source: Robert H. Jackson, "Epidemic Disease and Population Decline in the Baja California Missions, 1697–1834," *Southern California Quarterly* 63 (1981), pp. 339–40.

Appendix 4

Population of the Alta California Missions

Year	San Diego	San Carlos	San Antonio	San Gabriel	S. Luis Obispo	San Francisco	San Juan Capistrano
1773	76	163	131	71			
1774	97	242	182		101		
1779	642	373	413	409			231
1781	701	416	540	570	446		431
1782	743	521	557	549	464	181	352
1783	742	614	582	638	492	215	383
1784	786	645	774	739	479	260	431
1785	838	718	850	843	499	250	544
1786	890	694	886	855	524	354	544
1787	918	707	979	935	531	426	592
1788	914	720	1,028	983	556	426	656
1789	940	732	1,064	1,044	582	429	771
1790	933	712	1,092	1,078	599	518	765
1791	883	770	1,083	1,204	682	590	766
1792	862	800	1,074	1,219	736	622	822
1793	869	835	1,142	1,225	751	711	969
1794	879	861	1,159	1,260	803	913	976
1795	887	876	1,150	1,290	810	872	983
1796	908	839	1,168	1,335	814	790	994
1797	1,405	832	1,176	1,316	799	790	1,107
1798	1,526	738	1,123	1,311	792	645	1,107
1799	1,405	720	1,097	1,254	786	603	1,060
1800	1,511	747	1,114	1,136	726	635	1,043
1801	1,588	705	1,097	1,129	692	778	1,022
1802	1,559	688	1,152	1,047	697	814	1,013
1803	1,587	591	1,158	1,123	824	1,051	1,027
1804	1,589	591	1,203	1,294	832	1,103	1,024
1806	1,486	550	1,217	1,052	830	886	1,062
1807	1,571	562	1,140	1,097	795	828	1,109
1808	1,586	550	1,108	1,059	762	906	1,096
1809	1,560	533	1,114	1,174	731	1,010	1,114
1810	1,611	511	1,122	1,199	711	1,057	1,138
1811	1,583	485	1,103	1,550	686	1,214	1,209
1812	1,616	455	1,093	1,550	677	1,224	1,361
1813	1,537	448	1,074	1,678	663	1,205	1,249
1814	1,428	431	1,044	1,679	638	1,180	1,244
1815	1,386	423	1,008	1,667	610	1,113	1,198
1816	1,357	405	985	1,650	592	1,091	1,142
1817	1,430	402	962	1,701	570	1,060	1,138
1818	1,558	390	922	1,644	546	1,100	1,128
1819	1,425	397	902	1,596	531	1,163	1,078
1820	1,567	381	878	1,636	504	1,252	1,064
1821	1,622	374	875	1,626	482	1,801	1,050
1822	1,697	341	834	1,593	467	958	1,052

(Continued)

Year	San Diego	San Carlos	San Antonio	San Gabriel	S. Luis Obispo	San Francisco	San Juan Capistrano
1823	1,758	317	817	1,643	462	208	1,062
1824	1,829	306	806	1,644	423	265	1,060
1825	1,728	295	801	1,594	395	238	1,031
1826	1,704	277	751	1,565	361	232	1,043
1827	1,630	275	744	1,438	344	241	956
1828	1,576	234	710	1,386	328	236	947
1829	1,554	233	704	1,383	310	229	934
1830	1,544	229	681	1,371	283	219	926
1831	1,506	209	661	1,398	265	210	939
1832	1,455	199	600	1,320	231	204	900
1834	1,382	165	567	1,320	264	163	861
1835					253		
1837						210	
1838			520				
1839	780	50	270	388	170	89	61
1840		274	462			77	
1841			518?			78	
1842	500	40	150	500	81	50	100
1844	100			300			

Year	Sta. Clara	S. Buena-Ventura	Sta. Barbara	La Purísima	Sta. Cruz	La Soledad	San José	S. Juan Bautista
1777	13							
1778	91							
1779	111							
1780	270							
1783		22						
1784		53						
1785		120						
1786		144	27					
1787	647	230	183					
1788	672	303	260	95				
1789	787	380	425	151				
1790	910	419	407	278				
1791	957	462	499	434	89	9		
1792	1,001	478	504	510	158	118		
1793	1,062	508	541	546	233	213		
1794	1,418	516	440	656	332	193		
1795	1,514	557	569	743	507	240		
1796	1,433	725	642	760	523	289		
1797	1,364	736	782	842	495	322	33	85
1798	1,382	766	796	920	504	345	154	296
1799	1,343	747	792	937	468	444	189	347
1800	1,318	715	866	961	472	512	275	586
1801	1,322	711	1,022	956	442	565	515	723
1802	1,291	938	1,093	1,028	437	563	622	910
1803	1,291	1,078	1,792	1,436	437	627	776	976

(Continued)

Year	Sta. Clara	S. Buena-Ventura	Sta. Barbara	La Purísima	Sta. Cruz	La Soledad	San José	S. Juan Bautista
1804	1,240	1,107	1,783	1,520	461	687	779	1,073
1806	1,406	1,159	1,603	1,166	466	679	662	1,068
1807	1,390	1,205	1,539	1,124	492	651	637	1,072
1808	1,410	1,290	1,477	1,084	485	624	544	980
1809	1,398	1,288	1,477	1,031	449	595	578	902
1810	1,332	1,295	1,355	1,020	507	598	545	700
1811	1,371	1,260	1,325	978	462	575	961	666
1812	1,348	1,211	1,304	999	437	549	1,172	638
1813	1,347	1,169	1,269	1,010	398	547	1,151	633
1814	1,306	1,207	1,300	982	388	531	1,149	607
1815	1,306	1,186	1,240	1,019	365	500	1,298	580
1816	1,336	1,328	1,259	1,018	358	500	1,508	575
1817	1,336	1,277	1,226	958	408	527	1,576	608
1818	1,321	1,209	1,199	937	410	519	1,675	582
1819	1,313	1,172	1,159	888	381	417	1,670	660
1820	1,359	1,127	1,132	840	461	436	1,754	843
1821	1,388	1,092	1,039	808	519	450	1,754	1,093
1822	1,394	973	1,010	764	499	532	1,620	1,222
1823	1,395	935	962	722	474	536	1,746	1,248
1824	1,450	908	923	662	461	512	1,806	1,221
1825	1,403	865	885	532	429	454	1,796	1,166
1826	1,428	852	867	521	428	409	1,783	1,146
1827	1,462	833	847	471	410	373	1,800	1,108
1828	1,369	789	762	445	364	333	1,766	986
1829	1,269	765	737	406	333	327	1,641	969
1830	1,226	726	711	413	320	342	1,745	964
1831	1,184	703	679	404	298	336	1,886	928
1832	1,125	668	628	372	284	339	1,713	916
1834	800	626	556	407	238	300	1,229	858
1836						177		
1838				242		168		
1839	400	455	555	142	70	78	402	324
1840	344				102	68	1,322	992
1842	300	300	400	60	50	20	180	80
1844			287					
1845	130		264					

Year	San Miguel	San Fernando	San Luis Rey	Sta. Inés	San Rafael	San Francisco Solano
1797	27	55				
1798	185	135	212			
1799	277	191	279			
1800	362	312	337			
1801	536	501	452			
1802	612	614	532			
1803	908	820	615			
1804	928	985	636	225		

(Continued)

Year	San Miguel	San Fernando	San Luis Rey	Sta. Inés	San Rafael	San Francisco Solano
1806	949	955	961	576		
1807	970	986	1,025	587		
1808	963	976	1,110	587		
1809	962	965	1,121	603		
1810	871	963	1,517	628		
1811	964	1,081	1,601	611		
1812	968	1,056	1,733	611		
1813	1,048	1,043	1,815	607		
1814	1,076	1,053	1,846	588		
1815	1,050	1,014	1,866	636		
1816	1,052	1,025	1,913	768		
1817	1,025	1,045	2,269	720		
1818	995	1,024	2,246	681	386	
1819	996	1,024	2,585	647	509	
1820	973	1,028	2,603	635	590	
1821	956	1,018	2,631	604	696	
1822	926	1,001	2,663	582	830	
1823	918	961	2,721	564	895	
1824	904	957	2,767	516	839	692
1825	867	924	2,756	500	1,008	634
1826	852	911	2,869	487	1,051	641
1827	832	900	2,685	477	1,050	667
1828	747	832	2,736	455	1,026	704
1829	728	831	2,744	428	1,008	772
1830	684	827	2,776	418	970	760
1831	679	811	2,819	388	1,073	939
1832	658	782	2,788	360	300	996
1834	599	792	2,844	344	262	648
1836						547
1837				335		
1838	525				365	
1839	361	503	1,122	313	370	343
1840					93	144
1842	30	541	650	250	20	70
1844			400	264		
1845				270		

Source: Ms. Annual Reports, Archivo General de la Nación, México, D.F.; Ms. Annual Reports, the Santa Barbara Mission Archive-Library, Santa Barbara, California; and Ms. Mission Statistics, BLUC.

Appendix 5

Baptisms, Burials, and Population in Selected Alta California Missions

The tables in this appendix record the annual totals of baptisms of converts, births, burials, and population at seven of the twenty-one Alta California missions. The data has been abstracted from several sources, including the extant registers of baptisms and burials, and the annual reports. The parish registers are found in the diocese office of the Bishopric of Monterey, California. The Soledad mission burial register has not survived, so I have taken figures on burials from annual and biennial reports.

Population Baptisms, and Burials at San Carlos Mission, 1770–1840

Year	Baptisms of Converts	Births	Burials	Population
1770	3	0	6	
1771	20	0	1	
1772	7	2	2	
1773	131	3	2	163
1774	89	4	20	242
1775	89	8	21	327
1776	51	15	3	
1777	61	14	15	
1778	32	22	24	
1779	0	24	41	487
1780	14	16	42	
1781	5	15	55	
1782	76	22	71	521
1783	148	10	30	614
1784	54	23	44	645
1785	110	36	69	711
1786	22	29	69	694
1787	24	31	36	707
1788	5	17	19	720
1789	34	32	47	732
1790	50	31	101	712
1791	73*	41*	61	770
1792	63	51	78	800
1793	42	36	43	835
1794	33	48	55	861
1795	11	51	57	876
1796	11	19	59	839
1797	22	28	52	832
1798	12	40	47	738
1799	5	38	63	720
1800	0	37	21	747
1801	6	23	54	705
1802	5	16	84	688

(Continued)

Population Baptisms, and Burials at San Carlos Mission, 1770–1840 ***(Continued)***

Year	Baptisms of Converts	Births	Burials	Population
1803	0	21	57	591
1804	16	16	45	591
1805	19	21	44	587
1806	71	15	84	550
1807	21	19	41	562
1808	11	27	51	550
1809	0	19	54	533
1810	1	17	44	511
1811	1	23	47	485
1812	2	17	44	455
1813	1	19	27	448
1814	4	15	33	432
1815	2	26	30	423
1816	2	18	37	405
1817	1	25	29	402
1818	0	19	30	390
1819	11	30	22	397
1820	1	16	36	381
1821	1	20	26	374
1822	0	12	45	341
1823	0	20	35	317
1824	0	18	34	306
1825	1	17	29	295
1826	0	19	17	277
1827	0	11	13	275
1828	6	11	51	234
1829	1	13	15	233
1830	0	14	15	229
1831	0	7	9	209
1832	0	11	12	199
1833	1	13	10	182
1834	0	14	11	165
1835	0	11	8	
1836	1	14	10	
1837	15	18	8	
1838	4	11	20	
1839	13	29	15	50
1840	0	18	15	274

*Adjusted

(Continued)

Population, Baptisms, and Burials at San Antonio Mission, 1771–1840

Year	Baptisms of Converts	Births	Burials	Population
1771	19	0	3	34
1772	16	0	3	90
1773	126	5	2	131
1774	23	7	8	178
1775	146	10	17	259
1776	64	12	22	343
1777	46	10	46	322
1778	27	11	17	346
1779	59	20	11	415
1780	70	27	14	502
1781	51	21	38	540
1782	60	24	25	557
1783	107	26	34	582
1784	88	40	46	774
1785	114	40	77	850
1786	86	47	67	886
1787	38	42	30	979
1788	47	62	45	1,028
1789	12	64	34	1,064
1790	14	70	60	1,092
1791	24	47	109	1,083
1792	13	62	51	1,074
1793	30	67	41	1,142
1794	20	49	41	1,159
1795	13	35	48	1,150
1796	28	30	51	1,168
1797	40	37	50	1,176
1798	29	44	84	1,123
1799	55	39	89	1,097
1800	27	65	79	1,114
1801	23	44	70	1,097
1802	78	40	135	1,152
1803	135	49	82	1,158
1804	93	27	96	1,203
1805	137	69	94	1,296
1806	22	47	153	1,217
1807	4	52	113	1,140
1808	4	40	78	1,108
1809	9	65	68	1,114
1810	29	38	59	1,122
1811	0	59	79	1,103
1812	6	53	69	1,093
1813	0	55	73	1,074
1814	0	47	78	1,044
1815	0	45	82	1,008
1816	0	57	82	985
1817	0	41	64	962

(Continued)

Population, Baptisms, and Burials at San Antonio Mission, 1771–1840 *(Continued)*

Year	Baptisms of Converts	Births	Burials	Population
1818	0	33	75	922
1819	0	47	67	902
1820	0	37	61	878
1821	0	37	40	875
1822	0	37	78	834
1823	0	43	60	817
1824	0	35	45	806
1825	0	42	48	801
1826	0	34	83	751
1827	0	39	53	744
1828	0	22	54	710
1829	1	24	31	704
1830	1	22	46	681
1831	0	21	41	661
1832	0	17	38	640
1833	0	20	57	600
1834	13	17	61	567
1835	5	15	35	526
1836	16	17	48	
1837	9	11	32	
1838	23	9	34	
1839	0	14	53	
1840	0	10	26	

Population, Baptisms, and Burials at San Luis Obispo Mission, 1772–1838

Year	Baptisms of Converts	Births	Burials	Population
1772	1	0	0	
1773	33	0	0	
1774	59	1	4	96
1775	46	4	6	
1776	59	8	9	
1777	45	19	17	
1778	47	6	12	
1779	45	23	13	343
1780	54	19	12	
1781	29	21	12	446
1782	36	21	21	464
1783	<incomplete>		11	492
1784	<incomplete>		33	484
1785	20	34	27	492
1786	12	26	16	524
1787	12	16	24	531
1788	45	27	19	556

(Continued)

Population, Baptisms, and Burials at San Luis Obispo Mission, 1772–1838 *(Continued)*

Year	Baptisms of Converts	Births	Burials	Population
1789	5	24	22	582
1790	21	25	22	599
1791	109	21	55	682
1792	74	24	44	736
1793	14	22	20	751
1794	60	25	35	803
1795	31	26	52	810
1796	35	25	55	814
1797	33	20	47	799
1798	29	19	57	790
1799	26	33	80	786
1800	30	23	77	724
1801	25	28	79	697
1802	60	23	68	699
1803	239	37	71	824
1804	30	34	58	961
1805	22	34	47	789
1806	7	24	84	830
1807	2	28	63	795
1808	1	34	44	762
1809	3	25	53	739
1810	0	19	44	711
1811	0	31	55	678
1812	0	29	44	677
1813	27	22	60	663
1814	0	27	52	638
1815	0	24	50	610
1816	1	19	38	592
1817	0	16	38	570
1818	0	26	50	546
1819	0	27	37	531
1820	0	18	46	504
1821	0	13	28	491
1822	0	11	36	467
1823	0	12	29	462
1824	0	11	37	424
1825	0	5	43	395
1826	0	6	37	361
1827	0	4	26	344
1828	0	4	20	328
1829	0	6	26	310
1830	0	4	26	283
1831	0	9	27	265
1832	0	4	38	231
1833	0	5	30	203
1834	76	2	19	264

(Continued)

Population, Baptisms, and Burials at San Luis Obispo Mission, 1772–1838 *(Continued)*

Year	Baptisms of Converts	Births	Burials	Population
1835	93	11	46	
1836	3	10	27	
1837	3	11	16	
1838	3	11	39	

Population, Baptisms, and Burials at Santa Cruz Mission, 1791–1840

Year	Baptisms of Converts	Births	Burials	Population
1791	82	0	2	89
1792	73	1	5	158
1793	78	4	6	233
1794	119	11	27	332
1795	242	16	75	507
1796	97	14	91	523
1797	20	13	64	495
1798	72	16	64	504
1799	26	14	70	468
1800	41	11	51	482
1801	15	10	51	442
1802	42	14	61	437
1803	17	14	33	437
1804	63	12	49	461
1805	61	13	53	464
1806	90	15	105	466
1807	49	12	53	492
1808	31	15	49	485
1809	1	6	49	449
1810	120	11	61	507
1811	1	9	56	462
1812	0	9	30	437
1813	1	8	49	398
1814	10	6	26	388
1815	1	11	37	365
1816	15	12	34	358
1817	69	14	33	408
1818	29	21	31	410
1819	0	13	48	381
1820	94	19	33	461
1821	98	13	31	519
1822	0	20	39	499
1823	10	16	53	474
1824	13	16	48	461
1825	1	18	51	429
1826	19	12	32	428

(Continued)

Population, Baptisms, and Burials at Santa Cruz Mission, 1791–1840 *(Continued)*

Year	Baptisms of Converts	Births	Burials	Population
1827	1	10	29	410
1828	6	10	61	364
1829	7	3	41	333
1830	4	12	29	320
1831	1	9	33	298
1832	0	7	35	284
1833	2	6	16	261
1834	16	12	15	238
1835	3	3	19	
1836	1	4	18	
1837	3	4	16	
1838	4	7	49	
1839	3	5	9	71
1840	0	2	8	102

Population, Baptisms, and Burials at Soledad Mission, 1791–1834

Year	Baptism of Converts	Births	Deaths	Population
1791	9	0	0	9
1792	64	6	6	118
1793	63	12	10	213
1794	26	10	23	193
1795	26	10	12	240
1796	59	5	17	289
1797	48	8	27	322
1798	50	19	41	345
1799	105	18	45	444
1800	100	18	33	512
1801	92	8	50	565
1802	69	13	127	563
1803	86	10	40	627
1804	98	7	60	687
1805	100	9	72	688
1806	67	5	113	679
1807	26	11	64	651
1808	8	5	50	624
1809	16	4	38	595
1810	43	10	52	598
1811	20	7	50	575
1812	15	8	51	549
1813	19	11	30	547
1814	0	14	36	531
1815	8	11	48	500
1816	29	10	38	500

(Continued)

Population, Baptisms, and Burials at Soledad Mission, 1791–1834 (*Continued)*

Year	Baptism of Converts	Births	Deaths	Population
1817	42	17	32	527
1818	12	17	39	519
1819	3	10	46	417
1820	40	14	32	436
1821	13	5	27	450
1822	124	11	55	532
1823	9	25	29	536
1824	0	13	35	512
1825	0	13	56	454
1826	7	9	37	409
1827	0	5	31	373
1828	3	6	52	333
1829	4	5	18	327
1830	22	5	21	342
1831	17	5	35	336
1832	22	4	26	339
1833	49	5	47	346
1834	38	9	50	350

Population, Baptisms, and Burials at San Juan Bautista Mission, 1797–1840

Year	Baptisms of Converts	Births	Burials	Population
1797	84	3	7	85
1798	173	8	10	296
1799	58	20	33	347
1800	285	19	15	586
1801	151	17	33	723
1802	225	26	84	910
1803	116	42	103	976
1804	166	21	109	1,073
1805	143	63	108	1,112
1806	22	30	199	1,068
1807	69	57	95	1,072
1808	1	25	93	980
1809	0	25	78	902
1810	1	28	85	700
1811	4	27	63	666
1812	0	31	59	638
1813	11	33	52	633
1814	1	20	47	607
1815	2	34	62	580
1816	18	33	55	575
1817	29	40	35	608
1818	7	24	52	582
1819	107	40	69	660

(Continued)

Population, Baptisms, and Burials at San Juan Bautista Mission, 1797–1840 *(Continued)*

Year	Baptisms of Converts	Births	Burials	Population
1820	171	64	36	843
1821	296	64	102	1,098
1822	206	64	142	1,222
1823	61	53	88	1,248
1824	26	56	114	1,221
1825	12	31	101	1,166
1826	45	35	90	1,146
1827	18	32	81	1,108
1828	55	25	227	986
1829	12	33	58	969
1830	22	28	49	964
1831	7	28	81	928
1832	20	35	69	916
1833	6	43	95	902
1834	1	40	61	858
1835	1	47	64	
1836	1	40	54	
1837	6	38	68	
1838	6	68	159	
1839	5	50	55	
1940	8	57	54	

Population, Baptisms, and Burials at San Miguel Mission, 1797–1835

Year	Baptisms of Converts	Births	Burials	Population
1797	27	0	0	27
1798	154	3	16	169
1799	88	14	26	159
1800	87	11	8	366
1801	184	17	46	557
1802	126	16	74	614
1803	296	33	52	908
1804	59	33	70	928
1805	95	44	47	1,000
1806	15	18	84	949
1807	1	47	30	970
1808	10	31	53	963
1809	4	39	45	962
1810	18	36	47	971
1811	22	43	73	964
1812	12	34	41	968
1813	97	38	51	1,048
1814	48	28	52	1,078
1815	18	32	77	1,050

(Continued)

Population, Baptisms, and Burials at San Miguel Mission, 1797–1835 *(Continued)*

Year	Baptisms of Converts	Births	Burials	Population
1816	31	30	59	1,052
1817	0	43	69	1,025
1818	0	31	62	995
1819	0	49	49	996
1820	0	38	67	973
1821	9	34	60	956
1822	2	40	73	926
1823	0	39	46	918
1824	1	37	53	904
1825	4	21	60	867
1826	0	26	45	852
1827	0	28	46	834
1828	0	18	104	747
1829	0	31	50	728
1830	1	20	45	684
1831	0	23	51	679
1832	1	11	32	658
1833	6	18	83	596
1834	73	21	88	599
1835	181	13	74	

Appendix 6

A Chronology of Building Construction at Selected Alta California Missions, 1777–1832

The following year-by-year chronologies of building construction at selected Alta California missions record the types of structures built at the missions and the order in which the Franciscans requested different types of buildings to be built. Although not complete in every instance, because of gaps in the record or an incomplete registration of construction in some years, they document the relative importance of dormitories by the early construction date and the late date for the building of Indian housing.

Building Construction at Santa Clara Mission, 1777–1832

1777–1779: Temporary structures were built, including a chapel, a residence for the missionaries and servants, offices and a granary.

1779: A flood in early 1779 forced the relocation of the mission to a new site. Temporary buildings were constructed, including a chapel, a residence for the missionaries, and a dormitory or residence for some Indian converts. In the spring of 1779, the Franciscans directed the construction of additional structures, including a chapel, a granary, a residence for the missionaries, a kitchen, and offices.

1780: Buildings constructed in this year were a new residence for the missionaries, offices, and a granary.

1781: Several adobe buildings were built, including a granary, and the foundations were laid for a new church completed and dedicated in 1784.

1787: The central quadrangle of the missions reached completion with the addition of an adobe wing. The Franciscans did not record the use of the new structures.

1789: An adobe structure was built, and the missionary's residence was repaired.

1790: Residence for the *mayordomo* (overseer) was built.

1791: A granary was built.

1792: A granary and housing for Indian families were built.

1793: Housing for Indian families was built.

1794: Housing for Indian families was built.

1796: A barracks was built for the soldiers stationed at the mission.

1798: Housing for Indian families was built.

1813: New barracks were built for the soldiers stationed at the mission.

1818: A new [temporary?] church was begun to replace the structure completed in 1784.

1822–1825: A new church and central quadrangle were built to replace the structures built in the 1780s. The Franciscans provided little detail on the use of the new structures.

Building Construction at La Purísima Mission, 1787–1832

1788: Temporary buildings were constructed, including a chapel, a residence for the missionaries, a granary, and several other buildings.

1789: A church, a granary, and a kitchen were built.

1790: A wing was added to the central quadrangle.

1791: A granary and a kitchen were built.

1792: The Franciscans had the church and a granary enlarged.

1793: A wing was added to the central quadrangle, and contained a new residence for the missionaries, quarters for visitors to the mission, an office, and a storeroom for Indian clothing.

1794: A barracks was built for the soldiers stationed at the mission, and quarters for the *mayordomo*.

1795: A granary was built.

1796: Three storerooms were built.

1797: A new residence was built for the missionaries.

1798: A new barracks was built for the soldiers stationed at the mission, and the foundations were laid for a new church completed in 1802.

1799: Two adobe structures were built.

1800: A wing was added to the central quadrangle.

1804: A new barracks was built for the soldiers stationed at the mission.

1810: Several structures were built at a nearby livestock ranch.

1812: An earthquake in December of 1812 destroyed many mission buildings, including one hundred housing units for Indian families.

1813: The missionaries moved the mission to a new site, and directed the construction of temporary buildings, including a church.

1815: A long adobe structure was completed, and contained quarters for the missionaries and visitors to the mission, workshops, and a chapel.

1816: A long adobe structure was built, containing a barracks for the soldiers stationed at the mission and the *mayordomo*, and workshops. A hospital was built for sick converts.

1817: The foundations were laid for a new church. A fountain was built in the Indian village, which indicates that the dormitory for single women and the two large barracks-like structures with apartments for Indian families excavated in the 1950s and 1960s by archaeologists may already have been built.

1818: A new church was built.

1821: A bell tower was added to the church.

1823: Housing units were built for Indian families.

Building Construction at Santa Inés Mission, 1804–1832

1804: A single long adobe structure was built, containing a residence for the missionaries, a granary, and a church.

1805: An adobe wing was added to the central quadrangle.

1806: An adobe wing was added to the central quadrangle.

1807–1808: A new residence was built for the missionaries.

1810: A barracks was built for the soldiers stationed at the mission.

1811: A residence was built for the *mayordomo*.

1812: Eighty Indian housing units were built. An earthquake in December badly damaged many mission buildings, which were repaired in 1813 and 1814.

1813: The height of the missionary's residence was lowered. A granary was built or converted to serve as a temporary church.

1814: The foundations were laid for a new church completed in 1816.

1820: A grist mill was built.

1823: A tack room was built.

1825–1829: Buildings damaged or destroyed in the 1824 Chumash revolt were repaired or replaced, including the barracks for the soldiers stationed at the mission, a tack room, a hospital, a kitchen, and quarters for visitors to the mission.

1832: A granary was built.

Building Construction at San Rafael Mission, 1818–1832

1818: A long adobe structure was built, containing a residence for the missionaries, a dormitory for single women and girls, a chapel, a hospital, and quarters for visitors to the mission.

1819: Several buildings were added to the mission complex, including a new dormitory for single women, a kitchen, a hospital, a residence for the *mayordomo*, workshops, and a tack room.

1820: A new chapel, granaries, workshops, and a residence for the missionaries were added to the mission complex.

1821: A granary was enlarged.

1822: Housing units were built for Indian families.

1824: A new church was completed, and a barracks for soldiers stationed at the mission and a dormitory for recent converts were built.

1825: A kitchen and dormitory for single men were built.

1826: Housing units for Indian families and a dormitory for recent converts were added to the mission complex.

1827: Housing units for Indian families and a tanning vat were built.

1828: A granary was enlarged.

1829: A residence was built for the *mayordomo*.

1830: Housing units were built for Indian families.

1831: Housing units were built for Indian families, and the barracks for the soldiers stationed at the mission was enlarged.

Building Construction at San Francisco Solano Mission, 1824–1840

1824: Several adobe structures were built, including a *sala* (reception room), workshops, and a chapel.

1825: Several adobe structures were built, including a residence for the missionaries, a granary, and housing for Indians.

1827: An adobe wing, containing a new residence for the missionaries, was built. Construction began on a church, completed in 1832, and a granary, completed in 1828.

1829: An adobe wing was added to the central quadrangle.

1840: A chapel was built to replace the church completed in 1832.

Source: Annual Reports; Archivo General de la Nación, México, D.F., and the Santa Barbara Mission Archive-Library, Santa Barbara, California. References for the years 1799–1809 are taken from the individual mission histories written by Zephyrin Engelhardt, O.F.M.

Abbreviations

AF. Archivo Franciscano, Biblioteca Nacional, México, D.F.

APA. Altar Parish Archive, Altar, Sonora.

BLUC Bancroft Library, University of California, Berkeley, California.

DTCA Diocese of Tucson Chancery Archive, Tucson, Arizona.

GC Calvin Collection, Dublin, Ireland.

GLUSF Gleason Library, University of San Francisco, San Francisco, California.

Notes

Introduction

1. For a useful discussion of the origins and different views of contact population levels, see William Denevan, ed. *The Native Population of the Americas in 1492* (Madison, 1976).

2. For a general discussion of European demographic patterns in the early modern period, see Michael Flinn, *The European Demographic System, 1520–1820* (Baltimore, 1981). The most detailed and ambitious demographic study of any European regions is E. A. Wrigley and R. S. Schofield, *The Population History of England, 1541–1871: A Reconstruction* (Cambridge, 1981). Despite the impact of disease, the population of England experienced population growth during the early modern period.

3. Henry Dobyns, *Spanish Colonial Tucson: A Demographic History* (Tucson, 1976).

4. Peveril Meigs, *The Dominican Mission Frontier of Lower California* (Berkeley, 1935); and Homer Aschmann, *The Central Desert of Baja California: Demography and Ecology* (Berkeley and Los Angeles, 1959).

5. Sherburne Cook, "The Extent and Significance of Disease among the Indians of Baja California from 1697 to 1773," *Ibero-Americana* 9 (Berkeley, 1937).

6. Robert H. Jackson, "Epidemic Disease and Population Decline in the Baja California Missions, 1697–1834," *Southern California Quarterly* 63 (1981): 308–46.

7. The entire series of monographs, first published in *Ibero-Americana,* was republished in 1976 by the University of California Press under the title of *The Conflict between the California Indian and White Civilization.*

8. Sherburne Cook, *The Population of the California Indians, 1769–1970* (Berkeley and Los Angeles, 1976).

9. Published by the University of California Press in 1979.

10. See, for example, Francis Guest, O.F.M., "An Examination of the Thesis of S. F. Cook on the Forced Conversion of Indians in the Alta California Missions," *Southern California Quarterly* 61 (1979): 1–77; David Hornbeck, "An Assessment of S. F. Cook's Research on the 'Indian Versus the Spanish Mission,'" paper read

at the "Spanish Missions and the California Indians" symposium, Davis, Calif., March 2–4, 1990; and Bishop Thaddeus Shubsda, *The Serra Report* (Monterey, n.d. [1986]).

11. A notable example is John Johnson's detailed study of Chumash demographic patterns, summarized in "The Chumash and the Missions," in David Hurst Thomas, ed., *Columbian Consequences Archaeological and Historical Perspectives on the Spanish Borderlands West* (Washington, D.C., 1989), 365–75.

12. See, for example, Robert H. Jackson, "Patterns of Demographic Change in the Missions of Central Alta California," *Journal of California and Great Basin Anthropology* 9 (1987): 251–72; Robert H. Jackson, "A Utopian Paradise?: The Dynamic of Demographic Collapse in the California Missions, 1697–1840," paper read at the annual meeting of the American Historical Association, San Francisco, Calif., Dec. 27, 1989; and Robert H. Jackson, "La dinámica del desastre demográfico de la población india en las misiones de la bahía de San Francisco, Alta California, 1776–1840," *Historia Mexicana* 40 (1991): 187–215.

13. James Sandos, "Christianization among the Chumash: An Ethnohistoric Perspective," *American Indian Quarterly* 15 (1991): 65–89. Sandos's article is a series of observations on Chumash culture framed as an attack on the work of anthropologist John Johnson, rather than a coherent explanation of the process of cultural change in the missions established among the Chumash. Sandos's examination of the 1824 Chumash revolt, "Levantamiento! The 1824 Chumash Revolt Reconsidered," *Southern California Quarterly* 67 (1985): 109–33, is a more solid contribution to the ethnohistory of the Alta California missions. In "The Native Response to the Colonization of Alta California," in Thomas's, *Columbian Consequences,* 377–94, Edward Castillo provides important insights concerning forms of Indian resistance in the missions.

14. The debate began as a critique of Dobyns's book *"Their Numbers Become Thinned": Native American Population Dynamics in Eastern North America* (Knoxville, 1983), written by Dean Snow and Kim Lamphear and entitled "European Contact and Indian Depopulation in the Northeast: The Timing of the First Epidemics," *Ethnohistory* 35 (1988): 15–33. Dobyns responded in "More Methodological Perspectives on Historical Demography," *Ethnohistory* 36 (1989): 285–99.

15. Thomas Whitmore, "A Simulation of the Sixteenth-Century Population Collapse in the Basin of Mexico," *Annals of the Association of American Geographers* 8 (1991): 464–87. Daniel Reff, *Disease, Depopulation, and Culture Change in Northwestern New Spain, 1518–1764* (Salt Lake City, 1991), is a recent study that offers an analysis of the chronology epidemics and their impact on native peoples, in this case in northwestern New Spain.

16. Woodrow Borah, "Epidemics in the Americas: Major Issues and Future Research," *Latin American Population History Bulletin* 19 (Spring 1991): 2–13.

17. One exception is Robert H. Jackson, "Demographic Change in Northwestern New Spain," *The Americas* 44 (1985): 462–79.

18. For a useful summary of the literature on the historical demography of early modern Europe, see Flinn, *European Demographic System.*

19. See Ron Lee, "Estimating Series of Vital Rates and Age Structure from Baptisms and Burials: A New Technique with Application to Pre-Industrial Eng-

land," *Population Studies* 28 (1975): 495–512; and Ron Lee, "Inverse Projection and Back Projection: Comparative Results and Sensitivity Tests for England," *Population Studies* 39 (1985): 233–48; and Robert McCaa and James Vaupel, "How Well Does Inverse Projection Perform With Simulated Data?" *University of Minnesota Center For Population Analysis and Public Policy Working Paper*, no. 89-06-2 (1989). For studies that apply inverse projection to historical population, see Peter Smith and Shui-Meng Ng, "The Components of Population Change in Nineteenth-Century Southeast Asia: Village Data from the Philippines," *Population Studies* 36 (1982): 237–55; Robert McCaa, "The Female Population of Chile, 1855–1964: A Microcomputer Balance Sheet Method," *Latin American Population History Newsletter* 15 (Spring 1989): 9–14; Robert McCaa, "Benchmarks for a New Inverse Population Projection: England, Sweden, and a Standard Demographic Transition," in Roger Schofield and David Reher, eds., *Old and New in Historical Demography* (Oxford and New York, forthcoming); and Jackson, "La dinámica."

Chapter 1

1. On the policy of civil and religious *congregación* see Charles Gibson, *The Aztecs under Spanish Rule: A History of the Indians of the Valley of Mexico, 1519–1810* (Stanford, 1964); William Taylor, *Landlord and Peasant in Colonial Oaxaca* (Stanford, 1972); Murdo MacLeod, *Spanish Central America: A Socioeconomic History 1520–1720* (Berkeley and Los Angeles, 1973); Nancy Farriss, *Maya Society under Colonial Rule: The Collective Enterprise of Survival* (Princeton, 1984); and W. George Lovell, *Conquest and Survival in Colonial Guatemala: A Historical Geography of the Cuchumatan Highlands, 1500–1821* (Kingston and Montreal, 1985). In a three-volume historical geography of New Spain, Peter Gerhard documents the implementation of *congregación* throughout Mexico; see *A Guide to the Historical Geography of New Spain* (Cambridge, 1972); *The Southeast Frontier of New Spain* (Princeton, 1979); and *The North Frontier of New Spain* (Princeton, 1982).

2. For a detailed examination of *ancien-régime* Spanish rural village society, see Richard Herr, *Rural Change and Royal Finances in Spain at the End of the Old Regime* (Berkeley and Los Angeles, 1989).

3. For ethnohistoric and ethnographic overviews of the northern Pima population, see the essays on the Pimas and Papagos in Alfonso Ortiz, ed., *Handbook of North American Indians: Volume 10, Southwest* (Washington, D.C., 1983). The essays are Bernard Fontana, "Pima and Papago: Introduction," 125–36; Bernard Fontana, "History of the Papago," 137–48; Paul Ezell, "History of the Pima," 149–60; Robert Hackenberg, "Pima and Papago Ecological Adaptations," 161–77; and Donald Bahr, "Pima and Papago Social Organization," 178–92.

4. See, for example, the works of Peter Dunne, S.J.: *Pioneer Black Robes on the West Coast* (Berkeley and Los Angeles, 1940); and *Pioneer Jesuits in Northern Mexico* (Berkeley and Los Angeles, 1944).

5. Daniel Reff, *Disease, Depopulation, and Culture Change in Northwestern New Spain, 1518–1764* (Salt Lake City, 1991).

6. Luis González Rodríguez, *Etnología y misión en la Pimería Alta, 1715–1740* (México, D.F., 1977), 71, 177, 244.
7. Charles Polzer, *Precepts of the Jesuit Missions* (Tucson, 1976), 37.
8. Ms., Santa María Magdalena Mission Baptismal Register, BLUC.
9. Published in Ernest Burrus, S.J., and Felix Zubillaga, S.J., eds., *Misiones mexicanas de la compañía de Jesús, 1618–1745* (Madrid, 1982).
10. Ibid.
11. Francisco Alegre, S.J., *Historia de la Compañía de Jesús en Nueva España (1566–1766)*, 3 vols. (Rome, 1960), 3:505.
12. González Rodríguez, *Etnología y misión,* 64.
13. Ibid., 69–76.
14. Ibid., 81.
15. Ibid., 18.
16. John Donahue, S.J., *After Kino: Jesuit Missions in Northwestern New Spain* (Rome, 1969), 12, 66, 72.
17. Ms., San Ignacio Mission Baptismal Register, BLUC.
18. Donahue, *After Kino,* 69.
19. Peter Dunne, S.J., trans. and ed., *Juan Antonio Balthasar: Padre Visitador-General to the Sonora Frontier, 1744–1745* (Tucson, 1957), 4; and Donahue, *After Kino,* 112.
20. Donahue, *After Kino,* 80–82.
21. Ms., Jacobo Sedelmayr, S.J., to Juan Antonio Balthasar, S.J., Tubutama, May 10, 1751, GC.
22. Ms., Santa María Soamca Mission Baptismal Register, BLUC.
23. Henry Dobyns, "Indian Extinction in the Middle Santa Cruz River Valley, Arizona," *New Mexico Historical Review* 38 (1963): 173 and passim.
24. John Kessell, *Mission of Sorrows Jesuit Guevavi and the Pimas, 1691–1767* (Tucson, 1970), 146.
25. Henry Dobyns, *Spanish Colonial Tucson: A Demographic History* (Tucson, 1976), 18–19.
26. Donahue, *After Kino,* 142.
27. Ibid., 142.
28. Ms., San Francisco de Ati Mission Baptismal Register, BLUC.
29. Ms., San Antonio de Oquitoa Mission Baptismal Register, BLUC.
30. Dobyns, *Spanish Colonial Tucson,* 137.
31. Ms., San Ignacio Mission Baptismal Register, BLUC.
32. Dobyns, *Spanish Colonial Tucson,* 46.
33. Ms., Jacobo Sedelmayr, S.J., to Christoval de Escobar y Llamas, S.J., Tubutama, May 29, 1745, GC.
34. Donahue, *After Kino,* 118.
35. Ms., Jacobo Sedelmayr, S.J., to Juan Antonio Balthasar, S.J., Tubutama, March 22, 1747, GC.
36. Ms. San Ignacio Mission Baptismal Register, BLUC.
37. Quoted in Dunne, *Juan Antonio Balthasar,* 78.
38. Ms., José Mora, O.F.M., La Cieneguilla, June 12, 1793, "Plan de la Misión de Caborca y de sus pueblos de visita Pitic y Busanic," AF 36/795.
39. Ms., Jacobo Sedelmayr, S.J., Tubutama, 1750, "Relación de la entrada que se hizo el año de 1750 por el mes de Noviembre y Diciembre a las naciones del Río

Xila y Colorado por mi Jacobo Sedelmayr, Misionero Jesuita de Tubutama en la Pimería Alta," GC.

40. Quoted in Herbert Bolton, trans. and ed., *Kino's Historical Memoir of the Pimería Alta* (Berkeley and Los Angeles, 1948), 255.

41. Ms., Jacobo Sedelmayr, S.J., to Juan Antonio Balthasar, Tubutama, March 22, 1747, GC.

42. Ms., Jacobo Sedelmayr, S.J., to Christoval de Escobar y Llamas, S.J., Tubutama, May 29, 1745, GC.

43. Ms., Jacobo Sedelmayr, S.J., to Juan Antonio Balthasar, S.J., Tubutama, Jan. 9, 1751, GC.

44. Ms., Jacobo Sedelmayr, S.J., to Juan Antonio Balthasar, S.J., Tubutama, May 21, 1751, GC.

45. Ms., Bernardo de Urrea, Altar, Nov. 7, 1775, "Diario que manifiesta las operaciones practicadas por mi Bernardo de Urrea, capitán del presidio de Santa Gertrudis del Altar, en la marcha que emprendi al interior de la Papagueria . . . a fin de explorar los animos de los Papagos para reducirse a una o dos misiones," AF 34/729.

46. For a discussion of non-Indian settlement patterns in the Pimería Alta, see Peter Stern and Robert H. Jackson, "Vagabundaje and Settlement Patterns In Colonial Northern Sonora," *The Americas* 44 (1988): 461–81.

47. Ibid., 479.

48. For a discussion of the process of biological and cultural change in the Pimería Alta missions and the migration of mission Indians to mines and other settlements, see Robert H. Jackson, "Causes of Indian Population Decline in the Pimería Alta Missions of Northern Sonora," *The Journal of Arizona History* 24 (1983): 417–21. Stern and Jackson, "Vagabundaje and Settlement Patterns," 464–70, discuss mining camps in northern Sonora and patterns of seasonal labor. Caste terminology recorded in Sonora sacramental registers documents the advanced state of *mestizaje* in central and southern Sonora, although it is difficult to establish with precision the racial-ethnic origins of the Sonora population. Parish priest and missionary alike exercised subjectivity in the identification of the caste-ethnic status of newly born children, and in many cases, they demonstrated a preference in the use of specific terms. The following table summarizes the caste terms used most frequently in selected Sonora parishes.

Use of Caste Terms as Recorded in Selected Sonora Parish Polls, 1796–1814

Year	Community	Priest/Missionary	Caste Term(s)
1796	Cocospera*	Juan de Santisteban	Gente de Razón
	San José de Pimas	Diego Pozo	Español, Coyote, Mulato
	Yecora	Domingo Moreno	Español
	Aribechi	Francisco Tamajon	Coyote, Español, Moreno, Mulato
	Cumuripa	Salvador del Castillo	Español, Coyote
	Tecoripa	Ignacio Davalos	Español, Mestizo
	Cucurpe	Manuel Legarra	Español, Mulato, Mestizo
1801	Cocospera*	Joaquín Goita	Mulato

Use of Caste Terms as Recorded in Selected Sonora Parish Polls, 1796–1814 *(Continued)*

Year	Community	Priest/Missionary	Caste Term(s)
	San Ignacio*	Josef Pérez	Europeo, Español, Mestizo, Mulato
	Saric*	Bartolomé Soeze	Español
1814	Opodepe	Joaquín Goita	Español, Pardo
	Ures	Martin Pérez	Español Europeo, Español Americano, Pardo
	Bacerac	Luis Romero	Español, Negro, Mulato, Mestizo
	Cumuripa	Salvador del Castillo	Español, Pardo
	Matape	Pedro Martínez	Español, Mestizo, Pardo

*Primería Alta missions.

49. Peter Dunne, S.J., *Black Robes in Lower California* (Berkeley and Los Angeles, 1952), 222.

50. Clemente Guillen, S.J., Dolores, 1744, "Informe del principio, progresso, y estado presente de la Misión de N[uest]ra Señora de los Dolores," BLUC.

51. See, for example, Ms., Sebastian de Sistiaga, S.J., Comondú, November 1744, "Informe y padrón de la Misión de S[an] Joseph Comondú de California en noviembre de 1744," Mateu Collection, Barcelona, Spain. I would like to thank Fr. Charles Polzer, S.J., for giving me a typescript copy of this report.

52. Ms., Miguel Venegas, S.J., "Empressas Apostolicas de los PP Missioneros de la Compañía de Jesús, de la Provincia de Nueva España obradas en la Conquista de Californias," BLUC, 329, para. 1004.

53. Ibid.

54. Zephyrin Engelhardt, O.F.M., *Missions and Missionaries of California: Lower California* (Santa Barbara, 1929), 477.

55. On the congregation of the Baja California Indians in the Jesuit, Franciscan, and Dominican missions, see Peveril Meigs, *The Dominican Mission Frontier of Lower California* (Berkeley, 1935); Homer Aschmann, *The Central Desert of Baja California: Demography and Ecology* (Berkeley and Los Angeles, 1959); Robert H. Jackson, "Demographic Patterns in the Missions of Northern Baja California," *Journal of California and Great Basin Anthropology* 5:1–2 (1983): 131–39; Robert H. Jackson, "Demographic Patterns in the Missions of Central Baja California," *Journal of California and Great Basin Anthropology* 6:1 (1984): 91–112; and Robert H. Jackson, "Patterns of Demographic Change in the Missions of Southern Baja California," *Journal of California and Great Basin Anthropology* 8:2 (1986): 273–79.

56. Erick Langer and Robert H. Jackson, "Colonial and Republican Missions Compared: The Cases of Alta California and Southeastern Bolivia," *Comparative Studies in Society and History* 30 (1988): 295.

57. Sherburne F. Cook, *The Conflict between the California Indian and White Civilization,* repr. ed. (Berkeley and Los Angeles, 1976), 59–61.

58. Ibid., 245–50.

59. John Kessell, *Friars, Soldiers, and Reformers: Hispanic Arizona and the Sonora Mission Frontier, 1767–1856* (Tucson, 1976), 229.

60. Charles Hale, *Mexican Liberalism in the Age of Mora, 1821–1853* (New Haven, 1968), 221.

61. Romeo Flores Caballero, *La contra revolución en la independencia los españoles en la vida política, social y económica de México (1804–1838)* (México, D.F., 1973).

62. Michael Costeloe, *La primera república federal de México (1824–1835)* (México, D.F., 1975), chap. 14.

63. Kessel, *Friars, Soldiers, and Reformers,* chaps. 10–11; Jackson, "Causes of Indian Population Decline," 405–29; Cynthia Radding, "Las estructuras socio-económicas de las misiones de la Pimería Alta 1768–1850," *Noroeste de México* 3 (1979): 1–124; and Cynthia Radding, "La aumulación originaria de capital agrario en Sonora: Comunidad indigena y la hacienda en Pimería Alta y Opateria, 1768–1868," *Noroeste de México* 5 (1981): 15–46.

64. Robert H. Jackson, "Epidemic Disease and Population Decline in the Baja California Missions, 1697–1834," *Southern California Quarterly* 63 (1981): 308–46; and Aschmann, *Central Desert,* 253.

65. Aschmann, *Central Desert,* 251.

66. Ibid., 251.

67. Engelhardt, *Missions and Missionaries,* 1:661–64.

68. Meigs, *Dominican Mission Frontier,* 117, 159.

69. Engelhardt, *Missions and Missionaries,* 1:682–83; and Aschmann, *Central Desert,* 252.

70. Aschmann, *Central Desert,* 254–58; Meigs, *Dominican Mission Frontier,* 158–59.

71. On the inclusion of the Alta California missions in the general liberal discussion of church wealth in early republican Mexico, see Jan Bazant, *The Alienation of Church Wealth in Mexico* (Cambridge, 1971).

72. The Franciscan version of the secularization of the Alta California missions was presented by Engelhardt, *Missions and Missionaries.* Engelhardt argued the thesis that the rapacious "paisano" (Californio) politicians stole much of the wealth of the missions following what the author felt was the illegal proclamation of secularization in 1833, terminating the good work of the Franciscans and depriving the Indians of the material benefits of their labor in the missions. An early and relatively balanced view of the politics of secularization can be found in H. H. Bancroft, *History of California,* 6 vols. (San Francisco, 1887–1888). A more recent examination of secularization is Manuel Servin, "The Secularization of the California Missions: A Reappraisal," *Southern California Quarterly* 47 (1965): 133–49.

73. There are two exceptions. Clement Meighan, "Indians and California Missions," *Southern California Quarterly* 69 (1987): 187–201, argues that the mission economies collapsed with the implementation of the secularization decree, which, in turn, was the primary reason for the exodus of the Indians from the missions. George Phillips, "Indians and the Breakdown of the Spanish Mission System in California," *Ethnohistory* 21 (1974): 291–302, argues that the exodus of the Indians from the missions was a rejection of the mission regime.

74. Engelhardt, *Missions and Missionaries,* 3:239–41.

75. Ms., San Carlos Mission Annual Reports, 1827–1832, the Santa Barbara Mission Archive-Library, Santa Barbara, Calif. (hereafter cited as SBMA).

76. Zephyrin Engelhardt, O.F.M., *San Juan Capistrano Mission* (Los Angeles, 1922), 112–15, 121–23, 125, and 140–42.

77. Engelhardt, *Missions and Missionaries,*, 3:466–82.

78. Robert Jackson, Edna Kimbro, and Mary Ellen Ryan, "'*Como la Sombra, Huye la Hora*: Restoration Research, Santa Cruz Mission Adobe, Santa Cruz Mission State Historic Park," unpublished report on file with the State of California Department of Parks and Recreation, 64–69.

79. Engelhardt, *Missions and Missionaries,* 4:17.

80. The "Diario, Informe, y Borradores de Correspondencia" (cited here as Diary, Report, and Drafts) are preserved in BLUC.

81. José Anzar, O.F.M., and Andrés Pico, "Ynventario de los muebles raices semovientes en la Misión de Sta Cruz por la comisión nombrada pr el Excmo Sor Gobernador," BLUC.

82. Ms., San Rafael Mission Annual Report, 1840, SBMA.

83. Ms., San José Mission Annual Report, 1840, SBMA.

84. Ms., San Antonio Mission Annual Report, 1840, SBMA.

85. Ms., San Rafael Mission Annual Report, 1840, SBMA.

86. Ms., "Quaderno en donde consta las familias casadas, y sus hijos e hijas, los solteros y solteras, los huerfanos y huerfanas de esta Misn de Sn Anto de Padua," BLUC.

87. Ms., José Estrada, "Padrón general que manifiesta el numero de havitantes que ecsisten en la municipalidad de Monterey 1836," BLUC. In 1846, John Sutter employed a labor force of former mission Indians. There were 395 "tame/neophyte" Indians and 2,373 "wild/gentile" Indians in the lands of New Helvetia, and Sutter employed 103 "tame/neophyte" Indians in his different economic operations. See Albert Hurtado, *Indian Survival on the California Frontier* (New Haven, 1988), 66–67.

88. Ibid.

89. Ms., William Hartnell, Diary and Blotters of Correspondence, BLUC.

90. Ms., San Rafael Mission Annual Reports, 1818–1832, SBMA; and Ms., San Rafael Mission baptismal register, San Francisco Archdiocese Chancery Archive, Colma, Calif.

91. Reported in Ms., William Hartnell, Diary, BLUC. Hartnell reported that at San Rafael he had been told "that in the Russian fields there are many Mission Indians whom they [administrators?] claim."

92. Jackson, Kimbro, and Ryan, "*Como la Sombra . . . ,*" discusses long-term demographic trends at Santa Cruz mission and the post-secularization Indian populations in the Santa Cruz area.

93. Ms., San Juan Bautista Mission Annual Report, 1840, SBMA.

94. Ms., San José Mission Annual Report, 1840, SBMA.

95. Robert H. Jackson, "The Post-Secularization Dispersion of the Population of the Alta California Missions, 1834–1846," paper presented at the annual meeting of the Rocky Mountain Council of Latin American Studies, Flagstaff, Ariz., Feb. 26–28, 1991.

96. Ms., William Hartnell, Blotters of Letters, BLUC. In a letter dated November 8, 1839, Hartnell scolded the administrator of San Miguel mission for having given

one Indian one hundred lashes, although the mission administrators were authorized to apply no more than twenty-five lashes to converts.

97. William Hartnell recorded such complaints during his 1839 and 1840 inspection tours. Indians living at San Fernando, San Buenaventura, San Luis Obispo, San Miguel, Santa Cruz, San Francisco, and San Rafael registered complaints over the granting of mission lands to prominent Mexican settlers. Moreover, the Indians at San Juan Capistrano, Santa Cruz, and San Rafael requested the distribution of communal mission property and the conversion of the former missions into *pueblos de indios.* Finally, the Indians living at San Juan Capistrano objected to the plan of the Pico brothers to lease the mission, rather than distributing communal mission goods and property to the Indians. Hartnell attributed the petition presented by the San Juan Capistrano Indians to bad advice from settlers trying to manipulate them, but, as noted in a letter sent to Andrés Pico on July 24, 1840, the inspector general was confident that the Indians' request would be granted.

98. Jackson, Kimbro, and Ryan, "*Como la Sombra . . . ,*" 68.

99. Ibid., 68.

100. Ibid., 64–69, 104, 112–13, 137–56.

Chapter 2

1. Daniel Reff, *Disease, Depopulation, and Culture Change in Northwestern New Spain, 1518–1764* (Salt Lake City, 1991), 233.

2. Peter Gerhard, *The North Frontier of New Spain* (Princeton, 1982), 295; and Robert H. Jackson, "Epidemic Disease and Population Decline in the Baja California Missions, 1697–1834," *Southern California Quarterly* 63 (1981): 310.

3. Robert H. Jackson, "Demographic Change in the Missions of Central Baja California," *Journal of California and Great Basin Anthropology* 6 (1984): 93, 104.

4. Jackson, "Epidemic Disease and Population Decline," 310, 335.

5. Gerhard, *North Frontier,* 304.

6. Sherburne F. Cook, "Historical Demography," in Robert Heizer, ed., *Handbook of North American Indians: California* (Washington, D.C., 1978), 92.

7. Henry Dobyns, "Indian Extinction in the Middle Santa Cruz River Valley, Arizona," *New Mexico Historical Review* 38 (1963): 181; and Carl Sauer, "Aboriginal Population of Northwestern Mexico," *Ibero-Americana* 10 (1935): 32.

8. H. H. Bancroft, *History of the North Mexican States and Texas,* 2 vols. (San Francisco, 1884–1889), 1:524.

9. Henry Dobyns, *Spanish Colonial Tucson: A Demographic Study* (Tucson, 1976), 19–21.

10. Ibid., 20–21.

11. John Kessell, *Friars, Soldiers, and Reformers: Hispanic Arizona and the Sonora Mission Frontier, 1767–1856* (Tucson, 1976), 88.

12. Ms., Guevavi Mission Burial Register, DTCA.

13. Kessell, *Friars, Soldiers, and Reformers,* 170.

14. Ms., Caborca Mission Baptismal and Burial Registers; APA, and BLUC.

15. Jackson, "Demographic Change," 94–95.

16. Ibid., 95–98.

17. Ibid., 98–99.

18. Ibid., 101.

19. Ibid., 105.

20. Ibid., 105.

21. On the expansion of the missions into northern Baja California, see Peveril Meigs, *The Dominican Mission Frontier Of Lower California* (Berkeley, 1935); and Homer Aschmann, *The Central Desert of Baja California: Demography and Ecology* (Berkeley and Los Angeles, 1959).

22. On the establishment of San Fernando mission, see Carl Sauer and Peveril Meigs, "Site and Culture at San Fernando Velicata," *University of California Publications in Geography* 2:9 (1927): 271–302; and Aschmann, *Central Desert,* 38–41, 174–77, 226–30. On the motives for the expansion to the north and the presence of a permanent military garrison in the northern missions, see Meigs, *Dominican Mission Frontier,* 1–39, 148–50, and passim.

23. Robert H. Jackson, "Demographic Patterns in the Missions of Northern Baja California," *Journal of California and Great Basin Anthropology* 5 (1983): 132.

24. Ibid., 132.

25. Ibid, 133.

26. On the early problems at San Gabriel mission, see Edward Castillo, "Neophyte Resistance and Accomodation in the Missions of California," paper presented at the conference "The Spanish Missionary Heritage of the United States," San Antonio, Tex., Nov. 8, 1990.

27. Annual and biennial reports, Archivo General de la Nacion, México, D.F.; and the Santa Barbara Mission Archive-Library, Santa Barbara, Calif.

28. Ms., San Luis Obispo Mission baptismal and burial registers, Monterey Diocese Chancery Archive, Monterey, Calif., and Appendix 4.

29. Robert H. Jackson, "Patterns of Demographic Change in the Missions of Central Alta California," *Journal of California and Great Basin Anthropology* 9:2 (1987): 263–65.

30. Ibid., 265–69.

31. Ibid., 267–68; Ms., San Miguel Mission baptismal and burial registers, Monterey Diocese Chancery Archive, Monterey, Calif.; and Appendix 4.

32. Robert H. Jackson, "Gentile Recruitment and Population Movements in the San Francisco Bay Area Missions," *Journal of California and Great Basin Anthropology* 6:2 (1984): 225–28.

33. Ibid., 228–30.

34. Ibid., 231–34, 236.

35. Ibid., 234–35, 238.

36. Ibid., 230–32.

37. A number of scholars have examined, to varying degrees, the gender and age structure of the mission populations. See Dobyns, *Spanish Colonial Tucson,* 146–48, and Tables 17 and 18; Sherburne Cook, *The Conflict Between The California Indian and White Civilization,* repr. ed. (Berkeley and Los Angeles, 1976): 427–40; Aschmann, *Central Desert,* 199–203; Jackson, "Central Alta California," 254–58; John Johnson, "Chumash Social Organization: An Ethnohistorical Perspective,"

unpublished Ph.D. dissertation, University of California, Santa Barbara, 1988; and John Johnson, "The Chumash and the Missions," in David Hurst Thomas, ed., *Columbian Consequences Archaeological and Historical Perspectives on the Spanish Borderlands West* (Washington, D.C., 1989): 365–75.

Chapter 3

1. For examples of studies that document mortality patterns during other epidemic outbreaks in northwestern New Spain, see Robert H. Jackson, "Epidemic Disease and the Population of the Sonora Missions in the Seventeenth, Eighteenth, and Early Nineteenth Centuries," unpublished manuscript; Robert H. Jackson, "The 1781–1782 Smallpox Epidemic in the Baja California Missions," *Journal of California and Great Basin Anthropology* 3 (1981): 138–43; and Robert H. Jackson, "Epidemic Disease and Population Decline in the Baja California Missions, 1697–1834," *Southern California Quarterly* 63 (1981): 308–46. In most cases, the missionaries registering epidemic deaths did not record the specific ages of the victims, or the amount of time the victim had lived in the mission community. The 1769–1770 measles outbreak claimed the lives of young children and recent converts at San Ignacio, Santa María Magdalena, and Caborca in the Pimería Alta, the most susceptible segment of the population not previously exposed to the disease. In 1781, the majority of smallpox deaths at Tumacacori were of children and young adults under the age of twenty who had been born or brought to the mission since the last major smallpox outbreak in the 1760s. The specific references to the 1806 measles epidemic at San Francisco mission are from: Ms., Fr. Tomás de la Peña, San Francisco, April 28, 1806; and Ms., José Viader, San Francisco, May 29, 1806, BLUC.

2. In the 1780s, inoculation by variolation, the intentional infection of an individual with smallpox to build up immunity to the disease, was first practiced in northwestern New Spain and reduced smallpox mortality. In 1803, the Spanish government sent an expedition to the New World to introduce the Jenner cowpox vaccine, but it produced limited results. Smallpox continued to claim hundreds of lives in Sonora and the Californias, until at least the 1830s. Purging and bloodletting, commonly practiced in the eighteenth century, generally proved worse than the disease, while other popular treatments could prove useful. Concern with the spread of Asian cholera in the 1830s prompted the Mexican government to issue instructions for its treatment, which included measures to improve sanitation, and when carried out, such measures generally helped . For a discussion of some medical practices in northwestern New Spain, see Jackson, "1781–1782 Smallpox Epidemic," and Jackson, "Epidemic Disease and Population Decline."

3. On explanations given by missionaries for high rates of epidemic mortality, see John L. Phelan, *The Millennial Kingdom of the Franciscans in the New World,* 2d rev. ed. (Berkeley and Los Angeles, 1970). On the use of inoculation by variolation in Baja California in 1781–1782, see Jackson, "1781–1782 Smallpox Epidemic." The refusal to inoculate was also motivated by the fear of smallpox, and particularly by the idea of intentionally infecting an individual with a deadly

disease. Inoculation by variolation and the Jenner Cowpox vaccine both encountered opposition when first introduced in Europe in the eighteenth and early nineteenth centuries; and complacency over the decline of smallpox in the nineteenth century led to a resurgence of the disease in the 1850s and 1860s in the United States, when parents did not vaccinate their children. However, the millenarian ideology of the missionaries was an important factor in their passivity during epidemic outbreaks.

In the late eighteenth and nineteenth centuries, the Spanish and Mexican governments circulated reports on different forms of disease treatment, such as treatments for smallpox and, when it became a major problem in the 1830s, Asian cholera. These treatments, although not always effective, were made available to government officials and missionaries alike in northwestern New Spain, but they were not always acted upon.

4. See, for example, E. A. Wrigley and R. S. Schofield, *The Population History of England,* 1541–1871: A Reconstruction (Cambridge, 1981).

5. A number of the responses to an 1813 questionnaire sent to California by the liberal Spanish Cortes in Cadiz reported the spread of syphilis to the Indian populations living in the missions. The Franciscans stationed at San Gabriel mission reported:

> This last named [impurity in sexual relations—syphilis] has permeated them to the very marrow with [the] venereal malady. The consequence is that many children at birth already manifest the only patrimony which their parents give them [congenital syphilis]. Hence it is that of four born, three die in the first and second year of their [lives]; and that of the rest who survive, the most reach [only] the age of twenty-five.

Quoted in Zephyrin Engelhardt, O.F.M., *San Gabriel Mission and the Beginnings of Los Angeles* (San Gabriel, 1927), 104. The Franciscans stationed at San Buenaventura wrote in 1814:

> The most prevailing diseases are the *galico* [syphilis], consumption, and dysentery. . . . These [maladies] afflict them [the Indians] more forcibly in [the] spring and autumn. The number of births does not correspond with that of deaths; for in some years there are three deaths to two births.

Quoted in Zephyrin Engelhardt, O.F.M., *San Buenaventura: The Mission by the Sea* (Santa Barbara, 1930), 36. The Franciscans at Santa Barbara noted:

> The most pernicious [disease], however, and the one from which they [the Indians] suffer most in this region, is the *mal galico* [syphilis], or French disease. All are infected with it. . . . On this account few children are born, and of these many die soon after birth, so that the number of deaths exceeds that of births by three to one.

Quoted in Zephyrin Engelhardt, O.F.M., *Santa Barbara Mission: The Queen of the Missions* (San Francisco, 1923), 94.

6. In the response to the 1813 questionnaire, the missionaries stationed at Santa Clara mission reported that abortion was one of the principal vices of the Indians. See Erick Langer and Robert H. Jackson, "Colonial and Republican Missions

Compared: The Cases of Alta California and Southeastern Bolivia," *Comparative Studies in Society and History* 30 (1988): 302–3. In a recent study, Edward Castillo cited an Indian account of mission life that described how Ramón Olbes, O.F.M., stationed at Santa Cruz mission, examined the reproductive organs of one Indian women believed to be sterile, had the woman beaten when she resisted the examination, and made her stand in front of the mission church with a small wooden doll that represented a child not born as a form of public humiliation. Other accounts document similar practices at different missions. Castillo suggests that the missionaries suspected that sterile women practiced abortion, and that the beatings and public humiliation were designed to prevent this behavior. See Edward Castillo, "The Native Responses to the Colonization of Alta California," in David H. Thomas, ed., *Columbian Consequences: Archaeological and Historical Perspectives on the Spanish Borderlands West* (Washington, D.C., 1989), 1:380. Sherburne Cook argued that negative conditions in the missions, including poor diet, social control, and limitations on cultural expression and physical mobility contributed to the practice of abortion and infanticide in the missions. See Sherburne F. Cook, *The Conflict between the California Indian and White Civilization,* repr. ed. (Berkeley and Los Angeles, 1976), 112.

7. See, for example, Robert H. Jackson, "Patterns of Demographic Change in the Missions of Central Alta California," *Journal of California and Great Basin Anthropology* 9 (1987): 258–59. Cook outlined the importance of large-scale flight from the missions in his *Conflict,* 426 and passim.

8. Quoted in Langer and Jackson, "Colonial and Republican Missions," 301. Zephyrin Engelhardt, O.F.M., quotes a document that provides a graphic description of punishment at Santa Barbara mission.

> The punishments resorted to at Santa Barbara are the shackles, the lash, and the stocks, but only when we find that corrections and reproofs are unavailing. Seldom are the women punished with any of the above instruments but the stocks. . . . A man, a boy, or a woman runs away or does not return from the excursion, so that other neophytes must be sent after them. When such a one is brought back to the mission, he is reproached for not having heard holy Mass on a day of obligation. He is made to see that he has of his own free will taken upon himself this and other Christian duties, and he is warned that he will be chastized if he repeats the transgression. He runs away again, and again he is brought back. This time he is chastized with the lash or with the stocks. If this is not sufficient, as is the case with some who disregard a warning, he is made to feel the shackles, which he must wear three days while at work. This same punishment is meted out to such as are caught in concubinage.

Quoted in Engelhardt, *Santa Barbara Mission,* 80–81.

9. See Castillo, "Native Response," 383–84.

10. Ms., Diego de Borica, Monterey, June 30, 1797, "Noticias de las misiones que ocupan los religiosos de S. Francisco del colegio de San Fernando de México en dicha provincia," W. B. Stevens Document Collection, no. 9, University of Texas General Libraries, Austin. Borica apparently appended his observations on condi-

tions in the missions to a standard biennial report of the type generally prepared by the Father-President of the Alta California missions.

11. On the supply of food to the military garrisons, see Robert H. Jackson, "Population and the Economic Dimension of Colonization in Alta California: Four Mission Communities," *Journal of the Southwest* 33 (1991): 387–439. Between 1810 and 1830, for example, the Franciscans stationed at San Gabriel mission supplied food and clothing to the garrisons at San Diego and Santa Barbara, which, according to their own calculations, was worth 56,560 pesos. See Engelhardt, *San Gabriel Mission,* 134. Between 1785 and 1789, the missionaries stationed at San Gabriel mission stored between 50 percent and 100 percent of the wheat and corn produced at the mission in granaries. See San Gabriel Mission Annual Reports, Archivo General de la Nación, México, D.F.

12. Cook, *Conflict,* 45, 55.

13. Ann Stodder, *Mechanisms and Trends in the Decline of the Costanoan Indian Population of Central California* (Salinas, 1986).

14. Reported in David Huelsbeck, ed., *Lost and All But Forgotten: Archaeology and History at the Santa Clara Mission Site,* forthcoming from Coyote Press, Salinas, Calif.

15. Richard Herr, *Rural Change and Royal Finances in Spain at the End of the Old Regime* (Berkeley and Los Angeles, 1989), 191–93.

16. The Asisara account is available in translation in two articles edited by historian Edward Castillo: "The Assassination of Padre Andrés Quintana by the Indians of Mission Santa Cruz in 1812: The Narrative of Lorenzo Asisara," *California History* 68 (1989): 116–25, 150–53; and "An Indian Account of the Decline and Collapse of Mexico's Hegemony over the Missionized Indians of California," *American Indian Quarterly* (Fall 1989): 391–408. Sherburne Cook discussed the use of dormitories at the missions, and concluded that women and girls incarcerated in the dormitories slept in cramped quarters, with little room to sleep comfortably, facing a problem of incomplete disturbed sleep, poor ventilation, the accumulation of filth, and the emotional strain of limited mobility for a people used to considerable mobility. See *Conflict,* 88–90.

17. On the construction of Indian housing at specific missions and the chronology of the development of building complexes, see, for example, Robert H. Jackson, "A Chronology of Building Construction at Santa Clara Mission, 1777–1832," in Huelsbeck, *Lost and All But Forgotten.* The missionaries stationed at Santa Clara (established 1777) directed the construction of adobe Indian housing organized in rows in the 1790s. For a second example, see Robert H. Jackson, "A Chronology of Building Construction at the First La Purisima Site," *Prelado de los Tesoros* (1988) [the monthly publication of the La Purisima State Historic Park docents group]; Robert H. Jackson, "A Chronology of Building Construction at La Purísima Concepción Mission, 1788–1835," unpublished manuscript. The Franciscans stationed at La Purísima (established in 1787) had Indian housing built between 1798 and 1810. In 1812, following a devastating earthquake, the missionaries reported that one hundred Indian housing units had been rendered unusable because of earthquake damage. The missionaries relocated the mission to a new site, and had several large barracks-type housing units built. Both types of housing were built at Santa Cruz mission (established in 1791); row houses were built between 1800 and

1810, and large barracks-type housing between 1818 and 1822 to accommodate new recruits brought to the mission from the Central Valley. See Robert Jackson, Edna Kimbro, and Mary Ellen Ryan, "'*Como la Sombra, Huye la Hora,*' Restoration Research, Santa Cruz Mission Adobe, Santa Cruz Mission State Historic Park," manuscript of report in the possession of the State of California Department of Parks and Recreation, Sacramento, Calif. The Franciscans stationed at San Rafael mission (established in 1817) had Indian housing built between 1822 and 1831, although a part of the Indian population probably continued to live in traditional-style housing. There is a reference to Indian housing built at San Francisco Solano (established in 1823) in 1825. Again, though, a part of the Indian population probably lived in traditional-style housing. See Robert H. Jackson, "A Chronology of Building Construction at San Rafael and San Francisco Solano Missions," unpublished manuscript. Although incomplete, the record of building construction at Santa Inés mission (established in 1804) indicates that eighty Indian housing units were built in 1812, and probably had to be repaired following the earthquake in December of the same year. Notes on building construction at Santa Inés mission are found in extant annual reports, the Santa Barbara Mission Archive-Library, Santa Barbara, Calif. Maps prepared following secularization show that Indian housing at Santa Inés was organized in rows of multiunit buildings.

For other studies that outline the chronology of building construction at California missions and mention Indian housing see: Maynard Geiger, O.F.M., "New Data on Mission San Juan Capistrano," *Southern California Quarterly* 49 (1967): 37–45; Maynard Geiger, O.F.M., "The Building of Mission San Gabriel: 1771–1828," *Southern California Quarterly* 50 (1968): 33–42; and Harry Kelsey, "The Mission Buildings of San Juan Capistrano: A Tentative Chronology," *Southern California Quarterly* 69 (1987): 1–32. Curiously, although the author of the last article included a series of diagrams showing the development of the main quadrangle of the mission complex of buildings, Kelsey did not indicate the location or spatial organization of the Indian housing. Zephyrin Engelhardt, O.F.M., included data on building construction at the California missions in his series of individual mission histories published in the 1920s and early 1930s, including references to the construction of Indian housing.

Walls frequently surrounded Indian housing in order to limit the mobility of converts and, specifically, to prevent flight. For example, the barrackslike dormitory built at Santa Cruz mission between 1819 and 1822 to house recent Yokuts recruits was partially or completely surrounded by walls. The trail that led to the orchard described in the Asisara account, a possible escape route, may have been closed off by the construction of walls. Several maps of the Santa Barbara mission building complex, reproduced in Engelhardt, *Santa Barbara Mission,* show a long wall surrounding the Indian housing on three sides, with the fourth side opening to the main complex and the guardhouse of the soldiers stationed at the mission.

Plat maps were prepared in the mid-1850s for each of the missions when the properties were returned to the Catholic Church, but few record former Indian housing or walls in the building complexes that might have survived in the 1850s. A lack of maintenance and the removal of roofing materials resulted in the rapid physical deterioration of Indian housing between the mid-1830s and mid-1850s. Few examples of Indian housing survive today. The finest example is the 1820s barracks-style family housing unit built at Santa Cruz mission to house Yokuts converts from the Central Valley. The state of California is currently restoring the adobe structure as the central feature of the Santa Cruz Mission State Historic Park.

18. On this point, see Langer and Jackson, "Colonial and Republican Missions," p. 301. On the psychological disorientation of Indians living in the missions, see George H. Phillips, "Indians and the Breakdown of the Spanish Mission System in California," *Ethnohistory* 21 (1974): 291–302. In a similar situation, the Franciscans stationed in Baja California relocated a group known as the Guaicura, only marginally acculturated, to a mission with well-watered agricultural lands, and they attempted to force the Indians to work in sustained field labor for the first time, with negative results. The Indians engaged in active and passive resistance, including flight, work slowdowns, and the destruction of mission property. The Franciscans and civil officials used escalating levels of corporal punishment in an attempt to get the Indians to work, and they eventually had to hire non-Indian agricultural workers to work the land and oversee Indian laborers. See Robert H. Jackson, "Patterns of Demographic Change in the Missions of Southern Baja California," *The Journal of California and Great Basin Anthropology* 8 (1986): 273–79.

19. On fugitivism from Alta California missions, see Jackson, "Patterns . . . Central Alta California," 258–60. Cook was one of the first scholars to identify the significance of flight from the Alta California missions, in his *Conflict,* 426 and passim.

A rough estimate can be made of the net flight from selected missions by calculating the difference between the total number of baptisms, burials, and population. The maximum estimate of population loss due to flight would be the difference between the three figures. However, there are flaws in the methodology. For example, Indians could have been baptized or died when they were away from the missions, and thus they would not have been counted in mission censuses. Moreover, non-Indian baptisms were included in the summaries reported in the annual reports, thus inflating the estimate of the number of Indians who fled successfully. Nevertheless, the figures do indicate the degree of the problem. Finally, in the specific case of the four San Francisco Bay missions San Francisco, San José, San Rafael, and San Francisco Solano (Santa Clara is excluded), the estimate of the number of fugitives must be combined, since converts were relocated between the four establishments. Data from selected establishments are summarized below for the year 1832.

Several patterns emerge from an analysis of the estimates of the number of Indian fugitives. First, and most important, the missions located in central and northern Alta California experienced a more severe problem with fugitivism. This can be attributed to the fact that the contact populations in central and northern Alta California were smaller than in the southern part of the province, and the missionaries resettled recruits from a greater distance from the mission communities and jumbled together a large number of converts from distinct politico-cultural groups. The recruitment of Indians from the Central Valley initiated a phase of increased resistance to the mission regime, especially large-scale flight. Second, the problem of large-scale flight appears to have been greatest in the San Francisco Bay missions, which were relatively close to the Sacramento–San Joaquín River delta, which was an ideal location for hideouts for fugitives. Flight was less of a problem in culturally homogeneous areas, such as in the Chumash missions located on the

Santa Barbara Channel, until the 1824 revolt and revitalization movement which led hundreds of former converts to a new life in an isolated part of the Central Valley.

Estimate of Indians Having Fled from Selected Missions by the Year 1832

Mission	Total Baptisms to 1832	Total Burials to 1832	Pop. in 1832	Estimated No. of Fugitives
S. Fernando	2,784	1,983	782	19
S. Buenaventura	3,875	3,150	668	57
Sta. Inés	1,348	1,227	360	239*
La Purísima	3,256	2,633	372	251**
S. Luis Obispo	2,644	2,268	231	145
S. Miguel	2,475	1,862	658	45
S. Antonio	4,419	3,617	640	162
Soledad	2,139	1,705	339	95
Sta. Cruz	2,439	1,972	281	186
S. Juan Bautista	4,017	2,854	916	247
Four San Francisco Bay Missions	16,098	10,985	3,213	1,900

*Indicates that converts were transferred to the mission from another mission.
**A part of the difference can be attributed to the transfer of converts to another mission, most likely Santa Inés.
Source: 1832 Annual Reports, the Santa Barbara Mission Archives-Library, Santa Barbara, California.

20. Quoted in Jackson, "Patterns . . . Central Alta California," 259.

21. Quoted in ibid, 259.

22. For Indian raids into Spanish-Mexican territory and Spanish-Mexican military expeditions, see, for example, Sylvia Broadbent, "Conflict at Monterey: Indian Horse Raiding, 1820–1850," *Journal of California Anthropology* 1 (1974): 86–101; Robert H. Jackson, "Gentile Recruitment and Population Movements in the San Francisco Bay Area Missions," *Journal of California and Great Basin Anthropology* 6 (1984): 225–39; Cook, *Conflict,* esp. 245–51; and Albert Hurtado, *Indian Survival on the California Frontier* (New Haven, 1988), passim.

23. The annual reports record a general increase in production levels, both in grains and in the number of livestock. The Franciscans engaged in trade with foreign merchants, selling cattle hides and tallow in exchange for manufactured goods that were not produced in California. Goods supplied to the military increased in volume. See, for example, Jackson, "Population and the Economic Dimension." A major theme in the works of Zephrin Engelhardt, O.F.M., is the way in which the military exploited and abused the Indians, contributing to increased resistance by converts. However, Engelhardt ignores the fact that the missionaries generally worked in close concert with the military and political leadership of the province, especially after 1810. This interpretation is evident through a reading of correspondence between missionaries and garrison commanders, and the accounts of supplies provided to the military.

24. See Langer and Jackson, "Colonial and Republican Missions," 301–3. The answers to the 1813 questionnaire document what different missionaries knew about traditional Indian religious practices. The Franciscans stationed at San Gabriel noted:

> According to our observations it seems that the Indians have some superstitions, or rather some vain practices peculiar to recent converts . . .

Quoted in Engelhardt, *San Gabriel Mission,* 100. The missionaries at San Luis Obispo wrote:

> I have not observed that they adore the sun and the moon. What I did learn is that the pagans have a sort of oratory, but I have not been able to verify the report, not to whom they direct their supplications.

Quoted in Zephyrin Engelhardt, O.F.M., *Mission San Luis Obispo* (Santa Barbara, 1933), 50. Finally, the missionaries at Santa Barbara wrote:

> Though we tried hard, we have not been able to ascertain whether in their pagan state they practiced any formal idolatry or vane observations.

Quoted in Engelhardt, *Santa Barbara Mission,* 93.

25. Nancy Farriss, *Maya Society under Colonial Rule: The Collective Enterprise of Survival* (Princeton, 1984), 286–354. Farriss argues that the Yucatec Maya incorporated the Christian God and Saints into their own religion at different levels of worship. For example, specific Saints became transformed into the fertility god of the village, and the adoration of the Saint became the primary act of communal religious practice. The evidence from the Alta California missions suggests that some missionaries did not believe that the California Indians could have a complex religion and worldview.

26. Langer and Jackson, "Colonial and Republican Missions," 302–3.

27. Ibid., 302.

28. See Robert H. Jackson, "Demographic Change in Northwestern New Spain," *The Americas* 41 (1985): 462–79.

29. Phillips develops this interpretation in "Indians and the Breakdown of the Spanish Mission System."

30. Kieran McCarty, O.F.M., *Desert Documentary* (Tucson, 1976), 11–15.

31. Ms., Santa María Magdalena Mission Burial Register, BLUC.

32. Ms., Los Santos Angeles de Guevavi Mission Burial Register, DTCA.

33. Ms., Anonymous, "Breve resumen de los desastres, muertes, robos, y asatamientos acaezidas en la Provincia de Sonora . . . " AGN Temporalidades, 17–69.

34. Ibid.

35. Ms., Los Santos Angeles de Guevavi Mission Burial Register, DTCA.

36. San José de Tumacacori Mission Burial Register, DTCA.

37. The population of Sonora was exposed to epidemics prior to the establishment of missions in the seventeenth century. As such, the rate of demographic collapse due to epidemics was greater than the surviving eighteenth-century parish records would seem to indicate. On the early impact of epidemics in Sonora and surrounding areas, see Daniel Reff, "Old World Diseases and the Dynamics of

Indian and Jesuit Relations in Northwestern New Spain, 1520–1660," in N. Ross Crumrine and Phil C. Weigand, eds., "Ejidos and Regions of Refuge in Northwestern Mexico," *Anthropological Papers of the University of Arizona* 46 (1987): 85–94.

Chapter 4

1. On the relationship between population levels in the missions and the recruitment of converts, see Robert H. Jackson, "Demographic Patterns in the Missions of Northern Baja California," *Journal of California and Great Basin Anthropology* 5:1 and 2 (1983): 131–39; Robert H. Jackson, "Demographic Patterns in the Missions of Central Baja California," *Journal of California and Great Basin Anthropology* 6:1 (1984): 91–112; Robert H. Jackson, "Gentile Recruitment and Population Movements in the San Francisco Bay Area Missions," *Journal of California and Great Basin Anthropology* 6:2 (1984): 225–39.

2. See Noble David Cook, *Demographic Collapse: Indian Peru, 1520–1620* (Cambridge, 1981).

3. Nicolas Sánchez-Albornoz, *The Population of Latin America: A History,* trans. W. A. R. Richardson (Berkeley and Los Angeles, 1974), 44.

4. On demographic patterns in colonial Latin America, see ibid, chaps. 3 and 4.

5. José Gordillo and Mercedes del Rio, "La visita de Tiquipaya: Analisis de un padrón toledano (1573)," unpublished manuscript, 1989.

6. For a useful survey of European demographic patterns in the early modern period, see Michael Flinn, *The European Demographic System, 1500–1820* (Baltimore, 1981).

7. Ibid., 124–29.

8. Ibid., 130–37.

9. These preliminary conclusions are based upon the unreported results of an analysis of mission censuses that register the age of individual converts and family reconstitution for several mission communities, reported in Jackson, "Demographic Patterns . . . Central Baja California"; and Jackson, "Gentile Recruitment."

10. Norman Owen, *Prosperity without Progress: Manila Hemp and Material Life in the Colonial Philippines* (Berkeley and Los Angeles, 1984), provides a useful overview of the sociocultural and economic changes that occurred in one part of the Philippines as a consequence of the intensification of export-oriented commercial agricultural and a resulting deemphasis of traditional rice cultivation for consumption in local markets. Owen documents an erosion in the standard of living of the majority of the Filipinos in the region he studied, despite the outward signs of prosperity with the growth in the volume of exports.

Conclusions

1. Daniel Reff, "Old World Diseases and the Dynamics of Indian and Jesuit Relations in Northwestern New Spain, 1520–1660," in N. Ross Crumrine and Phil

Weigand, eds., *Ejidos and Regions of Refuge in Northwestern Mexico* (Tucson, 1987), 85–94; and Daniel Reff, *Disease, Depopulation, and Culture Change in Northwestern New Spain, 1518–1764* (Salt Lake City, 1991).

2. Ibid., 89.

3. For a discussion of stress and the process of demographic collapse in northwestern New Spain, see Robert H. Jackson, "Demographic Change in Northwestern New Spain," *The Americas* 44 (1985): 462–79.

4. Robert H. Jackson, "Demographic Patterns in the Missions of Central Baja California," *Journal of California and Great Basin Anthropology* 6 (1984): 91–112.

5. Robert H. Jackson, "Population and the Economic Dimension of Colonization in Alta California: Four Mission Communities," *Journal of the Southwest* 33 (1991): 387–439.

6. Punishment of sinful colonists was the rationalization most commonly used by missionaries and priests in central Mexico to explain epidemics. See John L. Phelan, *The Millennial Kingdom of the Franciscans in the New World,* 2d rev. ed. (Berkeley and Los Angeles, 1970).

Bibliography

Archival Sources

Archivo Franciscano, Biblioteca Nacional, México, D.F.
This document collection contains reports and censuses that relate to the history of colonial Sonora.
Archivo General de la Nación, México, D.F.
Documents from several *ramos* of this archive have been used in the preparation of this study. Annual and biennial reports for the Alta California missions from the 1770s through 1796 are found in the section Documentos para la Historia de México. Annual and biennial reports for the Baja and Alta California missions in the 1790s come from the section Misiones. A variety of sources on the history of colonial Sonora are found in the section Temporalidades of the Archivo Historico de Hacienda.
Asociación Historica Americanista, México, D.F.
This small private collection of documents related to the ecclesiastical history of Mexico contains original sacramental parish registers from Baja California missions, including those from San José de Comondú mission.
Bancroft Library, University of California, Berkeley, Berkeley, California.
A variety of documents from this repository deal with the demographic history of the mission communities of northwestern New Spain. The Colección de la Pimería Alta contains sacramental registers from selected Pimería Alta missions, including San Antonio de Oquitoa, San Francisco de Ati, San Ignacio, Santa María Magdalena, and Santa María Soamca missions. The Mission Statistics collection consists of abstracts of data, taken from original reports destroyed during the 1906 San Francisco earthquake and fire, on the population, vital rates, agriculture, and numbers of livestock at the Alta California missions and nonmission settlements in Alta California. Other collections contain documents on Colonial Sonora and the Californias.
Monterey Diocese Chancery Archive, Monterey, California.
This chancery office and archive houses the original sacramental registers of the Alta California missions that fall within the jurisdiction of the Bishop of Monterey, including Santa Cruz and San Juan Bautista missions.
Saint Albert's College, Oakland, California.

The archive of the college houses the original sacramental registers of San Fernando, Rosario, Santo Domingo, and San Vicente missions in northern Baja California.

Santa Barbara Mission Archive-Library, Santa Barbara, California. This archive houses annual and biennial reports, principally for the years 1810–1832; letters; and other documents that originally constituted the archive of the Father-Presidents of the Alta California mission chain.

Sonora Parish Archives.

Several projects from the University of Arizona microfilmed the parish archives, including sacramental registers, of a number of Sonora parishes, including Altar, Banamichi, Hermosillo, Magdalena, and the archive of the bishopric of Sonora.

W. B. Stevens Collection, General Libraries, University of Texas at Austin, Austin, Texas.

This large document collection contains documents on the Jesuit missions of northwestern New Spain, including several important general reports (visitas) on the missions of Sonora and the Californias.

Published Sources

Alegre, S.J., Francisco. *Historia de la Compañía de Jesús en Nueva España (1566–1766).* 3 vols. Rome: Jesuit Historical Institute, 1960.

Aschmann, Homer. *The Central Desert of Baja California: Demography and Ecology.* Berkeley and Los Angeles: University of California Press, 1959.

Bahr, Donald. "Pima and Papago Social Organization." In Alfonso Ortiz, ed., *Handbook of North American Indians: Volume 10, Southwest,* pp. 178–92. Washington, D.C.: Smithsonian Institute Press, 1983.

Bancroft, H. H. *History of the North Mexican States and Texas.* 2 vols. San Francisco: The History Company, 1884–1889.

———. *History of California.* 6 vols. San Francisco: The History Company, 1887–1888.

Bazant, Jan. *The Alienation of Church Wealth in Mexico.* Cambridge: Cambridge University Press, 1971.

Bolton, Herbert, trans. and ed. *Kino's Historical Memoir of the Pimería Alta.* Berkeley and Los Angeles: University of California Press, 1948.

Borah, Woodrow. "Epidemics in the Americas: Major Issues and Future Research." *Latin American Population History Bulletin* 19 (Spring 1991): 2–13.

Broadbent, Sylvia. "Conflict at Monterey: Indian Horse Raiding 1820–1850." *Journal of California Anthropology* 1 (1974): 86–101.

Burrus, S.J., Ernest. *Kino and Manje Explorers of Sonora and Arizona.* Rome and St. Louis: Jesuit Historical Institute, 1971.

Burrus, S.J., Ernest, and Felix Zubillaga, S.J., eds., *Misiones mexicanas de la Compañía de Jesús, 1618–1745.* Madrid, 1982.

Castillo, Edward. "The Native Responses to the Colonization of Alta California." In David H. Thomas, ed., *Columbian Consequences: Archaeological and*

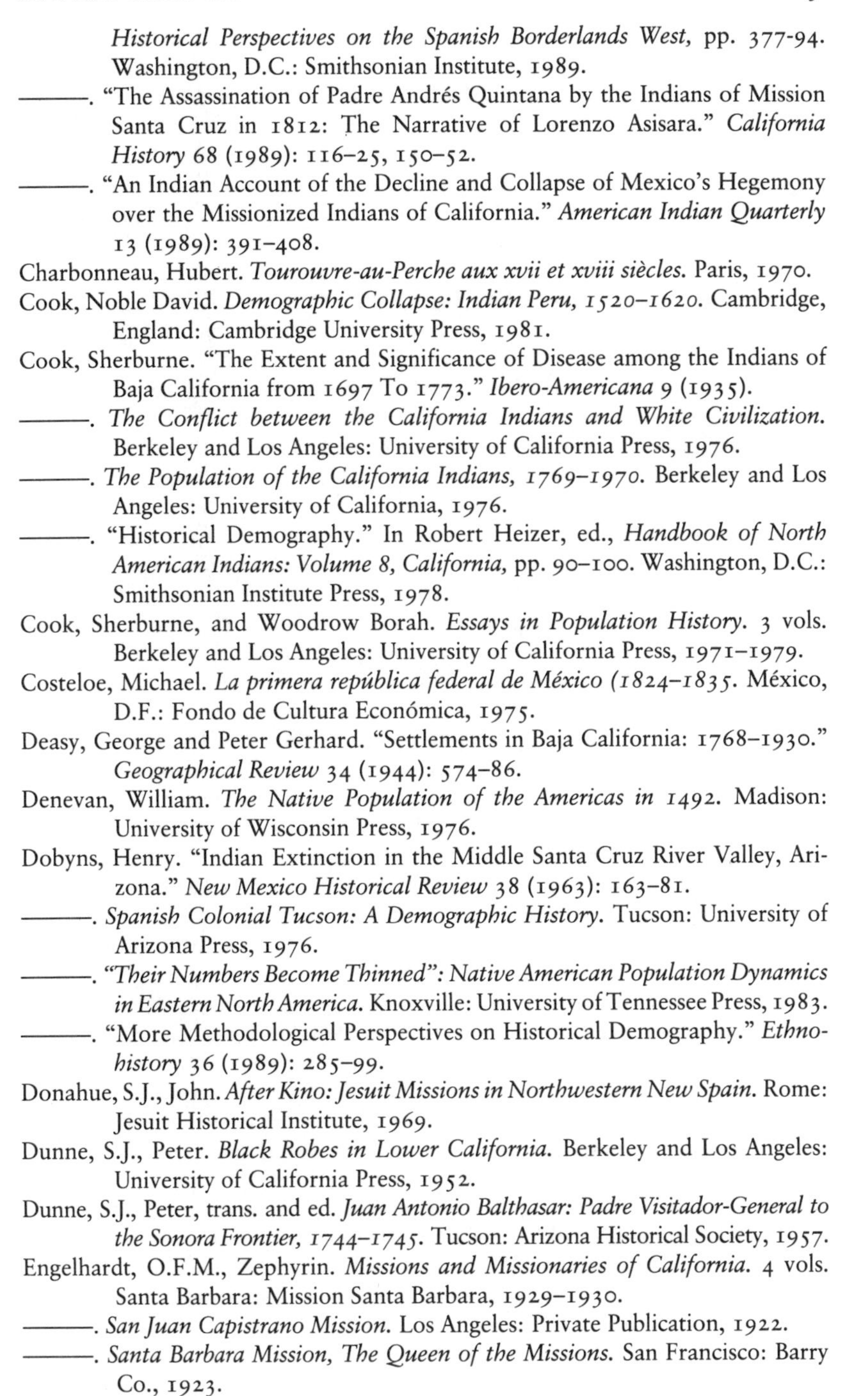

Historical Perspectives on the Spanish Borderlands West, pp. 377-94. Washington, D.C.: Smithsonian Institute, 1989.

———. "The Assassination of Padre Andrés Quintana by the Indians of Mission Santa Cruz in 1812: The Narrative of Lorenzo Asisara." *California History* 68 (1989): 116–25, 150–52.

———. "An Indian Account of the Decline and Collapse of Mexico's Hegemony over the Missionized Indians of California." *American Indian Quarterly* 13 (1989): 391–408.

Charbonneau, Hubert. *Tourouvre-au-Perche aux xvii et xviii siècles*. Paris, 1970.

Cook, Noble David. *Demographic Collapse: Indian Peru, 1520–1620*. Cambridge, England: Cambridge University Press, 1981.

Cook, Sherburne. "The Extent and Significance of Disease among the Indians of Baja California from 1697 To 1773." *Ibero-Americana* 9 (1935).

———. *The Conflict between the California Indians and White Civilization*. Berkeley and Los Angeles: University of California Press, 1976.

———. *The Population of the California Indians, 1769–1970*. Berkeley and Los Angeles: University of California, 1976.

———. "Historical Demography." In Robert Heizer, ed., *Handbook of North American Indians: Volume 8, California*, pp. 90–100. Washington, D.C.: Smithsonian Institute Press, 1978.

Cook, Sherburne, and Woodrow Borah. *Essays in Population History*. 3 vols. Berkeley and Los Angeles: University of California Press, 1971–1979.

Costeloe, Michael. *La primera república federal de México (1824–1835*. México, D.F.: Fondo de Cultura Económica, 1975.

Deasy, George and Peter Gerhard. "Settlements in Baja California: 1768–1930." *Geographical Review* 34 (1944): 574–86.

Denevan, William. *The Native Population of the Americas in 1492*. Madison: University of Wisconsin Press, 1976.

Dobyns, Henry. "Indian Extinction in the Middle Santa Cruz River Valley, Arizona." *New Mexico Historical Review* 38 (1963): 163–81.

———. *Spanish Colonial Tucson: A Demographic History*. Tucson: University of Arizona Press, 1976.

———. *"Their Numbers Become Thinned": Native American Population Dynamics in Eastern North America*. Knoxville: University of Tennessee Press, 1983.

———. "More Methodological Perspectives on Historical Demography." *Ethnohistory* 36 (1989): 285–99.

Donahue, S.J., John. *After Kino: Jesuit Missions in Northwestern New Spain*. Rome: Jesuit Historical Institute, 1969.

Dunne, S.J., Peter. *Black Robes in Lower California*. Berkeley and Los Angeles: University of California Press, 1952.

Dunne, S.J., Peter, trans. and ed. *Juan Antonio Balthasar: Padre Visitador-General to the Sonora Frontier, 1744–1745*. Tucson: Arizona Historical Society, 1957.

Engelhardt, O.F.M., Zephyrin. *Missions and Missionaries of California*. 4 vols. Santa Barbara: Mission Santa Barbara, 1929–1930.

———. *San Juan Capistrano Mission*. Los Angeles: Private Publication, 1922.

———. *Santa Barbara Mission, The Queen of the Missions*. San Francisco: Barry Co., 1923.

———. *San Gabriel Mission and the Beginnings of Los Angeles*. San Gabriel: San Gabriel Mission, 1927.
———. *Missions and Missionaries of California: Lower California*. Santa Barbara: Mission Santa Barbara, 1929.
———. *San Buenaventura, The Mission by the Sea*. Santa Barbara: Mission Santa Barbara, 1930.
———. *Mission San Luis Obispo*. Santa Barbara: Mission Santa Barbara, 1933.
Ezell, Paul. "History of the Pima." In Alfonso Ortiz, ed., *Handbook of North American Indians: Volume 10, Southwest*, pp. 149–60. Washington, D.C.: Smithsonian Institute Press, 1983.
Farriss, Nancy. *Maya Society under Colonial Rule: The Collective Enterprise of Survival*. Princeton: Princeton University Press, 1984.
Flinn, Michael. *The European Demographic System, 1520–1820*. Baltimore: The Johns Hopkins University Press, 1981.
Flores Caballero, Romeo. *La contra revolución en la independencia: los españoles en la vida política, social y económica de México (1804–1838)*. México, D.F.: El Colegio de México, 1973.
Fontana, Bernard. "Pima and Papago: Introduction." In Alfonso Ortiz, ed., *Handbook of North American Indians: Volume 10, Southwest*, pp. 125–36. Washington, D.C.: Smithsonian Institute Press, 1983.
———. "History of the Papago." In Alfonso Ortiz, ed., *Handbook of North American Indians: Volume 10, Southwest*, pp. 137–48. Washington, D.C.: Smithsonian Institute Press, 1983.
Geiger, O.F.M., Maynard. "New Data on Mission San Juan Capistrano." *Southern California Quarterly* 49 (1967): 37–45.
———. "The Building of Mission San Gabriel: 1771–1828." *Southern California Quarterly* 50 (1968): 33–42.
Gerhard, Peter. *A Guide to the Historical Geography of New Spain*. Cambridge, England: Cambridge University Press, 1972.
———. *The Southeast Frontier of New Spain*. Princeton: Princeton University Press, 1979.
———. *The North Frontier of New Spain*. Princeton: Princeton University Press, 1982.
Gibson, Charles. *The Aztecs under Spanish Rule: A History of the Indians of the Valley of México, 1519–1810*. Stanford: Stanford University Press, 1964.
González Rodríguez, Luis. *Etnología y misión en la Pimería Alta 1715–1740*. México, D.F.: UNAM, 1977.
Guest, O.F.M., Francis. "An Examination of the Thesis of S. F. Cook on the Forced Conversion of Indians in the Alta California Missions." *Southern California Quarterly* 61 (1979): 1–77.
Hackenberg, Robert. "Pima and Papago Ecological Adaptation." In Alfonso Ortiz, ed., *Handbook of North American Indians: Volume 10, Southwest*, pp. 161–77. Washington, D.C.: Smithsonian Institute Press, 1983.
Hale, Charles. *Mexican Liberalism in the Age of Mora, 1821–1853*. New Haven: Yale University Press, 1968.
Herr, Richard. *Rural Change and Royal Finances in Spain at the End of the Old Regime*. Berkeley and Los Angeles: University of California Press, 1989.

Huelsbeck, David, ed. *Lost and All But Forgotten: Archaeology and History at the Santa Clara Mission Site.* Salinas: Coyote Press, in press.

Hurtado, Albert. *Indian Survival on the California Frontier.* New Haven: Yale University Press, 1988.

Jackson, Robert H. "Epidemic Disease and Population Decline in the Baja California Missions, 1697–1834." *Southern California Quarterly* 63 (1981): 308–46.

———. "The 1781–1782 Smallpox Epidemic in the Baja California Missions." *Journal of California and Great Basin Anthropology* 3 (1981): 138–43.

———. "Population and the Economic Dimension of Colonization in Alta California: Four Mission Communities." *Journal of the Southwest* 33 (1991): 387–439.

———. "Causes of Indian Population Decline in the Pimería Alta Missions of Northern Sonora." *The Journal of Arizona History* 24 (1983): 405–23.

———. "Demographic Patterns in the Missions of Northern Baja California." *Journal of California and Great Basin Anthropology* 5 (1983): 131–39.

———. "Disease and Demographic Patterns at Santa Cruz Mission, Alta California." *Journal of California and Great Basin Anthropology* 5 (1983): 33–57.

———. "Gentile Recruitment and Population Movements in the San Francisco Bay Area Missions." *Journal of California and Great Basin Anthropology* 6 (1984): 225–39.

———. "Demographic Change in the Missions of Central Baja California." *Journal of California and Great Basin Anthropology* 6 (1984): 91–112.

———. "Demographic Change in Northwestern New Spain." *The Americas* 44 (1985): 462–79.

———. "Indian Demographic Patterns in Colonial New Spain: The Case of the Baja California Missions." *PCCLAS Proceedings* 12 (1986): 37–46.

———. "Patterns of Demographic Change in the Missions of Southern Baja California." *Journal of California and Great Basin Anthropology* 8 (1986): 273–79.

———. "Patterns of Demographic Change in the Missions of Central Alta California." *Journal of California and Great Basin Anthropology* 9 (1987): 251–72.

———. "A Chronology of Building Construction at the First La Purísima Site." *Prelado de los Tesoros* (1988): 3–4.

———. "The Demographic Consequences of Spanish Indian Policy in Baja California, 1768–1782." *University of Minnesota Working Papers in Early Modern History* (April 6, 1989).

———. "La dinámica del desastre demográfico de la población india en las misiones de la Bahía de San Francisco, Alta California, 1776–1840," *Historia Mexicana* 40 (1991): 187–215.

Johnson, John. "The Chumash and the Missions," In David Hurst Thomas, ed., *Columbian Consequences: Archaeological and Historical Perspectives on the Spanish Borderlands West,* pp. 365–75. Washington, D.C.: Smithsonian Institute Press, 1989.

Kelsey, Harry. "The Mission Buildings of San Juan Capistrano: A Tentative Chronology." *Southern California Quarterly* 69 (1987): 1–32.

Kessell, John. *Mission of Sorrows: Jesuit Guevavi and the Pimas, 1691–1767.* Tucson: University of Arizona Press, 1970.

———. *Friars, Soliers, and Reformers: Hispanic Arizona and the Sonora Mission Frontier, 1767–1856.* Tucson: University of Arizona Press, 1976.

Langer, Erick, and Robert H. Jackson. "Colonial and Republican Missions Compared: The Cases of Alta California and Southeastern Bolivia." *Comparative Studies in Society and History* 30 (1988): 286–311.

Lee, Ron. "Estimating Series of Vital Rates and Age Structure from Baptisms and Burials: A New Technique with Application to Pre-Industrial England." *Population Studies* 28 (1975): 495–512.

———. "Inverse Projection and Back Projection: Comparative Results and Sensitivity Tests for England." *Population Studies* 39 (1985): 233–48.

Lovell, W. George. *Conquest and Survival in Colonial Guatemala: A Historical Geography of the Cuchumatan Highlands.* Kingston and Montreal: McGill University Press, 1985.

MacLeod, Murdo. *Spanish Central America: A Socio-Economic History 1520–1720.* Berkeley and Los Angeles: University of California Press, 1973.

Matson, Daniel, and Bernard Fontana, trans. and eds., *Fray Bringas Reports to the King.* Tucson: University of Arizona Press, 1977.

McCaa, Robert. "The Female Population of Chile, 1855–1964: A Microcomputer Balance Sheet Method." *Latin American Population Newsletter* 15 (Spring 1989): 9–14.

———. "Benchmarks for a New Inverse Population Projection: England, Sweden, and a Standard Demographic Transition." In Roger Schofield and David Reher, eds., *Old And New In Historical Demography.* Oxford, England, and New York: Oxford University Press, forthcoming.

McCaa, Robert, and James Vaupel. "How Well Does Inverse Projection Perform with Simulated Data?" *University of Minnesota Center for Population Analysis and Public Policy Working Paper,* no. 89-06-2 (1989).

McCarty, O.F.M., Kieran. *Desert Documentary.* Tucson: Arizona Historical Society, 1976.

Meigs, Peveril. *The Dominican Mission Frontier of Lower California.* Berkeley: University of California Press, 1935.

Owen, Norman, *Prosperity without Progress: Manila Hemp and Material Life in the Colonial Philippines.* Berkeley and Los Angeles: University of California Press, 1984.

Phelan, John. *The Millennial Kingdom of the Franciscans in the New World.* 2d rev. ed. Berkeley and Los Angeles: University of California Press, 1970.

Phillips, George. "Indians and the Breakdown of the Spanish Mission System in California." *Ethnohistory* 21 (1974): 291–302.

Polzer, S.J., Charles. *Precepts of the Jesuit Missions.* Tucson: University of Arizona Press, 1976.

Radding, Cynthia. "Las estructuras socio-económicas de las misiones de la Pimería Alta, 1768–1850." *Noroeste de México* 3 (1979): 1–124.

———. "La acumulación originaria de capital agrario en Sonora: Comunidad indígena y la hacienda en Pimería Alta y Opateria, 1768–1868." *Noroeste de México* 5 (1981): 15–46.

Rawls, James. *Indians of California: The Changing Image.* Norman: University of Oklahoma Press, 1984.

Reff, Daniel, "Old World Diseases and the Dynamics of Indian and Jesuit Relations in Northwestern New Spain, 1520–1660." In N. Ross Crumrine and Phil Weigand, eds., "Ejidos and Regions of Refuge in Northwestern Mexico." *Anthropological Papers of the University of Arizona* 46 (1987): 85–94.

———. *Disease, Depopulation, and Culture Change in Northwestern New Spain, 1518–1764.* Salt Lake City: University of Utah Press, 1991.

Sánchez-Albornoz, Nicolas. *The Population of Latin America: A History.* Translated by W. A. R. Richardson. Berkeley and Los Angeles: University of California Press, 1974.

Sauer, Carl. "Aboriginal Population of Northwestern Mexico." *Ibero-Americana* 10 (1935).

Sauer, Carl, and Peveril Meigs. "The Site and Culture at San Fernando Velicata." *University of California Publications in Geography* 2 (1927): 271–302.

Servin, Manuel. "The Secularization of the California Missions: A Reappraisal." *Southern California Quarterly* 47 (1965): 133–49.

Shubsda, Thaddeus, ed. *The Serra Report.* Monterey: N.P., N.D. [1986].

Smith, Peter, and Shui-Meng Ng. "The Components of Population Change in Nineteenth-Century Southeast Asia: Village Data from the Philippines." *Population Studies* 36 (1982): 237–55.

Stern, Peter, and Robert H. Jackson. "Vagabundaje and Settlement Patterns in Colonial Northern Sonora." *The Americas* 44 (1988): 461–81.

Stodder, Ann. *Mechanisms and Trends in the Decline of the Costanoan Indian Population of Central California.* Salinas: Coyote Press, 1986.

Swann, Michael. *Migrants in the Mexican North Mobility, Economy, and Society in a Colonial World.* Boulder: Westview Press, 1989.

Taylor, William. *Landlord and Peasant in Colonial Oaxaca.* Stanford: Stanford University Press, 1972.

———. *Drinking, Homicide, and Rebellion in Colonial Mexican Villages.* Stanford: Stanford University Press, 1979.

Whitmore, Thomas. "A Simulation of the Sixteenth-Century Population Collapse in the Basin of Mexico." *Annals of the Association of American Geographers* 8 (1991): 464–87.

Wrigley, E. A., and R. S. Schofield. *The Population History of England, 1541–1871: A Reconstruction.* Cambridge: Harvard University Press, 1981.

Unpublished Sources

Castillo, Edward. "Neophyte Resistance and Accommodation in the Missions of California." Paper presented at the conference "The Spanish Missionary Heritage of the United States," San Antonio, Texas, November 8, 1990.

Gordillo Claure, José, and Mercedes del Rio. "La visita de Tiquipaya: Analisis de un padrón toledano (1573)." Cochabamba: typescript, 1989.

Hornbeck, David. "An Assessment of S.F. Cook's Research on the 'Indian Versus the Spanish Mission.'" Paper read at the "Spanish Missions and the California Indians" symposium, Davis, California, March 2–4, 1990.

Jackson, Robert H. "Demographic and Social Change in Northwestern New Spain: A Comparative Analysis of the Pimería Alta and Baja California Missions." Master's thesis, University of Arizona, 1982.

———. "A Utopian Paradise?: The Dynamic of Demographic Collapse in the California Missions, 1697–1840." Paper read at the annual meeting of the American Historical Association, San Francisco, California, December 27, 1989.

———. "The Dynamic of Indian Demographic Collapse in the San Francisco Bay Region Missions, 1776–1840." Paper read at the "Spanish Missions and the California Indians" symposium, Davis, California, March 2–4, 1990.

———. "Epidemic Disease and the Population of the Sonora Missions in the seventeenth, eighteenth, and early nineteenth Centuries." Unpublished manuscript.

———. "A Chronology of Building Construction at La Purísima Concepción Mission, 1788–1835." Unpublished manuscript.

———. "A Chronology of Building Construction at San Rafael and San Francisco Solano Missions." Unpublished manuscript.

———. "The Post-Secularization Dispersion of the Population of the Alta California Missions, 1834–1846." Paper presented at the annual meeting of the Rocky Mountain Council of Latin American Studies, Flagstaff, Arizona, February 26–28, 1991.

Jackson, Robert H., Edna Kimbro, and Mary Ellen Ryan. "'*Como la Sombra, Huye la Hora*': Restoration Research, Santa Cruz Mission Adobe, Santa Cruz Mission State Historc Park." Manuscript of report in the possession of the State of California Department of Parks and Recreation, Sacramento, California.

Johnson, John. "Chumash Social Organization: An Ethnohistorical Perspective." Ph.D. dissertation, University of California, Santa Barbara, 1988.

Index

About the Book and Author

Indian Population Decline
The Missions of Northwestern New Spain, 1687–1840
Robert H. Jackson

This new ethnohistory of missions in California, Arizona, and northwest Mexico seeks to answer questions long debated about how Indians fared when relocated and placed under the Church's care. Drawing on extensive and scattered archival sources, Jackson produces a sophisticated demographic analysis that permits evaluation of the causes, manifestations, and regional variations of the demographic collapse of mission Indians.

The central finding is that diseases are only part of the explanation of population decline. In addition to deaths due to such illnesses as measles and smallpox and to psychological trauma, we must consider the effects of declining fertility among Indian women manifested in abortions, miscarriages, and death in childbirth. The unhealthy conditions in missions frequently resulted in nine of ten children dying before age eight. Missionaries often rationalized such high mortality rates as divine retribution for "repeated apostasy and transgressions."

Robert H. Jackson, a history professor at Texas Southern University, is a Latin Americanist and Borderlands specialist.